W9-DDD-680

Ethics, Morality, and the Media

Reflections on American Culture

Humanistic Studies in the Communication Arts

Ethics, Morality and The Media

Reflections on American Culture

Compiled and Edited
by LEE THAYER

With the assistance of
Richard L. Johannesen
and Hanno Hardt

COMMUNICATION ARTS BOOKS

Hastings House, Publishers
New York 10016

5219676

4-90

Library of Congress Cataloging in Publication Data
Main entry under title:

Ethics, morality, and the media.

(Humanistic studies in the communication arts)
(Communications arts books)
    Bibliography: p.
    Includes index.
    1. Mass media — United States — Moral and religious
aspects — Addresses, essays, lectures.   2. United
States — Popular culture — Addresses, essays, lectures.
I. Thayer, Lee   II. Johannesen, Richard L.
III. Hardt, Hanno.
P94.E8   301.16′1′0973   79-9479
ISBN 0-8038-1957-9
ISBN 0-8038-1958-7 pbk.

Published simultaneously in Canada by Copp Clark Ltd., Toronto

Designed by Al Lichtenberg
Printed in the United States of America

9 8 7 6 5 4 3 2

Contents

Contributors

Ashmore, Harry S., President, Center for the Study
of Democratic Institutions

Bagdikian, Ben H., Writer and Professor, Graduate School
of Journalism, University of California

Clark, Peter B., The Evening News Association—Detroit

Crichton, John, President, American Association of
Advertising Agencies

Crist, Judith, Film Critic

Edelstein, Alex A., Director, School of Communications,
University of Washington

Fox, James F., President, Fox Public Relations, Inc.

Fox, William Price, Novelist, TV and Film Writer

Gallup, George, Chairman, the Gallup Poll
American Institute of Public Opinion

Hardy, David Keith, Film Producer

Harris, T. George, Magazine Editor

Jones, Jenkin Lloyd, Editor and Publisher, *The Tulsa Tribune*

Koop, Theodore F., Retired Washington Vice President, CBS

Lacy, Dan, Senior Vice President, McGraw-Hill Book Company

Lasch, Christopher, Professor of History,
University of Rochester

Levitt, Theodore, Professor, Harvard University
Graduate School of Business Administration

MacDonald, Kenneth, Newspaper Editor

Mayer, Martin, Author and Journalist

Morăn, Terence P., Media Ecology Program, New York University
Newman, Edwin, NBC News
Rubicam, Raymond, Co-Founder, Young & Rubicam
Safford, E. S., President and Publisher, Mountain Empire Publishing, Inc.
Scanlon, T. Joseph, Professor, School of Journalism,
    Carleton University
Stone, Leslie C., Current Affairs Commentator, BBC
Thayer, Lee, Professor of Communication, University of
    Wisconsin-Parkside
Vanocur, Sander, National Public Affairs Center for Television
Wasilewski, Vincent T., President, National Association of
    Broadcasters

Editors' Preface

In this book, 27 authors and respondents — mostly practitioners — explore the major ethical and moral issues which confront us today in our uses of, and in our attempts to assess the performance of, modern mass communication systems. For all of those who have an interest in mankind's present state and future prospects, it would be difficult to imagine a more important, more provocative, inquiry.

In 1975, there were more than 1,700 daily newspapers, with a circulation in excess of 60 million. There were 7,500 radio stations broadcasting to potentially more than 300 million receivers. There were 1,000 television stations broadcasting to more than 125 million receivers. There were 3,400 cable systems with approximately 10 million subscribers. Motion picture receipts were already above $5 billion in 1972. In the same year, more than 30,000 books were published in the United States, making the book business a $3 billion plus industry. There are more than 8,000 magazines published regularly in the United States. And, in 1975, more than $28 billion was spent on advertising.

As arresting as *these* figures are, we know that the record industry is now, in dollars and cents, the *largest* of the "mass" media. We know that Americans invest more time in watching television than any other life activity except work. If we add to these research, educational, publicity, and other activities that together comprise the "knowledge" and "information" industries, then we are looking at the dominant economic and social force of the twentieth century.

In Europe, these are sometimes referred to collectively as the "consciousness" industry. It is an apt term. It is increasingly the case that our very consciousness of the world in which we live is made up of pieces which are *manufactured* for us by one or another component of the "consciousness" industry.

And, for humankind, as our consciousness goes, so we will go. What *is* "happening" to us in our steadily increasing immersion in the products of the "consciousness" industry? What do our present uses of the mass media — whether as "producers" or as "consumers" of those media — portend for our present state and our future prospects?

Just to ask that question — and how could we avoid asking it? — is to point to the kinds of issues which are raised and explored in this book. For what our authors and respondents investigate in this book are questions of right and wrong, of good and bad. Are the ways in which we are presently using our mass media — both as "producers" and as "consumers" — the ways we *should* be using them? Are those ways good for us or bad for us? How can we know what *is* right and wrong about our uses of the media, or about the myriad circumstances of working in them? What are the obstacles to our doing what is "right," avoiding what is "wrong"? And if something is "wrong" or "bad" for us, who or what is to blame? And how do we go about making adjustments to the system, or of making the users of the mass media more "moral" or "ethical" than they may now seem sometimes to be? How do we correct those ills and faults that we can see and identify? And what about the ones that we cannot, or will not, see?

What sense of right and wrong *should* a reporter or a broadcaster or an advertiser or a novelist or a "consumer" have? And where is it to come from?

These and a great many like questions are explored in this book. It is a fascinating, a vital, inquiry. And our authors and respondents have searched themselves and their own experiences as tenaciously as they have analyzed the larger scene. So this book presents a spectrum of personal inquiries as well as a social analysis, and thus provides a unique perspective on some of the most vital and important issues of our present human circumstances.

The idea for this book first emerged some years ago. At that time, a year-long series of colloquia on ethical and moral issues in communication and mass communication was held at the University of Iowa. An earlier book, based in part upon those proceedings, has already been published.* That volume represents the thinking of a wide range of philosophers and academicians on the matter of "right" and "wrong" behavior in communication systems.

In this book is represented the thinking of an equally wide range of professionals and practitioners involved in various aspects of mass communication — from journalists to movie critics, from magazine editors to

---

* Lee Thayer (ed.), *Communication: Ethical and Moral Issues* (N. Y.: Gordon and Breach, 1973).

public opinion research executives, from filmmakers to newspaper publishers, from advertising executives to public broadcasters.

Some of the papers included here were originally presented at the Iowa colloquia, and these have been revised and updated for this volume. Others were commissioned especially for this book, and still others are reprinted here from other sources — simply because no better treatment of one particular set of issues could be had. The "Conversations with . . . ," which comprise Part III, were developed from interviews, correspondence, and tape transcripts of discussions held at one place or another, at one time or another. In addition to the appeal of the question-and-answer format of this Part of the book, we felt that some issues are raised here which could not have been raised in more formal "papers" on the subject.

The Introductory Essay is intended to provide a conceptual foundation, of some breadth and depth, for looking at the evaluating the many issues of ethics and morality involved in contemporary mass communication systems. While it focuses mainly upon the American culture, and thus provides a context for understanding these issues, it is readily applicable to other of the Western cultures. It is intended to be "heuristic" — that is, to provoke further questions and to guide the discovery of some of the more subtle aspects of our theme that might otherwise be overlooked. For all readers, it is addressed to the question: How shall we *think* about all such matters?

One of the disadvantages of a book of this sort, it is sometimes believed, is that it may have no single unifying scheme. Rather than being a disadvantage in this case, we feel that this is a distinct advantage. If there were already a universally-agreed upon set of principles about our subject — a single "theory," perhaps — then such a book as this might be an inefficient way of going about things. But in the absence of a fixed set of principles, or where, in fact, we are trying to discover what those principles might be, then a book which approaches the central questions from a wide range of points of view offers the advantage of actually "opening-up" the reader's experiences and perspectives on our theme. Letting this well-informed and thoughtful set of practitioners speak for themselves we believe to be the best approach here, where we seek mainly to explore, to begin to understand, what the key questions — the central issues — are.

Another advantage is that this book can be read in any order the reader prefers. Every paper and every "Conversation" is self-contained, and can therefore be read independently. Even the Introductory Essay need not be read before getting involved with one or another of the papers included here. One might want to read it first, or last, or even interspersed with the reading of other sections of the book. Or, it too can be read independently.

The appended list of further reading on the subject of this book is not intended to be exhaustive, but merely suggestive.

We are grateful to all of our authors and respondents for their cooperation, their patience, and their considered thoughtfulness in their individual contributions to this book. Whatever value it has can only reflect upon them individually.

In part, there is something of the legacy of the late Malcolm MacLean in this book, for he was instrumental in our earliest efforts to undertake the inquiry that culminated here.

Lee Thayer
Richard L. Johannesen
Hanno Hardt

Foreword

Shortly after World War II, college and universities in the United States began to broaden the bases and extend the reach of their academic offerings that were related, in one way or another, to the mass media of communications. Somewhat reluctantly, Schools of Journalism recognized that much news was now being disseminated by radio, and that the newfangled television gizmo might also hold out some sorts of similar promise. A few courses in broadcasting techniques were accordingly added to their curricula.

At about the same time, undergraduate departments of Speech and English, already famous for their onion-like divestitures of related disciplines (like Theatre and Linguistics), also began to offer courses — eventually departmentalized and thereafter sometimes glorified into Schools—in broadcasting, cinema appreciation and mass media production that developed into a varied menu of more or less academic ventures into what, for the lack of a better name, were finally called "communication arts" or "communication studies." Their course content was at first (and still is to a degree) determined by the interests and talents of whatever instructors were around to teach them and availability of capital that could legally be appropriated for the hardware and/or software necessary to sustain them. Not to be outdone by their colleagues, other colorful groups of mercenaries rode off onto collegiate turf along with them: school teachers (now called "audiovisual specialists"), political and social scientists and psychologists (now "communications researchers and theorists"), to say nothing of occasional assorted anthropologists, philosophy teachers, foot-loose administrators, engineers, photographers and poets.

The result in all its magnificent plurality and heterogeneity was the variegated assortment of events on the campuses of this nation's institutions of higher learning that make some kind of disciplinary claim to "communications." They are not much different today from what they were in the early 'seventies, the 'sixties and the 'fifties, except that there are many more of them and some of their names have changed. To the outside observer, they are, across-the-board, widely and wildly different one from the other for reasons which are rarely intellectual or rational but almost entirely pragmatic and have to do entirely with university politics, tradition and economics—none of which are usually intellectual or rational.

If one communal thread runs through each and every Department or School of Communications on the American campus, however, it has been, up to the present anyway, the presence of one course — or possibly two — entitled something like *Mass Communications and Contemporary Society; Mass Media: Cause and Effects; Enduring Issues in the Media Society; Systems and Issues in Mass Communication* (or similar words in some other crazy combination) that has been wedged into a curriculum somewhere between instruction in how to operate zoom lenses and the history of the animated cartoon.

These courses — or *this course,* in fact — are all pretty much the same. Students are handed a textbook containing essays by various notables concerning the "great issues" in mass communications today and are instructed henceforth to think deeply about them. These "great issues" are always the same: violence in television and films, the "fairness doctrine" in broadcasting, a reporter's right to protect his sources, whether movies reflect culture or vice-versa, a couple of hazy laments that center on the abuses rather than uses to which our modern instruments of communication have been put, and an essay on the excellence of press councils in England and/or similar attempts somewhere in Nebraska.

As I say, these "conscience courses" (as I enjoy calling them) have been part of the graduate and undergraduate communications curriculum up to the present. But I think I now detect winds of change. I just have counted *twenty-three* introductory anthologies designed for such intellectual adventures packed cheek-to-cheek in my bookcase. All of them are still in print. I believe it was Parkinson (of the law, not the disease) who once said that when any human endeavor reached institutional proportions, it became moribund, sunk, finished! *Twenty-three* separate volumes composed largely of the same batch of poorly edited essays bespeaks a high degree of literary institutionalization to me. I think I hear a bell tolling somewhere for these ever-present but invariably despised "conscience courses." Queasy consciences, of course, require something more concrete than one thirty-hour course in "great issues" by way of appeasement. One by one, these silly obeisances to phony intellectual honesty are at present being tossed aside, replaced largely by superior specialized academic efforts to grapple merely with *one* "issue" per course in sufficient detail and depth to justify calling it "great."

When these courses are boiled down to their essences and the anthologies summarized to their pith, the skeleton motive of the entire diversionary caper from the start becomes distressingly clear. (As a young graduate student in a communications department at one of the first universities to offer such courses, my x-ray eyes spotted this simple truth more than a quarter of a century ago — although teachers of extraordinary sensitivity, in my case Charles Siepmann — took extraordinary pains to emphasize that the general study of mass communications served mainly as a metaphor for a critical examination of modern culture.)

The object under the microscope is no mystery. The theme that runs through all the essays and all the notes of countless bored professors and students is simply the consideration of human *ethics*. There is a *right* way to do everything (including communicating by print one's deep concerns about the crispness of potato chips), and there is a *wrong* way. Severing the right from the wrong was — and is — the major question to which all ethical concerns are addressed. And problems of ethics are among the most difficult that men and women face, because they are subject to the enormous stress of individual need on one side and the general welfare of society on the other — both of which occur at the identical moment.

I think that, after decades of experience, we are at last coming to realize that most of our older, time-honored constructions of "communication ethics" were mostly straw men, in much the same way that the clear-sighted have figured out that "medical ethics" are also a fraud. Destroying a motion picture's artistic integrity by allowing a mongoloid to edit it for television is as unethical to me as keeping someone I love alive in a vegetable state by means of complex, expensive technology. Pressures of time and schedules in the broadcasting industry in the first place, and demands by shiny new inventions to be used in the second, have nothing to do with the issue. Remember that Hippocrates himself was not concerned with "medical ethics": he was worried about the kinds of behaviors people trying to help other people might indulge in to achieve their ends. The beginning and end of ethics, he knew, was *respect*. And respect is much the same when and wherever it appears: a lawyer's respect for the law, society and his client; a physician's respect for his art, science and his patient; a journalist's respect for his tradition, constitutional protection and reader; a broadcaster's respect for the owners of his channel of communication, the regulatory agency operating on their behalf and his viewers and listeners. (If he respects the latter, he will naturally not edit films for video but transmit them in their entirety or not broadcast them at all!)

Dr. Lee Thayer belongs to the same generation of communication scholars and teachers as I do, and none of this is a secret to him. *Humanistic Studies in the Communication Arts* is proud to open its presses to him and his associates. In this present — and fascinating — book about ethics, various individuals involved with communication set themselves, sometimes easily and sometimes uncomfortably, sometimes sagely and sometimes foolishly, to untangling the twisted strings of right and wrong that are wound into their professional and intellectual concerns. Dr. Thayer has, cleverly I think, given us a volume that yields *in toto* a rich and multifaceted view of contemporary society and its ideas of good and bad, right and wrong.

I do not think I would rush to Vincent T. Wasilewski with any manner of ethical problem that is bothering me, but neither would I seek counsel from Martin Mayer, and he is my blood cousin. What I would want to do is listen to both in order to take their measures as human beings, before I turned my attention to any matters of right and wrong, much less the complicated issues in *Ethics, Morality and the Media.* By virtue of clever selection and editing — as well as comments along the way — Lee Thayer has accomplished a similar task in this volume, compiled with more than a decorous respect for his reader in a wide range of contexts, all of which serve as measures of individual personality in the end.

George N. Gordon
Muhlenberg College
Cedar Crest College

PART ONE

Introductory Essay

Ethics, Morality, and the Media:

NOTES ON AMERICAN CULTURE

LEE THAYER

The wife of a convicted murderer is offered a
small fortune for the "rights" to her story of his
life. Is this ethical?

A celebrity is offered a great deal of money to
"endorse" a particular product. Is it ethical for
her to do so, even if she herself thinks the product
is okay?

Pollsters know that you can ask people questions
in such a way that they appear to have a real
opinion on a topic they know little or nothing,
and probably care less, about. When the "results"
are reported, the irrelevance of such data is
overlooked. Is this ethical?

A teenage film idol is offered a profitable film
role. The script calls for him to say to his cinema
mother, "God damn you!" Is there any sense in
which his doing so is immoral?

A famous newscaster knows that some film that will be used during his broadcast was staged to appear to be the real event, but is not. Is this ethical?

An advertiser knows that the way a television commercial was made does not accurately reflect the product. Is this ethical?

In answer to their critics, spokesmen for the television industry reply, "We're only giving the public what it wants." Is this ethical?

A newspaper editor shortens a story to fit the space available. In doing so, the import of the story is changed somewhat. Is this ethical?

A company manufactures a product known to be superior to a competing product. The competing product is very cleverly, and extensively, advertised. Has this company an ethical obligation to attempt even more persuasive advertising in order to promote its product over the other?

A movie critic believes a new film to be technically superior but potentially a negative social influence. Should she praise or pan the movie?

A successful political "image-maker" rationalizes his subtle deceptions with the argument: "If I don't do it, someone else will." Is this ethical?

A popular novelist writes a vivid, arousing scene of rape, an act which seems clearly gratuitous to the rest of the novel. Is this ethical?

Reporters often find it easier to use prepared news releases than to take the time and make the effort to develop a story directly. Is this unethical, or is it merely lazy?

A head of state, presuming that widespread knowledge of the "truth" about a certain matter would be detrimental to the cause of "peace," says something to interviewers that is not "true." Is this ethical?

A television script is altered to add a role for a representative of a "minority" group, of no relevance to the story. Is this ethical?

A magazine publisher attempts to increase subscriptions (and profits) by presuming to further the cause of some social movement, some "good" cause. Is this ethical?

A radio personality is offered a free trip and other amenities by a company seeking better publicity. Is this ethical?

Some of those involved in the "Watergate affair," on one side or the other, have parlayed their media-produced fame into fortunes. Is this ethical? Is it ethical for those who own and operate the media to capitalize on this sort of thing? But media audiences clearly want "more." Are *they* ethical?

A popular recording star is "marketed" much like every other mass-produced product. But his or her fans believe that the star is pursuing a cause, not money. Which is the ethical course, to allow them to persist in this false illusion, or to disillusion them?

An influential disc jockey is offered certain "gifts" if he will "push" a particular stable of recording artists. Is this ethical? Assuming the D.J. believes in the quality of all of those artists who might gain thereby, would it be moral for him to accept?

A politician has discovered that he has more media appeal if he changes his hair style and speaks in a more "roundabout" manner. Is this ethical?

The editor of a large book firm knows that, in
their popular novels, sex "sells." Would he be
immoral to make this a key criterion in selecting
manuscripts to be made into future novels? How
about the writer who writes her books in just
such a way that they *will* sell? And what about
the reader who buys only "best sellers," not
caring whether they are of any real literary
quality or not?

A television viewer knows that she is not really
interested in the program she is watching, and
that she "should" get up and do something more
useful. But she doesn't. Is this moral? Is the local
merchant from whom she bought the television
subject to any charge of complicity in her
behavior?

An intellectual — a critic — "puts down" the
American people because they would seem to
prefer "entertainment" to what he feels is more
"serious" media fare. Is his position a moral one?
What, after all, is the relationship between taste
and morality? Between preferences and ethics?

I

The list of questions that could be asked about matters of ethics and
morality in mass communication is, seemingly, endless. Is it possible that it
all just "depends" — upon the situation, upon intentions, upon current
social tastes in such matters?

We (Americans particularly) often fail to remember that the components of mass communication systems are *interdependent*. No one part of
the system is independent of the others. We wouldn't have the television
programming we have were it not for the fact that they have the audiences
they have. At the same time, those audiences wouldn't exist if those kinds
of programs were not made available. Without passing judgment on its
merit one way or the other, we can agree that there would be no "pornography" if there were no one who wanted it. Yet how would those who
"want" it know they wanted it if it did not exist?

Where, then, is the "cause" of the "effects" we wish to attribute to
the mass media? Who *is* responsible? Is the consumer blameless, beyond
any question of ethics or morality? Are there not indeed social "forces" for

which no individual, and no one set of individuals, can be held accountable?

Some of the issues are as old as mankind's selfawareness: Do the ends "justify" the means? Others are very modern: Do the means (i.e., the technology) "justify" their own ends (e.g., a "global village")?

The "mass media" are a phenomenon of the twentieth century. Does this mean that whatever moral or ethical standards are to be applied to their use (by either the "producers" or the "consumers") must also be invented in the twentieth century? Or are there principles of human behavior which are just as applicable today as they were two or four thousand years ago? Is an Aristotle, is a Confucius, less pertinent to our moral or ethical dilemmas today then is a Walter Benjamin, a George Steiner?

The issues are indeed complex, profound. It is not just that modern communication systems are exceedingly complex — economically, technologically, politically, legally, symbolically. It is that the dynamisms which guide our use of them are deeply imbedded in our culture, in the values and interests and perspectives of Western civilization. "The media" are not something separate from the social and cultural contexts of their users — their "producers" and their "consumers." They are an intricate, inextricable part of the social and cultural contexts of those who participate in them, whatever their role may be. They can, finally, be understood only as an aspect of the larger human context of which they are a part.

The issues are not only complex, they are profound. They are no more readily, no more certainly, understandable than is man himself. Without an ultimate, definitive theory of man, there could hardly be a definitive "theory" of mass communication. For the ways in which a people behave with and toward their media of communication can be understood only in terms of those people.

So where does this leave us? Does all this make the task of gaining some substantial understanding of the ethical and moral issues involved in modern mass communication an impossibility?

No, it does not. But it does mean that we cannot indiscriminately accept all of what has been said and written about mass communication in recent years. There are, in fact, a number of good reasons for being skeptical.

One reason has already been suggested. It is that much — if not most — of what has been said and written about mass communication in the modern world, whether by journalists or social "scientists," assumes the phenomena to be explained are more independent of the social/cultural context in which they occur than they actually are. For example, if "the media" are "commercial," as in some Western countries, the ultimate criterion is an economic one. If they don't make enough money to cover costs, they won't be around any longer. If "the media" are "public" (i.e., a function of government), as in some European and other countries, the ultimate criteria are ideological, if not political. In either case, to consider the ethics or the morality of "the media" apart from the larger social and cultural contexts within which their "producers" and their "consumers" use them is to risk missing the most salient facts.

Much of what has been said and written about mass communication in the modern world also misses another fact of even greater human import. Wherever there are *mass* media, one central question is always this: Shall the public be given only what it *should* have, or shall it be free to do as it wishes? Is that merely a question of expediency? Or is there something of much greater long range human import implied? One does not need to take a position with respect to which arrangement is intrinsically "better" than the other to see clearly at the outset that *any* assumption of "should" in assessing the performance of "the media" is inevitably and inescapably a *moral* one. It is never merely one of making "social policy" or of regulation. Nor is it merely "scientific" or merely factual. What "should" be the case is a moral issue itself.

And thus the moral dilemma which lies at the heart of this and like matters in our uniquely democratic and "open" society: If people are free to choose how they will "spend" their leisure time, and in someone's view do not do so in a manner which that someone believes to be most beneficial for them, then *who* is to decide what is to be done about it?

Many — if not most — of those who comment and do "research" on the media presume a detachment from this dilemma. If they do acknowledge it, they rarely acknowledge it for what it is — a *moral* dilemma.

A second reason for being skeptical of the bulk of what has been said and written about "the media" in recent years is that the arguments have been based in one or the other of two kinds of appeals. One uses a false stereotype — that of "science" as the ultimate authority. It plays upon our belief in "science." The other plays upon our susceptibility to the dramatic, the ease with which we "understand" things if they are put into the form of the "good" guys versus the "bad" guys. Both are irrational.

Our faith in "science"

Westerners generally, Americans particularly, have for years held the belief that "science" constitutes the primary — if not the exclusive — authority for "knowledge." Whatever can be supported "scientifically" is at once what is worth knowing, and what is "true." Any other basis for knowing or believing or making social decisions is less prestigious, often subject to suspicion and doubt.

Whatever the justifications for that faith pro and con may be — and it would take us too far afield to consider them here — one relevant fact remains. It is that whenever large numbers of people have such faith only in "science," those people will have an unusual susceptibility to any appeal that appears to be "scientific." It is therefore more possible to influence those who have this faith by appealing to the "scientific" nature of the facts or the opinions which someone thinks they "should" know. A shameful proportion of the extensive social and behavioral "research" on mass communication in the West can be gainsaid on this basis.

On the one hand, there is the ever-present temptation, for the researcher, to present his data, and his conclusions, as being more "scientific" than they really are. Using formulae and statistical arguments for their own sake, and using sociological or psychological jargon, are examples. Using prestigious references to support one's opinion is another. These are appeals to the presumed authority of "science," which has its source in a public belief. That belief is itself in no way "scientific."

The researcher or journalist may, out of his own hubris, come to believe that his tenuous and equivocal findings are indeed "true." He may then feel compelled to persuade others to his conclusions. So he waxes even more "scientific"-sounding, becomes himself an authority figure and, with the help of a gullible public and a handful of disciples, sets out to right the world.

It is not that science itself does not sometimes operate in this way.[1]* But it is not often that science uses a public arena to settle its disputes. Social and behavioral "scientists" often do; journalists almost always do. And when they do, both they and the public are misled.

The social and behavioral "sciences," at least in most of the Western world, have based themselves upon a highly-romanticized and much-outdated image of how science works. Science proceeds by questioning "the truth." The social and behavioral "sciences" attempt to proceed by *proving* "the truth." The difference is the difference between science and scientism. The latter is guided by the belief that the power of scientific inquiry is to be had in its trappings and accessories and not, as Einstein said, in a disciplined imagination.

As a result, those social and behavioral researchers who make pronouncements on mass communication in the modern world are likely to presume considerably more certainty for their findings than their procedures or their facts would justify. The bulk of the research on the "effects" of violence on television is a case in point. Being at all certain that television is the "cause" of any subsequent "violent" behavior would require, among others, a clear demonstration that such behavior could *in no case be attributed to any other cause.* So far, this has not been unequivocally demonstrated in *any* case.

One difficulty is the misguided assumption that specific human behaviors have specific "causes," and that these "causes" precede their "effects," thus laying claim to them. While such "cause-and-effect" relationships can be demonstrated in a laboratory, things are not so simple in the "real" world. Except for certain special applications, physicists have long ago

* References and notes throughout this book are collected in a section at the end of each chapter.

abandoned such simplistic and naive views of causation where complex phenomena are concerned.[2] Are the phenomena involved in the uses of the mass media by "producers" and "consumers" any less complex than what the physicist seeks to explain?

It may be easier for the rest of us to "understand" something complex if someone explains it to us in very simple cause-and-effect terms. But is that sufficient justification for doing so, when it is usually obvious that such explanations grossly distort the facts, and thereby mislead us into thinking we understand something when we don't? Does the politician "cause" the public to see him as they do; or do they "cause" him to present himself in the way he does? Does advertising "cause" people to be the way they are; or does the way people are "cause" advertising to be the way it is? Popular songs come and go. Only a few really "succeed." Do the ones that "succeed" do so because they "cause" us to like them? Or are they the way they are "because" we like them that way? Just to ask the question in this way is to reveal that the answers are not as simple or as directional as we would want to believe.

So we have good reason for being skeptical of much that has been written and said about the "mass media" in recent years — especially when the appeal is to some aspect of our faith in "science."

Our (cultural) penchant for the dramatic

Culturally, Americans have little interest in the complexities of life or of social issues — unless they can be explained simply. And we are most likely to have that warm glow of "understanding" if what others say to us is put in dramatic form — that is, in the form of a "story." Yet we do not understand all kinds of "stories" equally well. We seem to prefer those in which the "good" guys are clearly pitted against the "bad" guys — or "us" against forces that would do us in. So it is not coincidental that the most popular books about the mass media are those which cast the media — particularly television — as the "villain." It is simply easier for us to understand that "they" are out to do us in, and that we have to pull together to protect ourselves from "them," even though the facts are that we "consumers" are as guilty as "they" are of whatever it is that is supposed to be doing us in.

In thus attempting to muster the forces of "good" (everyone who agrees with the author) against the forces of "evil" (everyone who doesn't see it what way), such writers may, ironically, be accused of doing much the same thing that they accuse "the media" of doing: exploiting audience susceptibilities. Is it even possible that a book entitled *Media Sexploitation* is not itself exploitative?

The matter does not begin and end there, of course. Americans typically operate from an archetypal "plot": If something is "bad," it is because someone or something is out to get us; if something is "good," it is something we have brought about by ourselves. Our whole social fabric is infused with this philosophy. So it makes very good sense to us when applied to "the media."

This is the reason why, undoubtedly, "the news" in America is usually presented in highly oversimplified, dramatic form. Since we would find it difficult, if not impossible, to understand the whole range of economic and social forces involved in poverty, we identify the "villain" and "wage war" on poverty. It is no accident that Americans much prefer "story" programs over documentaries. Nor is it any accident that commercial advertising on television is presented in dramatic form: as in fiction, there must always be some "tension," some person with whom we can identify faced with difficulty or a crisis. Dirt? It's "Mr. Clean" to the rescue of the hapless but dedicated housewife. So you want to be as sexy as a glamorous international movie star? It's easy; all you have to do is use the perfume she uses.

But note that the critics of the media may have to use the same form if they want to win public approval of their criticisms. Do you feel guilty because you allow your child to watch "too much" television? Let's get together and do "battle" with the "enemy" — those who would ruin our children's minds. Most of the critics of the media know that the situation is not that simple. But they also know that they are not going to get their message across unless they keep it simple and in this dramatic form. How is what they do different from what they accuse "the media" of doing?

And isn't there something suggestive about the fact that it is often those who claim not to watch television at all who campaign most actively against its evils? Those who would save us from "pornography" appeal to our sense of propriety: if such "evil" is allowed to circulate, people will be demoralized; sex crimes will become commonplace. There is no evidence for this. There is even some evidence for the contrary, in the same way that there is evidence that viewing violence on television actually reduces violent behavior.[3] Even so, the appeal of the "villainy" perpetrated on us by "the media" is so compelling that we Americans have a generally negative attitude toward them, especially toward television. Even those who watch television most, and enjoy it most, are likely to say that television is "bad" for people. The facts will not support such widespread negativism. We have to attribute at least part of it to our susceptibility to the kind of story in which we are being victimized by conspiratorial forces, and by which we are thereby victimized.

II

Future historians of the twentieth century will have a difficult time deciding which was the more remarkable — the phenomena of the mass media, or the passionate causes that were mounted against them. Perhaps we forget our own history. The same kinds of campaigns were once waged against books that are now being waged against television. How readily we seem to forget, or overlook, the fact that the early critics of radio saw the same demoralizing, dehumanizing consequences of radio as are now being prophesized for television — over-exposure, sapping the brain, commercial exploitation, brainwashing, deteriorating literacy, weakened morals, and so on.

The very fervor with which such critical campaigns have been mounted against each new "mass" medium as it has emerged and become popular suggests there may be a deeper motive. We seem to have some special fear or anxiety about *mass* communication media that makes us an easy mark for the doomsaying critic. Why *are* we Americans so willing to be suspicious of "the media"? Is it merely a matter of a cultural elite being offended by their "popularity"?

Apprehensiveness about the "power" of communication

As a people, Americans would seem to have more interest in the back side of the moon than in the process by which we all become human, and in which we pattern our future. I am speaking, of course, of the process of communication itself, Perhaps because it is something that most of us engage in "naturally," we have a curious disinterest in communication — the most vital process of all. We seem to be afraid of "knowing" too much about communication, an apprehensiveness that must surely enter into every consideration of the ethical and moral issues in mass communication.

Perhaps our fear is "archetypal" — some predisposition inherited from our primitive ancestors. What records and interpretations we have of the earliest human cultures [4] would seem to suggest that people everywhere have always been (more or less) apprehensive of the "power" of language and of communication, and even fearful of exposure to any radical changes in means or modes of communication. Given that "communication metabolism" is to the life of the mind what energy metabolism is to the life of the body, there is considerable intuitive wisdom in such apprehensiveness.

It is not irrelevant that the first taboos were verbal taboos — having to do with the sensed "magic" of communication and the evils that would befall one and his people from the misuse of words. It was considered a violation of the social structure — itself sacred — for one to hear what one should not hear, or for one to say what one should not say. Nor is it mere coincidence that the words "speak" and "sperm" share the same root meanings — such as "to sprout" and "to scatter." A society is ordered — in order — only to the extent that its "sproutings" and its "scatterings" are controlled by social sanctions such as taboos. Sexual and verbal taboos seem interrelated, in this respect. Even in our own society, it was long considered sinful for a person "to lie" with any other than the one officially sanctioned by society. Now, it seems, our relaxed attitudes with respect to "lying" about have their parallel in our increased freedom to "lie" about one thing or another.

A human society is in basis — underlying all of its manifest characteristics — a complex set of rules governing who can say what to whom about what, when, in what manner, where, with what expectations, etc. There is a very real sense, then, in which *traditional* societies have a structure which derives from moral concerns. This is much less so for nontraditional or "modern" societies. It is only in our most "modern" societies, where there is increasing social and verbal (*viz.,* "symbolic") permissiveness, that the notion of "situational ethics" could arise.

The peoples of less "modern" societies are openly afraid of cameras and tape recorders and transistor radios. In our "sophistication," we have lost much of our intuitive fear of gadgets that amplify and store and display human communication. Even so, radical changes in the *means* of human communication always lead to changes in social patterns and social structures. It seems likely that there are still vestiges of that "primitive" fear in historical reactions to the emergence and spread of the media of mass communication.

When we reflect upon our modern "media," it is instructive to recall that many of the Greek thinkers expressed considerable concern that the spread of *literacy* would demoralize the people and bring down the whole civilization. Perhaps they were right. Writing was early considered to be a "magical" or a "sacred" act, and could be entrusted only to the shaman or the priest or, occasionally, the emperor. In a modern, literate, permissive society, we want to believe that people may write what they want to write, say what they want to say. And yet, we wonder: may this not "depend" upon the size of the audience? Isn't there something awesome about an audience of 30 million persons? Can we even comprehend an audience of that size?

Is there any more evidence that television is "bad" for us than that literacy or the book have been "bad" for us? If there have been "effects," those effects are *evolutionary,* and not immediate. Major changes in the form or the means of communication may have altered the course of history or, since they alter the forms and the reach of our consciousness as a species, may influence our human future in ways we can only guess at.[5] Thus, to know that television is "bad" for us in some immediate, psychological or sociological sense would require that the critic *know* what, in fact, our evolutionary future is *supposed* to be. A physical scientist does not approach the world as if he knew the way it is supposed to be arranged. The social "scientist" often does. *Are* the media "bad" for us in some way? Just to put the question in that form is to ask not a "scientific" but a moral question. Yet we seemingly can not, in our "scientized," secular, indulgent society, even admit to that. Is it possible that we simply fear those unknown, unknowable alterations in our consciousness and in our human trajectory into the future, and attempt to cloak our irrational attacks under the guise of doing "science"? In doing so, are we — all of us who comment upon the present state of mass communication in our society — assuming the appropriate moral burden ourselves?

Our denial of choice

What would we need to know — in order to be certain about matters of ethics and morality in mass communication systems in the modern world? Since we are faced with the prospect of solving our problems with the same mentality with which we created them, what can we know about the way we are in our culture that might bear upon our inquiry?

Here we will consider but one more aspect of American culture that bears heavily upon our present concerns. It is as subtle as it is pervasive.

Undoubtedly in part because the scientific view of the world is now our dominant cultural view of the world,[6] there has been over the course of time a slow shift from the assumption that wrongdoing is a matter of human choice (or at least culpability), to the assumption that wrongs and social ills are "caused" by external or internal forces over which people individually — and often collectively — have little or no control.[7] Substandard living conditions are seen to "cause" crime; our "age of anxiety" is seen to be the "cause" of all sorts of mental and social aberrations; "capitalism" is the "cause" of most of the world's problems; clever advertisers "cause" us to buy things we don't need; poor "teaching" "causes" students not to learn; and so on and on.

We used to blame people for their "sins" — both for their wrongdoing and for the human or social consequences of their wrongdoing. Now we blame some abstraction or other — e.g., "society." Is it that we have lost our grasp on what would constitute wrongdoing? Or is it that we are, indeed, making "progress"? And, if we are emancipating ourselves from the yoke of an archaic morality, why is it that we don't feel good about our new-found freedom from it? What do we have that might take its place, since science is by definition *amoral*?

We are so caught up in this new worldview that it almost makes sense to us when someone says that the "media" are "unethical" or "immoral." After all, if disease is "caused" by an impersonal pathogen of some sort, why do we not seek the "cause" of our social ills in some sort of impersonal social pathogen? We persist in this way of thinking, even though we know that the so-called civilizational diseases — cancer, hypertension, ulcers, etc. — have a very complex etiology, and one which involves a great many life choices that the individual has made over time. But our faith is apparently stronger than the facts. We see this predisposition to hold people blameless, and to blame some abstraction, all about us in American society: in our courts, in education, in public services, even in our "conscious-raising" industries. And we see this predisposition at work in research on, and critical evaluations of, the "mass media," where it is assumed that people are not choosing, for example, to sit before the television set as much as they do, but are being "caused" to do so by forces over which they have no control.

This is not to say, however, that there are not specific pathogens of certain diseases, or that one's background does not have any bearing on his criminal behavior, or that students may not really be disadvantaged, or that people can not fail out of circumstances beyond their control, or that people may not, in fact, spend time with television for reasons they may not be aware of, or be capable of overcoming. All of these possibilities exist, and occur.

The point, here, is not whether such things occur or not. It is a matter of the general attitude with which we approach — and attempt to solve — such "social" problems. The point is that those who assume that people are not to be held responsible for their condition and their behavior co-opt that responsibility. Whatever their motives, they have now insinuated themselves into responsibility for others, and must now try to manage their lives in some way. The one who assumes certain others are not responsible for their own condition and behavior now subjects them to *his* values and beliefs about the way things "ought" to be, and thus victimizes them. How do we *know* that some people are not to be less teachable than others? Or simply have other tastes?

Given the worldview by which we arrive at this paradoxical situation, it seems inevitable that the only way to save people from victimization by others is to victimize them ourselves. But what this reveals is a flaw in that worldview, not in either the victim or the victimizer. And to whom or what do we then lay accountability? The difficulty here is that the assumption is self-fulfilling. If we design our social institutions and our laws on the assumption that "consumers," at least, are not responsible either for how they "spend" their time or how they spend their money, and must therefore be "protected," then it will become increasingly impossible for people to behave responsibly. We've already had some previews of things to come. If someone commits a crime, what does it portend that that person can sue the television station for airing the program from which he or she "got the idea" for the criminal act?

Let us be clear: The point is not that the "producers" of mass media fare should be free to be as irresponsible as they could be. They should, indeed, be responsible for what they do and do not do. But can they be responsible for any one individual of that "mass"? There was a great deal more casual violence in the Europe of our ancestors. They had no television; few could even read. How were people turned on to violence before television?

The assumption of non-responsibility which is brought to the situation by social "science" researchers and media critics is more dehumanizing than is commercialism as such. The media exploit our hopes and dreams, or our tastes. The insinuation of non-responsibility denies us the freedom to exercise them. Those who would "save" us from the evils of the media are undoubtedly well-intentioned. But are intentions enough? Undoubtedly those who write for and act in television commercials are equally well-intentioned. And so is the manufacturer and so is the advertising agency. But are intentions enough?

The question, of course, is simple: Whose choice shall prevail? Who is responsible for a "persuasive" advertisement: its creator? The advertising company that produced it? The technicians who maintain the equipment? The actors who acted in it? The television station that broadcast it? The FCC? Society? Or the one who is "persuaded"?

If it is not a "sin" to be gluttonous, can it be a "sin" to cater to gluttons? If it is not a "sin" to be slothful, can it be a "sin" to encourage sloth? If it is not a "sin" to be envious, can it be a "sin" to play upon our envy of what our neighbors have? If, on the other hand, it were illegal or unethical to play upon our enviousness in "the media," would we thereby not be envious of what our neighbors have?

So who is responsible? And for what? What we are faced with, like it or not, is the fact that morality cannot be legislated. No amount of legislation would make it impossible for a given "consumer" of mass media fare to put that fare to immoral or unethical use, or to be deceived or manipulated by it as one's tastes and preferences predispose. Even Jesus and Martin Luther King, Jr. were misused. How "good" would a source have to be to prohibit misuse of a message by a person or a public?

It is, ultimately, the "consumers" who determine whether a system of mass communication is moral or not. In denying the "consumer's" choice and thus responsibility, we make the problem of media morality insoluble. If we shift responsibility to the politician or the bureaucrat, we still have to ask, do we not: And what is his or her motive? Montaigne said, "God save us from those who would save us." But where there is no longer a God but only government functionaries to "save" us, have we eliminated the problem of immorality or unethical behavior? Or merely compounded it? "The more the law protects against fraud," one observer pointed out, "the more people think the law protects against fraud . . . There is probably more deceptive advertising when laws on fraud exist than when they do not."[8]

It is thus that our cultural tendency to deny choice and responsibility in consumer behavior soon turns against us. But, the counter-argument goes, it makes sense to presume choice (and therefore responsibility) only where that choice is "informed" — that is, only in those situations where the consumer has sufficient and clear enough information to make an "intelligent" choice. If every brand of aspirin is the "best" and the "strongest," how is the "average" consumer to make an "informed" choice? Quite so. But is the consumer's competence to make choices, even in the face of a torrent of claims about this or that product, enhanced if someone else makes the choice for her? And aren't we then right back at the question of whose choice will prevail?

The dilemma is a dilemma of our evolving culture. Can people have a "right" to freedom of choice in all such matters, but delegate the "responsibility" to some other agency? And are not many questions of ethics and morality in mass communication confounded by that dilemma? And does that dilemma not remain to haunt us no matter how clear a situation might otherwise seem to us? And we should notice, too, the following: On the part of those who assume responsibility for us, the reason is that we "people" are willy-nilly influenced by forces over which we have no control, may not even be aware of. But if those who declare that "people" are so readily manipulated are themselves (apparently) immune, why don't they simply immunize us?

III

Our mass communication systems are an integral part of the larger cultural system we know as "American" civilization. They are both influenced by and influence the continuing evolution of that civilization. Moreover, we know that larger social systems have irreversible inertial forces of their own: manufacturers of "mass"-produced products cannot *not* advertise, in the same way that Iowa farmers cannot *not* fertilize. Not, that is, unless they wished to fail. To do away with advertising altogether would have somewhat the same consequences as would doing away with fertilizing altogether: a great many of us would starve.

Nor are our mass communication systems in any way independent of such socio-economic intricacies of our way of life. Such considerations may seem to take us afield. But they are at the heart of every question of ethics and morality in the media.

For example, we could hardly be unimpressed by the sheer speed and spread of the technologies involved in the "mass media." Some would even have these as the "villain" in the story.[9] But "technology" is not in itself problematic. There is evidence, for example, that other cultures — such as the Mayan — had the wheel and other pivotal technologies, but did not exploit them as we have. Thus whatever transportation and pollution problems we may have in the West are not attributable solely to the technologies involved, but to the unique *interaction* of certain technological possibilities *with* certain cultural proclivities or predispositions. Our mass communication systems would not be the way they are, in short, if people were not the way they are in our culture.

One can find even in Plato's speculations about social and economic arrangements the prediction that ours would be the consumption-oriented, commercialistic, materialistic society it is; and advertising and television were no part of his argument. New techniques (as of advertising) may intensify certain predispositions in people. But they do not in themselves create those predispositions. Those are cultural. They are therefore not subject to direct manipulation. But they are therefore subject to exploitation.

A beautiful model can seemingly "sell" almost any "glamorous" consumer product. But Americans believe the story of the "ugly duckling": we *know* that an ugly duckling can grow up to be a beautiful swan — *If. . . .* And that's where the beautiful model and her pitch come in. We cling to the myth of the "power" of "the media" to manipulate people. And yet, when cigarette advertising was banned, there was no appreciable long-term effect on the sale of tobacco products. The Hershey Company enjoyed the lion's share of the chocolate confections market long before they did any national advertising at all. There are now instances of politicians being elected to office by *avoiding* the media. And approximately eight out of ten new products fail, regardless of the level of promotion. In all such matters, our cultural "myths" about "the media" get in the way of our understanding them.

Nor are the ethical and moral problems of "the media" unique to them. Until fairly recently, most Americans seemed to believe that exposure to "education" can make the less "intelligent" person just as "intelligent" as the more "intelligent" person. But the facts are that the gap does not narrow with "education"; it widens. What is the ethical course here? Should those who have a vested interest in the educational establishment continue to speak of "education" in such a way that those who are interested might infer that "education" lessens the gap between the more "intelligent" and the less "intelligent"? Or would it be even less ethical to disillusion the hopefuls, since there are indeed exceptions to the rule?

Or consider the medical establishment. Physicians know (a) that most of the complaints they treat refer to conditions that would get better by themselves; and (b) that most people in American society believe that it is the doctor and modern "medicine" that makes them well. Is the physician who capitalizes on these two facts being ethical? Or should she attempt to disillusion her patients? Could she?

The ethical and moral issues involved in mass communication systems in our civilization are not unique. They bear a family resemblance to every other kind of ethical and moral issue in our culture, because they have the one source in common: the culture itself. It is the *interaction* between certain technological possibilities and certain cultural predispositions that give rise to those ethical and moral issues, wherever they arise. The myriad problems that claim our attention today cannot be attributed to the "technics" media "producers" use, nor to the cultural predispositions of their "consumers," but only to the peculiar interaction of the one with the other.

IV

One of our cultural predispositions is the urge to modernity. We want to be "modern." But to be "modern" means to disdain the "traditional." How has this predisposition affected the kinds of moral and ethical problems that arise?

In a traditional culture, the test of whether or not a given act is moral or ethical required referring that act to a *principle* or an *ideal* which is itself independent of the persons involved. One could determine whether one was doing the right thing or not by referring to an ideal state, or to a set of prescriptions for attaining that ideal state. One knew that one should not steal because there was a commandment against it.

In a traditional culture, people do not themselves invent those principles of conduct. They are given from the past — from God, from the wisdom of the Ancestors, from the Source. Such principles of conduct serve two key functions: (1) they restrain people from getting involved in situations for which they have no traditional guides to conduct; and (2) they provide guides to conduct for all the situations a member of that culture is likely to encounter.

To be "modern" means moving out into those spaces — geographical, social, psychological — which are "forbidden" in a traditional culture. The "modern," therefore, is one who frequently finds himself or herself in a situation for there are no ready principles. To be "modern" implies a willingness to make up those principles as we go along. In "liberating" ourselves from traditional restraints on what to do or how to be, we have cast ourselves adrift from the certainties and securities of the traditional culture. We do not know what we *should* be doing. I may be "OK" because you say so, and you may be "OK" because I say so, but there is something vaguely unsatisfactory about the *ad hoc* nature of this kind of morality. "I'm OK. You're OK." But *compared to what?*

One characteristic of the "modern" mind is the belief that everything that happens is unprecedented. It is true that most of the now very sophisticated skills and technics required to create, develop, produce, and broadcast a television show (or commercial) have been developed and refined within the past two or three decades. But not out of whole cloth. Do the technics change the function? Who produced the great spectacles of the Roman amphitheaters? And were the very sophisticated technics required unrelated to the same functions today?

We also like to think of the television viewer's situation as "unique." But is it, in function? Gathering to listen to "persuasive" speeches is ancient. Is the role of the consumer of television fare unprecedented?

It seems more likely that we *define* these situations in such a way as to make them seem unprecedented, so that we can appear to be "modern." And thus our problems of ethical and moral behavior are made to seem "new," without instructive precedent. But are they all that "new"? Are lying or deception or persuasion or credulousness inventions of the twentieth century? Or sloth or envy or avarice?

Is it not possible — even probable — that we exaggerate the "uniqueness" of our contemporary situation in order to further obviate the relevance of traditional moralities and ethical principles? We can make "sin" seem irrelevant to the present situation by defining that situation as being "modern" or even "postmodern." We are not "sinners" because we do not "sin," but because we are "modern."

It is true that more of us have more "leisure" time to "spend" than would seem to be the case with any other people in Western history. But ours is not the only way of life. In some cultures, what we would call "leisure" is what people have mostly at their disposal. By definition, our "leisure" is time left over from work. And we know that our "work ethic" is unique. Thus our "leisure" is the opposite of "work," an opposition that is inconceivable to other, less "modern," peoples of the world.

What is the proper way to "spend" that increasing "leisure"? The Greek thinkers believed that leisure time should be used for learning and self-improvement — i.e., for becoming "thinkers." The early church leaders thought that leisure time should be spent in spiritual reflection and activities. Modern aestheticians believe that leisure should be devoted more to the pursuit of aesthetic sensibilities. But most of us don't want to "work" at our "leisure." Since it is something we "deserve," we want to "spend" it indulging ourselves. Perfecting oneself is "work." Indulging oneself can be done with ease. Being told by others what to do, or being compelled by our own consciences to do, what we do at work is "communication pain," as Stephenson put it. Consuming television because we don't "have to" do so is "communication pleasure." [10]

Will all of those prophesized ills befall us if we watch television instead of visiting an art museum? Will we be brainwashed into even higher levels of consumerism? Will our minds begin to resemble the "pap" that we consume there? Will media "literacy" displace every other form of "literacy"?

Surely it is in part because of our unique conceptions of "work" and of "leisure" that Americans in large numbers seem to prefer "entertainment" to "education" from the mass media. But when was this not the case in our civilization? "Learning" and "education" are "work"; therefore, by definition, to avoid learning is play or pleasure. The first books to have a "mass" market were "entertainment," as were the first magazines and the first radio stations. So was the first theater that had a "mass" market. The clarity with which we equate leisure with "entertainment" is so potent that even "the news" must be made entertaining in order to capture and hold our attention. Is our preference for "entertainment" rather than "education" via the media an immoral one? Or is serving that preference the only immorality? And if certain interest groups bring about legislation or censorship of what we seem to prefer in our books and on our television screens, is *that* act moral? Or is it merely ideological?

Again, when we ask the question, "Whose preferences are to prevail?" in our culture, we come to another paradox. If we look at the implications of one kind of argument that is often made, what seems to be the case is that there is a "high" culture and a "popular" culture,[11] and that "high" culture is somehow superior to "popular" culture and should therefore displace "popular" culture wherever and whenever possible. But if the one defines the other, then something can be "high" culture only if it is *not* "popular," and something is "popular" not only because large numbers of people are "into" it, but also because it is *not* "high" culture. And what does this mean for the behavior of the respective "consumers"? People value and consume that which identifies them as belonging to one group or the other. Thus those who want to be seen as having membership in "high" culture will not only exhibit a preference for what is valued by that "high" culture, but by exhibiting or expressing a distaste for that which is "popular." And vice versa: Those who see themselves as a part of "popular" culture will not only exhibit a preference for what is valued and preferred by that culture, but by exhibiting or expressing a distaste for that which is considered "high" culture.

Turning away from a "documentary" or a "serious" television program, like avoiding "intellectual" books or magazines, is not therefore primarily a vote against the program or the book. It is primarily a sign that one belongs to the "silent majority" of "popular" culture. It is a sign, a message to one's fellows, that one is with them, and is not a "highbrow." The criterion is not the "quality" of the media fare as such. It is the preference that one has to exhibit in order to become or maintain oneself as a "member" of the one "taste public" or the other.

And the "popular" writer who is acclaimed at some point by "high" culture critics will be dropped by the "popular" culture, in the same way that a "high" culture celebrity who becomes "popular" will be dropped by the "high" culture. And what evolves from this paradox? If the "high" culture spokesmen were correct, that the availability of "superior" media fare would eventually drive out the "inferior," then "public" broadcasting would already have the largest audiences. On the other hand, if, in a "democratic," commercial society, the "bad" drives out the "good," what then?

What is preferred in "high" culture is no less a matter of *fashion* than what is preferred in "popular" culture. The one culture is as "modern" as the other, and is therefore controlled by fashion. And fashion is no less a master than tradition. It is just more changeable, arbitrary, *ad hoc*.

Fashion as a primary means of social control within "taste publics" is a phenomenon of our peculiar kind of democracy — of our egalitarianism. Is what "people" dictate to be right and proper via changing fashions inherently more or less "moral" than the individual himself? If not, and given that neither individual "producers" nor individual "consumers" of mass media fare have any direct control over what is fashionable, who then *is* responsible for resolving the apparent moral and ethical problems that arise?

V

For people, there are always two levels of "reality." There is the level of "what-is-going-on" — all of those physical and human and social phenomena which constitute the context in which we have our existence. Then there is the level of "what-it-means-to-humans" — all of the ways in which we assign meaning or significance or utility to our perceptions of "what-is-going-on." It is in the nature of our being human that we cannot consciously have direct contact with "what-is-going-on." We must give it a name, or otherwise conceptualize it, before we can have contact with "what-is-going-on." What this means is that what we have in our heads is not a copy of "what-is-going-on" in the world, but a set of possible interpretations of all that according to what it means to you and me.

How people interpret "what is going on" — that is, translate it into what it is supposed to mean to humans — depends, in a traditional culture, upon sacred or revered principles. In a "modern" culture, it depends upon you and me, upon what we want to or what is expedient for us to make of it.

But not every possibility obtains for us. The language we speak both enables and constrains our interpretations. Beyond that, how we interpret "what-is-going-on" depends upon "what-it-means to" all of the other humans upon which our psychological existence and continuity depend. People who interpret "what-is-going-on" in the same ways, and who value the same ways of seeing and knowing the world, constitute what is called an "epistemic community." What "what-is-going-on" means to humans depends upon which epistemic communities they "belong" to. A "liberal" sees certain things differently than does a "conservative," not because they are looking at two different worlds, but because where they are "coming from" — their epistemic communities — are different in certain significant respects.

Now all of this is largely forgotten when we come to consider the media and their "messages." It is a commonplace, for example, that our "mass" media are "one-way." By this, we mean that "messages" are broadcast or otherwise transported (like a film in its "can") to the place where we "consume" them, but that there is no regular communication channel between us "consumers" and those who have had some part in the complicated business of producing those "messages" or entertainments. We could crudely diagram that situation thus:

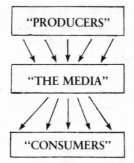

Fig. 1. Our "one-way" media.

The direction of flow is "one-way." But this is merely a data-transmission system. A *communication* system, by contrast, always "resolves" — that is, always involves two-way communication between or among people. Thus, the mass *communication* system involved would minimally consist of the following:

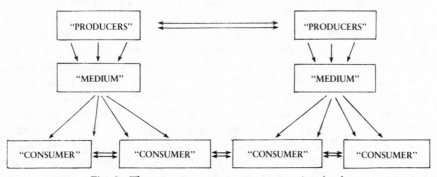

Fig. 2. The mass *communication* system involved.

What should be perfectly obvious to us, but which we seem to be unable to see, is that

a. The very uses to which a technique or technology will be put is neither "caused" nor determined by that technique or technology. How we will use "the media" is a matter of social norms and values; people alone determine what will be the appropriate use of a medium of communication. As we have already seen, some of the same pivotal technologies upon which Western industrial civilization has been built existed for other cultures, but were simply not exploited — not "used" — in the same ways we have normatively come to "use" those technologies in our own culture. This is no less true for the technologies that bring us records or television.

b. Secondly, no human artifact — such as a "message" or a song or a story — has intrinsic meaning or value. Whatever meaning they may have is the meaning attributed to them by those who would speak of them, or otherwise "use" or consume them. Which is to say, unequivocally, that whatever interest people have in a television program, and whatever meaning or value or import that program has for them, have their source not in that program, but *in* the communication of the people who want to share that experience in some way. What people will attend to, what they will prefer, how they will value those experiences, and what they will do with them — all of these are *social* realities (or norms), created and maintained by people *in* communication with one another — directly or indirectly, overtly or tacitly.

We can see as well, in Figure 2, that the *communication* system at the "producers" end resolves itself in all of those direct and indirect communication channels which connect the "producers" with one another. What this means is simply that the norms which guide the decisions and the conduct of the "producers" emerge mainly in *their* communication, in the same way that the norms which guide the choices and preferences and values of the "consumers" are products mainly of *their* intercommunication.

If we enlarge the schematic somewhat, as in Figure 3, we can see that the same is true generally for all of the components of the mass communication systems of which "the media" are but one technological link. The hatched lines represent communicative interactions for mainly *business* purposes. The solid lines represent communicative interactions for purposes of establishing and maintaining the *social* realities of those "epistemic communities" or groups. The dotted line represents the only formal channel of "feedback" in the system — that which serves the purposes of the "producers" as far as their business interests are concerned; its use is almost exclusively to tell them how they are "doing" in the market.

This scheme is admittedly crude and incomplete. It does not, for example, include such external regulative agencies as the Federal Communications Commission, or such internal agencies as the Radio and Tele-

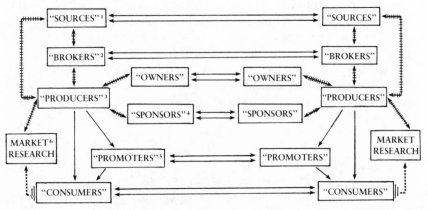

Fig. 3. The several communication systems involved in mass "communication."

[1] Artists, writers, politicians and other "newsmakers," etc.
[2] Agents and other "middle-men."
[3] All of those who are involved in the "production" of media fare under control of the "producer" — reporters, directors, cameramen, editors, graphics experts, etc.
[4] Those who buy time or space in "the media" to promote their wares. For simplicity, we include here the advertising agencies that create and produce the ads that we eventually see and hear.
[5] All of those who "broker" media fare in some way: including critics, teachers, publicity people, etc.
[6] Included here, again for simplicity, are all of those who provide rating services, public opinion and market research, etc., for the "producers."

vision News Directors Association. Every group has its own union and/or professional association except, of course, the "consumers." But they "compare notes" on products and programs and newspaper stories, and this amounts to much the same thing, although only informally.

But it is sufficient for our purpose here. And that is to make clear that whatever the ethical or moral issues that may arise, they do not have their source nor can they be "fixed" *in* the media themselves, or *in* their fare. They have their source exclusively in the communication systems within which the various *people* components of the larger system create and maintain their social realities. For ethics and morality are matters of value and of preference — of right and wrong. Whether novelists are "moral" or not depends upon the values of the "epistemic community" or the "reference group" to which they refer the appropriateness of their work; and this group is not the "consumers," not even the critics. This group is ultimately all of the other novelists and artists with whom the one will speak of his work, and pass judgment on the work of others. Morality, like ethics, cannot be legislated. Moral or ethical sanctions are normative, not legal. Consumer preferences and consumer behavior are guided and sanctioned by other consumers. There is no way to make "the media" moral or ethical. Mass communication systems will be no more, no less, moral and ethical than the "epistemic communities" of which they are comprised. As a group, are magazine consumers ethical? Moral? If not, can they be made so by constraints on the magazines and their advertisers? The answer, of course, is no — a fact which confounds our best intentions. But it is a fact which cannot reasonably be overlooked.

VI

Having made clear that the meaning, the value, and the appropriate uses to which media fare may be put are matters of social norms created and maintained in communication *within* "epistemic communities" — such as an audience or a "taste public," we have still to acknowledge that there are "forces" in all such social systems which are not under the control of, or controllable by, those persons or any others. In a complex society such as our own, there are social "forces" which are neither directly created nor directly controlled by any group or person or "epistemic community." They emerge from the complex structure of our society itself, and have their own *inertia*.

For example, anyone who makes his living or has his identity in a particular social system will have a vested interest in that social system. Even those who are the most passionate critics of contemporary television, for example, have a vested interest in its continuing along the path it is on; otherwise, they lose the vital meaning this has for their own lives. The ancients knew this: that the more vociferous the attack on the *status quo,* the more entrenched the status quo would become. Its operations may simply become more covert, more discreet.

We have seen how this paradox may function with respect to advertising. The more laws there are, the more deceptive advertising there is likely to be. It simply becomes cleverer, less obvious. The "Watergate Affair" did not drive the surreptitious gathering of political "intelligence" from the scene. The same activities, which were carried on prior to that incident,[12] are still being carried on. They are simply carried out more discreetly, with much less likelihood of being detected.

There is a certain inexorableness about social systems once set in motion. Influential lobbying groups may achieve some legislation that brings about changes on the face of things — e.g., the group known as Action for Children's Television. But underneath, everything remains much the same. This is so because in social systems we are *interdependent;* "consumers" have as much of a vested interest in the way television is programmed as do the "producers." Things don't change much because if a radical change were made somewhere else in the system, the rest of us would have to make a radical accommodation. And even minor changes are anathema to most of us.

Then there are the "laws of large numbers." Decisions about television programs and about the content of *Reader's Digest* are made on the basis of the interest of the largest number of viewers and readers. One may achieve "two-way" or "interactive" television via cable. But each channel will, necessarily, be responsive only to the largest number of its public. No one "consumer" is going to be that influential as to change such decisions, no matter how "interactive" the system may be technologically. The fact that most television viewers and record buyers by far are "satisfied" with what they get seals the consequence: they will get more of what they are getting, and more of the same. Democracy in any of our social domains is not without its difficulties.

What does seem likely for the future is that television will become more diverse, more specialized, more pluralistic — in order to serve increasingly diverse, specialized, and pluralistic "taste publics" and audiences. This has been the fate of all of the "mass" media to date. There have been steadily fewer and fewer "mass"-audience magazines, for example, and steadily more and more magazines for special-interest audiences. This has been the case with books, as well, and with radio. There is no reason to believe it will not be so for television and the cinema. There is already evidence, in fact, that this is precisely what is happening to both.

Will these changes clarify or confound the issues we are concerned with here — i.e., the moral and ethical issues involved? In one sense, they may mitigate those issues. At least they may seem to do so, for we are typically concerned about "the media" only to the extent that they reach a "mass" or a prurient audience — i.e., "those" others who are either not intelligent enough or tasteful enough to avoid being victimized by low-quality fare. But has anyone ever seen an attack on the "immorality" of golfing magazines or books? We seem to be concerned only when what is consumed seems to be purely "entertainment," having no obvious utility. Can this be in part our "Protestant ethic" asserting itself in some other guise? Is it possible that only that media fare which has some utility can receive the stamp of approval of our intellectuals and protectionists? Why a documentary about "abortion" is more acceptable than a treatment of the same subject in "All in the Family" tells us more about our culture than it does about the nature of morality, does it not? When there is a television cassette "club" for every taste, our apprehension about the "mass" part of the mass media may be put at ease. But we will still have to be on guard against those consumers who may have socially-unacceptable interests, will we not?

There is another "force" at work which is, as a matter of practicality, beyond anyone's control. Ellul is one of those who attributes to technology (*la technique*) its own motive force. One aspect of his argument is that,

given the peculiar nature of Western civilization, whatever is technologically possible is sufficient justification for its existence. Whether this is the
case or not, there is clearly an increasing "mismatch" between the sheer
capacity of our media — our knowledge and our entertainment industries — and our human capacities for their output. Communication media
and techniques in a traditional society will not be developed in capacity or
in reach beyond what is socially *necessary*. It is only in "modern" societies
that communication technologies are developed in capacity or in reach
limited only by *possibility* and/or economic feasibility and/or political ex-
igency, etc. Without our modern media of communication, we would be
both time- and space-bound psychologically and emotionally — as are the
peoples of traditional and "primitive" cultures. With them, we can transcend both time and space. We can read a book written by someone who
lived in another era, even another civilization. We can "see" the other side
of the moon. We can store more "knowledge" on a small wafer than one
person could digest in years of study, and we can transmit more information per second than any human could possibly "consume."

It is remarkable, indeed, that our ability to acquire and store and
deliver "information" to people expanded in almost inverse proportion to
our need for it. We say we have a "need" for it, but do we? Do we have a
"need" to know what is going on everywhere in the world, immediately?
If that were an aspect of "human nature," people of traditional and
"primitive" cultures would also exhibit it. They do not. Our "needs" are
mainly fashionable; they are not vital. It is merely fashionable to want to
know so much that we have no personal use for.

The power and the capacity of our media of communication have
been increased manyfold. But has there been a comparable increase in our
human capacities for information, for ideas, for images, for "entertainment"? It is said that 1500 advertising messages alone are put to our
senses every day. Can a human "process" that much information "intelligently"? And, if not, isn't it possible that whatever the moral issue involved, it is as beyond our control as this surfeit of "truth" is beyond our
grasp, beyond our capacity to digest?

There is another aspect of this. Whether fueled by economic or ideological mechanisms, this cancer-like growth in the power and reach and
capacity of "the media" brings us as well to an international confrontation
of a special kind. There has been growing concern in many other parts of
the world about the media encroachment of the West, though few Americans have ever heard anything about it. The problem stems from the sheer
power and reach of Western media. The "have" nations have overrun or
infiltrated the "have-not" nations with their whole arsenal of media fare.
How ethical, several of the "Third-World" nations have debated at
UNESCO meetings, is it to broadcast or otherwise distribute one's own
way of life into the lives of people of another culture? Does the fact that it

can be done — via satellite, for example, or videotape — or that it can be paid for, make that "invasion" of another culture ethical? And if those other people should misunderstand the Western way of life because of the popular media forms in which it is presented, shall the blame be laid to those alien "consumers"? Or is there some additional moral culpability involved?

And if the great reach and power of our own "news"-gathering apparatus bring us little tidbits from here and there, but do not or can not provide enough information for any true understanding of foreign situations, where shall that fault be laid? Our daily media bring us "news" from the far reaches of the globe. Then there is the question of the time and the distance required for wisdom to distill. Can anyone really gain a perspective on history *as it is happening*? If the events and the cultural artifacts of peoples around the world have to be simplified and abbreviated and put in a form which the curious everywhere can understand, but whose understanding is thereby misguided, who is to be held blameless?

If media "consumers" have a curiosity about this or that, which they would have no access to apart from the media, is catering to their curiosities ethical? Or, since no one is required to disqualify himself or herself as a consumer of media fare on the grounds of incompetency, is it even *possible* for those who produce that fare to be idealistic — in the best sense of that term?

One final consideration about media *capacity*. Is it not also possible that the more and more brought to us by our media becomes less and less simply because there is so much of it? At the very least, is it not possible that what is humanly most important gets lost in that continuous flood of words, sounds, and images? An overloaded circuit disconnects itself. This is the way a "primitive" would avoid what has been called "information overload." But we seem not to be wired that way. We accommodate the overload by diminishing everything. As with inflation, we cope by depreciating everything. But given that we diminish ourselves in leveling all else, is there not some moral question implicit? And what is to be done? The capacity — the power and the reach — of our media increases every day. What *is* the cure for cancer of the media?

VII

And what may be relevant about the role of *language* in all of this?

Given the awesome power and magic that must have been imputed to the word — to speaking, communication — by its first users, it is likely that concern about the uses and misuses of language was one of mankind's first "philosophic" concerns.[13] We know that this concern, this caution, reaches from at least Confucius (5th century B.C.) to the present day. Confucius was asked: "If the ruler of Wei should put you in power, how would you begin?" "I would begin with establishing a correct usage of terminology," Confucius replied.

> If the terminology is not correct, then the whole style of one's speech falls out of form; if one's speech is not in form, then the proper forms of . . . social intercourse cannot be restored; if the proper forms of . . . social intercourse are not restored, then legal justice in the country will fail; when legal justice fails, then the people are at a loss to know what to do or what not to do.[14]

How modern Confucius's concerns seem even today. If words are misused, society will suffer. We know that such concerns about the uses and misuse of language are reflected in our own Bible ("If any man offend not in word, the same is a perfect man, and able also to bridle the whole body." — James 3:2), in the Chinese *Tao Tê Ching*, and in other great texts of every human civilization.[15]

And why is language so important? We know that ". . . the symbol is the basic unit of all human behavior and civilization," as Leslie White put it.[16] Because we have our human existence *in* words, *in* communication, we are, in large, what our uses and misuses of language enable us to be. A human society has its source — and its destiny — in what people do and do not say, can and cannot say, for we cannot do what we cannot say. And if people misuse words, the social institutions which exist to give us meaning will misuse us.

To every means, to every end, language is central. But just how careful are we, how conscious of this central fact of our human existence? "Where *things* are exalted," wrote Richard Weaver in *Language Is Sermonic*, "words will be depressed."[17] But it could have been the other way around: that where words are depressed, misused to the point of general untrustworthiness, then *things* will be exalted. It is possible that our pervasive materialism stems from a long-term misuse of words in our civilization. And, in turn, that materialism misuses and devalues us.

What we know is that there are some quite complex, yet quite subtle, relationships between our language and our thought and feeling — between our uses and misuses of language and the nature of the society in which we live. Pascal, the great French mathematician, felt that "Thought makes the whole dignity of man; therefore endeavor to think well — that is the only morality." For those who have spent so much of their early lives with "the media," and so much more exchanging notes about media experiences, can we expect the kind of thought that makes for human dignity?

One characteristic of a "modern" society is that constraints on the uses and misuses of language are relaxed, just as they are relaxed for other aspects of everyday social life. Language mores are relaxed just as sexual mores are relaxed. In a society such as our own, there is a further "democratization" or permissiveness with respect to language: anyone can say anything to — or about — anyone. In a traditional society, one might harbor a strong opinion about a public figure; but one would never say so publicly. One would be polite, courteous, as if doing so were somehow vital to the workings of the society. In our own society, speaking out publicly against a high-placed person may or may not represent a studied opinion. It is more likely to represent "public opinion," a source of "truth" and rationalization for all sorts of extreme behavior. Many Americans have expressed an opinion about the celebrities of the "Watergate Affair." But those same Americans would be unlikely to know any of the names associated with the "Hydrogen Bomb Affair." Is that because the former is that much more important to our lives and our future?

Not many years ago, even a mild "damn" would have been taboo in the cinema. Now every expression that was once taboo is not only permitted; they have become *la mode*. What shall we make of this? What does it portend? Is there some deeper question of morality involved?

Closely related is the matter of the "permissible lie." If it is "permissible" not to tell someone that he or she is dying of cancer, is it "permissible" not to tell thousands of teenage girls that they are never going to be "beautiful" like the commercial models they see — no matter what they eat, or what makeup they use, or perfume they buy? If it is "permissible" to bend the truth a little if one's intentions are good, is it "permissible" for a politician to bend the truth a little in order to get elected, given his conviction that he would benefit the people more than his opponent would? If it is "permissible," as in many television programs and the "news"-papers, to pretend that there is mainly evil in the world, why is it not as "permissible" to pretend that there is "good" — or, for that matter, a God — in the world?

What we can see in our "modern" ways of describing the world to ourselves and others, is not that all taboos have disappeared. We simply have a different set. To avoid seeming overly-priggish or prudish, a public figure may feel compelled to the use of an occasional four letter word in public. For the movie "anti-hero," it is currently taboo *not* to swear. The politician and his contituency share a taboo *against* the telling of certain truths. The truth may be that the everyday envy and greed and gluttony of Americans contribute greatly to our problems. But can a politician say so? How many of us want to hear the truth about such matters as may reflect negatively upon our own character? What is the "truth" about products we buy for our own aggrandizement? Most of the cosmetics we pay so dearly for may, in fact, be largely worthless. Can one say so and still "sell" one's product? Or is the truth that one can sell one's product only by playing upon our vanities and narcissism? Why are *both* truths taboo? There is a conspiracy here, all right: it is the conspiracy between the advertiser and the consumer, and it inheres in the ways in which we do and do not speak of things.

Somehow, pushing a button that may remotely obliterate thousands of people the button-pusher has never seen doesn't carry the same burden of guilt or culpability as does inflicting slight injury upon a friend. The difference is that the remote "enemy" is anonymous and, therefore, a "thing" or a statistic. One can be wholly indifferent to people one does not personally know or care about. In order to justify injuring one's friend, one would really have to be angry *at him.* Pushing the button — Dr. Strangelove notwithstanding — requires no particular feeling one way or the other.

The parallel, of course, is that the audiences of the "mass" media are anonymous: meaningful individually only as a statistic. Do we assume something of the same sense of *a*morality here as does the button-pusher? The reporter says: "I am simply 'doing my job.' " If someone's life is inadvertently affected, she is unlikely to feel "guilty" (unless the story involves a friend). Those who write novels for popular consumption could not know personally more than a handful of those thousands — a national newscaster proportionally fewer yet of the millions of his audience. We presume less culpability where the audience is anonymous. Where face-to-face communication systems are "self-corrective," and therefore carry at least an intuitive moral burden, we do not sense that *mass* communication systems carry the same burden. Where one is not constrained by either the past or the future, where the relationship is not reciprocal, one has little or no moral obligation to use language "properly." Everything becomes a matter of expediency — in our culture, economic expediency perhaps, in another culture, perhaps ideologic expediency. One may have a sense of moral obligation to a few others. But to 30 million at once? We have no "natural" or intuitive sense of morality or ethics where such size along with anonymity are involved.

Another aspect of language is simply that where everything is exaggerated, there is a kind of "inflation," which brings in its wake the devaluation of all words. The more, and the more casually, words like "new" or "fantastic" are used, the less they are worth. We could much less accuse the commercial media of "causing" us to want more and buy more, than of bringing about a relentless "inflation" of language. Where words are misused by being overused, they lose their quality, their integrity. And, as words are diminished, so are we, for we have our lives in *how* we speak of things.

Nor is the language we speak the only language we use — or misuse. The language of poetry is different from the language of prose. Music has its own language, as does art, photography, and the cinema. Even newspapers have their own language — which is to say, not merely their special use of our speaking language, but the *form* into which things are forced. Every medium — and every genre within every medium — has a somewhat unique kind of "grammar." The forms and structures and rules of progression — of what follows what, and of what accounts for what — which over time become the most easily "consumed" by audiences, become the "conventional" modes, will be those most followed by writers, creators, directors, editors. A news story has a special form, one which is expected by the consumer and more or less enforced by the editor or director. This form does not grow out of the fact that the newswriters speak English, but out of the fact that they learn to "speak" (and to write) "news." Movies of the same genre (e.g., "cowboy" movies) have more or less the same form, which has little to do with the fact that they are made in Italy or Tokyo or Hollywood. Those of us who "consume" movies can readily comprehend only what is "properly" expressed. And this becomes the "grammar" of movies.

These underlying structures or "grammars" may constitute — often do — the great myths and metaphors that define and inform an age. With 100 million copies in circulation at any one time, "the comics" clearly undergird and sustain a sizable sub-culture of American civilization. The heroes and the villains are important; but they are important only for what they *represent*. They symbolize a very complex and sophisticated sense of what is "good" and what is "bad." The pictures and the dialogues are important; but they are important only because they support an underlying structure or form, which is itself an extended metaphor or myth — e.g., "good" sets out to eliminate "evil," gets caught in a series of crises, the situation begins to appear hopeless, but at the last moment "good" prevails over "evil." In the same way, popular music and the "true" confessions type of magazine undergird and sustain sizable, though perhaps somewhat different, sub-cultures. Television commercials are often patterned after the mythic structures predominant in one or more American sub-cultures. The visuals and the sound are there to support the underlying mythic structure, and not the other way around.

So, know it or not, like it or not, "the media" are very much in the culture business. While, to the present time, at least, "the media" do not *create* the myths and metaphors by which we live, they are necessarily very much engaged in the exploitation, confirmation, and modification of our cultural predispositions and predilections. Violence on television is "surface" language. Whether, in the underlying form, crime does or does not "pay," is "deep" language. In our criticism of the media, we point almost exclusively at "surface" language. Mind-shaping and soul-shaping occurs only at the "deep" level. Do we not need some way of evaluating the ethics or the morality of these "deep" languages of the media? Can the news be literally "true" if it is presented in metaphoric (e.g., the forces of "evil" against the forces of "good") form? Or does it make any difference, one way or the other? If it does make a difference, who is deceiving whom? With what consequences? These are questions we have only recently begun to ask.

There is one final aspect of the languages of mass communication to be considered here. It is that the languages of experience are not the lan-

guages of communication. And the languages of communication are not
necessarily the languages of mass communication. The spread of literacy
radically expanded Western man's consciousness — i.e., his capacity for
vicarious experience, for thought. As our forebears became literate, they
could read about things — people, places, ideas, happenings — that would
never have been a part of their immediate interest. Increasingly, their
images of the world took on the form of the media by which they informed and "entertained" themselves. Do the electronic media provide the
same radical expansion in our consciousness — in our capacity for "me-
diated" experiences — as Walter Ong has argued? [18] What about "heavy"
television users? Is their understanding of the world — the way they *see*
the world — increasingly like the ways in which television "sees" the
world, or not? Such changes as may be occurring in our consciousness
since the advent of the electronic media will not be detectable in any one
individual — or perhaps in any given generation. But evolutionary time
frames are wholly relative. This does not mean those changes are not occurring in an inexorable way. [19]

Languages both enable and constrain thought. A person whose total
perspective on the world had been *solely* derived from newspaper reading,
for example, would presumably be conscious of the world in a manner
consistent with the way newspapers are "conscious" of the world. He
would presumably think like a newspaper and talk like a newspaper. But
this is conjectural, for one learns the languages and the values that one
uses within a *human* culture — that is, in interaction with other people.
Thus far, there is no case of an individual being socialized by the media,
with no human contact.

As it is in the normal course of events, most of us most of the time
think like our sub-cultural peers and talk like our sub-cultural peers. We
"register" the world and report on the world as we have been socialized to
do so, and as we receive human confirmation for doing so. If we are
socialized mainly by our parents and our friends and our peers, we will either think and talk much as they do — or else rebel against their way of
thinking or their way of talking. There are those who direly predict that
"the media" will become our major source of socialization. But this seems
unlikely, since the media of mass communication would seem rather to
privatize than to *socialize* those who are psychologically most dependent
upon them. And if "the media" do in fact have the effect of desocializing
those who are addicted to them, to whom shall the responsibility be laid,
since by definition the addicted person in our society is not responsible?

Or will there simply be a dialectic, as there is between parents and
children? Children gain their autonomy in our culture in part by rebelling
against the values and mores of their parents. Would they not do the same
if "brought up" by television? How shall we interpret the following: In the
1950's, a group of artists and writers in California, fearful of the further
spread of "McCarthyism," coincidentally made this prediction — that,

since "the media" are owned and operated by business interests, within a decade we would all be "brainwashed," would all have the same "business" mentality as the owners and operators of "the media." If anything, the opposite occurred. There is today a higher level of *anti*-business attitudes in America than there was at that time. And we may have a higher level of anti-business attitudes than in many other areas of the world, where the media have been owned and operated by "the government." What shall we make of this?

Every language — which is to say, every way of seeing and thinking and comprehending the world — carries with it both a set of possibilities for thinking and understanding, as well as a set of possibilities for countering, for reacting *against* that way of thinking. If we were to constrain, by one means or another, certain ways of imaging the world in "the media," would we not thereby be eliminating the very antidote for it that would be most effective? There is an interesting paradox here: If we immunize ourselves against infectious diseases, the body no longer manufactures those specific antitoxins. Our progeny then have to be immunized, for they have no natural immunity. This makes us, in the long run, rather more susceptible than less so — if for any reason our pharmaceutical "hothouse" could not supply us. Is there a parallel with respect to censorship and every other form of constraint of the mass media?

VIII

The issues, as we have seen, are complex — and profound. Yet, no matter what aspect of the total situation we focus upon, we are always brought back to the vital component of mass communication systems — people.

In attempting to assess the ethicality or morality of mass communication systems — or of large social systems of any kind — we are likely to attribute to "human nature" much more than is factually justified. To say that people do not have one common "nature," but that peoples have different histories, is but one way of recognizing what even Confucius knew: that "By nature, men are nearly alike; by practice, they get to be wide apart." Unlike all other creatures, every human has to be born twice: once physically, and once symbolically. The indispensable midwife to that second birth — the one that makes us human — is some human culture. Unless we are "mad," we have no choice but literally and figuratively to *see* the world through the lenses of the culture and the sub-cultures into which we are socialized, within which we are in-formed. For it is only *in* a culture that humans become "human" — i.e., "symbolic." Thus the context in which we come to have the "nature" we have is our more or less peculiar cultural context. History is the track that a culture or civilization makes in human space and time. In one sense, any individual human is but a manifestation of a cultural process spanning the present from the past to the future.

The implications for the study and understanding of people in mass communication systems are straightforward enough. Whether as "producers" or as "consumers," people will relate to and use "the media" as they are enabled and constrained to do so by the cultures within which they have been in-formed. There are great variations in the ways people of different cultures relate to and "use" the media. An Indian community at the base of the Grand Canyon, for example, has very little use for newspapers or radio or television, even though these are readily available. Why? Because they believe that they know everything that is of interest and value to them through local "gossip." Some Americans have almost no use for television or radio or newspapers or movies. Why? They are "different" because they belong to a different sub-culture, a different "epistemic community." They simply value other uses of their attention and time more highly. Thus, the uses to which the media are put are not a function of "human nature." Rather, they reflect the values and the interests of the cultures and sub-cultures to which the "users" belong, to which they refer their behavior for confirmation and legitimacy. And, as we have already seen, there can be no question about the morality of "the media" as such. For whatever the ethical or moral problems that do arise, do so because of the *uses* or the *misuses* to which their "producers" and their "consumers" put the media.

We use the term "mass" communication. But adding the word "mass" does not alter or obviate the central facts of human communication. We are inclined in Western culture to think of communication as something that someone *does to* someone else. This is consistent with our power and control orientations. But it is not consistent with the facts. The facts are that human communication is, necessarily, at least mutual: there is no communicator without a communicatee, just as there is no lover without a lovee. A receiver can decode and interpret a "message" only as it is possible and consistent for him to do so. Thus what can be expressed to someone depends upon what that person can comprehend. What it is possible to "persuade" people of depends not upon the kinds of appeals that are employed, but upon the kinds of appeals those people are susceptible to, or to the kinds of ends they acquiesce in. A prideful person will be susceptible to appeals to his pride. And so on. It is impossible for "the media" to "do something to" people. That illusion arises from the underlying complicity of those people in that situation. Where people will use media fare in a particular way, and where the appeal is to that use, it will appear that the appeal has "caused" the use. This is no more true than it is to say that the intended use "caused" the appeal. The appeal is never independent of what people will do with that media fare which carries it. How people "use" media fare, on the other hand, can be independent of any appeal or intent, as is true of all human communication.

No person is born knowing what to *do,* or how to *be,* what to *think,* and how to *believe.* All this each must be "socialized" into doing properly. The more homogeneous the culture which endows us with our recipes for being and doing, the less interest we will have in what people of other cultures or sub-cultures are doing, or being. But, as David Riesman pointed out some years ago, the more "modern" or non-traditional we are — which is to say, the more capricious those recipes seem to be — the more "need" we feel to be "other-directed." Where we cannot reliably look inwardly for the answers to doing and being, we must follow the expediencies of looking outwardly — at other people. What is "right" is whatever seems to be in *fashion.*

The more "modern" the society, the more the currency of fashion rather than the immutability of tradition serves as the engine of social control. We live in houses that are in fashion, drive cars that are in fashion, wear clothes that are in fashion, eat what is in fashion surrounded by the furnishings and decor that are in fashion. And we do those things that are in fashion to do with our leisure time, as our finances allow, and as our need to be seen as "belonging" to one or another sub-culture dictates. We think the thoughts that are in fashion, and we hold the beliefs that are in fashion. And, if we want to engage in those conversations that are in fashion, we will have to be "up" on certain topics, more and more of which are drawn from the "mass" and from the sub-culturally specialized media. Our heroes and celebrities are those who are familar to us through the media. Most Americans no longer live in small interlaced communities where gossip constitutes the main "news" of the day — the topics of conversation. We live in urban areas, where one may neither know nor — safely — care to know his neighbor. For those Americans who are "into" the media, what is going on in "Constantinople" is of greater social utility than what is going on across the hall. It has more social utility because the celebrities and the other happenings connected with the media — or media "news" — is what is going to be talked about.

Even though what was a life or death matter to us yesterday will become tomorrow's "trivia," these fashions are no trivial matter. They are increasingly the sole source of social order in America. If one wants to participate in one or another sub-culture of our society, one *has to* be "tuned in" to the appropriate media.

Ortega y Gasset once characterized our age as one in which "People say what is said." If they didn't, they couldn't be *in* this society. Variations on this theme would include: "People attend to television because other people are attending to television." If one does not watch the "Super Bowl" game, how can one participate in the casual social conversations of the next day? "Young people listen to this week's top pops because other young people are listening to this week's top pops." And so on.

We are more curious about the personal lives of media celebrities than we are about the lives of our friends or relatives. There is a good explanation for this: It is unlikely that anyone will want to talk much about the lives of our friends or relatives, except they themselves; and they will more likely want to talk about the celebrated topics and personages of the media.

The media do not create these celebrities, any more than they create fashions in clothes or in cars or in thought. Rather, theirs is largely complicity in our own search for meaning, for significance, for being *in* our own social lives. One "belongs" by knowing what others know; by being the way others are; by thinking and talking the way others think and talk; by liking what others like and hating what others hate. That much has never changed. What *has* changed is the *source* of these convenants of society. What earlier had its source in the past now has its source in the present — in current fashion. And who controls these fashions? No one controls fashions, because everyone does. Whatever is "in" will attract people who want to be "in." People go to see the "in" movies, or attend the "in" galleries, because they want to be "in."

It is as simple, and as utterly complex, as that. Here is the rather involved question that emerges: If people in a permissive, egalitarian, affluent society such as our own are more guided by fashion than by principle; and if fashion derives its authority not from reason but from mere currency; and if no one controls fashions because "everyone" does; and *if* there are likely to be untoward consequences for the people involved, or for their children; then where do we lay the ethical or moral charge? Are people to blame? Or shall we lay whatever happens to the idiosyncracies of our culture? And, if so, what could we possibly do to change *that?*

If a charge could be laid to "people" in this regard, it would be that they are not as competent as they should be as consumers in general, and as consumers of the mass media in particular. When, earlier in this century, it became apparent that automobiles were going to be our major mode of transportation, the decision was made that it was not the automobile manufacturers, but the drivers, who needed licensing — some minimal evidence of operator competence. Have our orientations changed that much? One needs no license to operate a television set or a transistor head-set. Yet, if they are as dangerous to our social health and welfare as some critics seem to believe, why isn't it necessary for their users to be licensed?

Can we assume that we will just "naturally" be competent consumers of the media, which are themselves anything but "natural"? Herbert Read once remarked that "The discipline required of the reader is as great as the discipline required of the writer (i.e., the poet)." This is undoubtedly true. But, if less and less discipline is required of the writer, can we hold the reader accountable for any greater degree of discipline? If the principles by which we value art and literature are not "bigger" than we are, then everything becomes "relative." And "cultural relativism (which shades indistinguishably into cultural uncertainty, thus into cultural inflation)," as one observer put it, "renders many people tolerant of scandalous amateurism and barefaced ineptitude in the arts." [20] Can consumers demand higher quality than they are competent to discriminate?

Certain uses of the media seem to be "addictive." Is there something about being passive consumers of media fare that satisfies something very deep in our make-up? It has often been observed that competence and morality are two aspects of the same thing. If this is so, then how many of the moral or ethical problems of our mass communication systems have their source in the relative incompetence of the consumers *as* consumers?

An old saying has it this way: "See no evil, hear no evil, speak no evil." But how is one to avoid hearing or seeing evil if one does not assume one's responsibility for being competent to judge the evil from the good? For a television consumer, is not knowing (or caring) when to push the "OFF" switch as immoral an act as anything that the producer or advertiser might do? For a pop music consumer, is preferring certain performers *only* because they are the most popular as immoral an act as anything which the recording "star" or the company's hype-sters might do? For a respondent of a public opinion poll, is the failure to say, "I haven't really made any effort to learn anything about this subject and should therefore disqualify myself" any less immoral than anything the pollster might do? For the newspaper reader, is being unable to comprehend beyond the 10th grade level any less immoral than anything the publisher might do?

Few Americans would consider such behaviors "immoral." But aren't they? Can we be as lazy and as indolent and as indifferent and as incompetent as suits us, and still believe that we can inject morality or conscientiousness or diligent concern by legislation at the other end? Those who produce the fare of the mass media are people; and those who consume the fare of the mass media are people. To make one set of people responsible for the other set of people by declaring that other set of people "non-responsible" is a form of victimization by whatever name it is called. If a free people make the wrong choices — for whatever the reason — they may fail, their society may fail. But if they are not free to choose, they are not free. We (consumers of the mass media) may be so incompetent (as consumers of the mass media) as to behave stupidly from time to time. But would denying us the choice to do so be a moral act?

IX

Every human society has "laws." The more traditional it is, the more those laws will be tacit, an integral part of the culture. The more "modern" it is, the more those laws will be rationalized, reflecting the political, economic, or social exigencies that prompted them. As community has disappeared in America, giving way to "urbanity" and "modernity," Americans have looked increasingly to "legislation" as the solution to every sort of social and economic and political problem. Certainly the ideals of law and justice are deeply rooted in Western civilization.

What belongs to us is "protected" by law, and we are "guaranteed" certain rights by law. We employ law to control and distribute scarce resources, as when we legislate who may be allowed to broadcast on what frequencies, since the usable spectrum is finite, and since such legislation is "in the public interest."

Most civil laws are laws of "outlawry": that is, if a person or other legal entity does such-and-such an "illegal" thing, the punishment will be so-and-so — if the "outlaw" is caught and can be proven "guilty." "Outlaws" are by simple definition people who are acting outside of the law. All the rest of us are "inlaws." The more laws there are, the more difficult it is for an "inlaw" to avoid breaking a law inadvertently, and the easier it is for an "outlaw" to operate just outside the law. The paradox here is that the more elaborate and extensive our laws are, the more likely the innocent are to be caught up in the "letter" of the law, while the more possible it will be for the "outlaw" to manipulate the "letter" of the law for his own purposes. Thus one can read in Chapter 57 of the ancient Tao Tê Ching: "The more rules and precepts are enforced,/The more bandits and crooks will be produced."

There is a great difference between law and morality. The motorist who loses his life because the driver of the car that smashed into his was incompetent to be driving — is not "protected" by the law. His survivors merely have recourse. The killer may or may not be "punished." A moral person would not endanger other people by driving his car when he was incompetent to do so, for whatever reason. Morality protects a way of life by inhibiting an immoral action before it gets under way. Laws provide recourse only after the illegal act has been committed.

Our ingenuous belief that we can protect ourselves from unethical or immoral acts in mass communication systems by enacting and enforcing laws is therefore pathetically misguided. A "Freedom of Information" act does not convert "outlaws" into "inlaws." It merely defines which one is which. The "Code of Conduct" of the Radio and Television News Directors Association does not "protect" it or us from immoral or unethical acts. It merely provides us with recourse, should we be able to convict someone of "breaking" the Code in some obviously harmful way.

The simple truth is that morality — or ethical behavior — cannot be legislated. "The trouble about man is twofold," Rebecca West once said. "He cannot learn truths that are too complicated; he forgets truths that are too simple." This is one that we forget.

Nor should we be so quick to believe that our system of doing things is all wrong. The noted physicist-philosopher Henry Margenau made a pertinent point:

> . . . most accounts of ethics dwell on its *unsolved* problems, upon the reasons why it is not and cannot be authoritative, as cogent in its ap-

peals to men as is science; upon its lack of uniformity, its so-called relativity; upon the conflicts it is unable to resolve; upon its helplessness without religion. Rarely is there an acknowledgement today of the patent fact that human societies would be impossible except for the order and uniformities ethics has indeed achieved, or of the usefulness of ethics as that singular accomplishment which elevates man above nature. . . .[21]

There is an "ethic" in our mass communication systems, and it enables them to work, more often than not to our pleasure and satisfaction. For if what is "bad" about our media makes us "bad," then what is "good" about our media will make us "good." Those who own and operate American media have no vested interest in our being "bad." On balance, they are in their own lives ethical and moral persons, and would thus, on balance, have a vested interest in that direction. If there were more consumer interest in "goodness" than in "badness," that is what we would get more of. The "ethic" in our system is the most democratic, the most responsive one yet devised.

Yet, if violence on television "causes" violence, why does not kindness on television "cause" kindness? If we are so readily "persuaded" by advertisers that a certain product is "good" for us, why has it been impossible for those same advertisers to "persuade" us that a certain product is "bad" for us — hazardous, in fact, to our health?

Is it possible that we are trying to solve the wrong problems? Durkheim said that ". . . morality is the logic of action." Given that we don't believe all that much in "morality," what shall the logic of our action be?

And, for those who for one reason or another have an interest in all such matters, it may be well to close by recalling one more simple truth. Aristotle said:

We are not inquiring merely in order to know what excellence or virtue is, but in order to become good; for otherwise it would profit us nothing.

NOTES AND REFERENCES

[1] As, for example, described by Thomas S. Kuhn, *The Structure of Scientific Revolutions,* 2d ed. (University of Chicago Press, 1970); and Arthur Koestler, esp. *The Case of the Midwife Toad* (London: Macmillan, 1971), and *The Act of Creation* (N.Y.: Macmillan, 1964).

[2] Mario Bunge, *The Myth of Simplicity* (Englewood Cliffs, N.J.: Prentice-Hall, 1963); and Fritjof Capra, *The Tao of Physics* (Boulder, Colo.: Shambhala, 1975).

[3] On the latter conclusion, see Seymour Feshbach, *Television and Aggression* (San Francisco: Jossey-Bass, 1971). An interview with Professor Feshbach exploring some reasons for his contrary findings will appear in *Communication.*

[4] As suggested, e.g., by Clifford Geertz, *The Interpretation of Cultures* (N.Y.: Basic

Books, 1973); Victor Turner, *The Forest of Symbols* (Cornell University Press, 1967); and Ernst Cassirer, *Language and Myth* (N.Y.: Dover, 1946).

[5] Cf. Harold A. Innis, *Empire and Communication* (University of Toronto Press, 1972); and Walter J. Ong, S.J., *Interfaces of the Word* (Cornell University Press, 1977).

[6] For one description of this state of affairs, see Michael Polanyi and Harry Prosch, *Meaning* (University of Chicago Press, 1975), esp. pp. 24–25. Cf. Hans-Georg Gadamer, in *Truth and Method*, 2d ed. (N.Y.: Seabury, 1975), esp. p. xvii: "The methodological spirit of science permeates everywhere."

[7] The physician-novelist-philosopher Walker Percy put it thus: "The mark of the age is that terrible things happen but there is no 'evil' involved," in *Lancelot* (N.Y.: Farrar, Straus & Giroux, 1977), p. 139.

[8] Phillip Nelson, "Advertising and Ethics," ch. 11 in Richard T. DeGeorge and Joseph A. Pichler (eds.), *Ethics, Free Enterprise, and Public Policy* (N.Y.: Oxford University Press, 1978). p. 193.

[9] Herbert J. Muller, *The Children of Frankenstein* (Indiana University Press, 1970). Cf. Jacques Ellul, *The Technological Society* (N.Y.: Knopf, 1964).

[10] William Stephenson, *The Play Theory of Mass Communication* (University of Chicago Press, 1967).

[11] For discussions of these two (or more) cultures, see Dwight MacDonald, "A Theory of Mass Culture," in B. Rosenberg and D. M. White (eds.), *Mass Culture: The Popular Arts in America* (Glencoe, Ill.: Free Press, 1957), pp. 59–73; and Herbert J. Gans, *Popular Culture and High Culture* (N.Y.: Basic Books, 1974).

[12] See, e.g., Victor Lasky, *It Didn't Start with Watergate* (N.Y.: Dial, 1977).

[13] As suggested, for example, in Ernst Cassirer (see note 4); and Paul Radin, *Primitive Man as Philsopher* (N.Y.: Dover, 1952).

[14] The source for this particular quote is long since lost. But much the same idea can be found in Lin Yutang's translation, *The Wisdom of Confucius* (Modern Library Edition, 1938), esp. the section on "Ethics and Politics."

[15] Some recent studies are Richard M. Weaver, *The Ethics of Rhetoric* (Chicago: Regnery, 1953); Richard L. Johannesen, *Ethics in Human Communication* (Columbus, Ohio: Merrill, 1975); and Lee Thayer (ed.), *Communication: Ethical and Moral Issues* (N.Y.: Gordon & Breach, 1973).

[16] In *The Science of Culture* (N.Y.: Farrar, Straus & Cudahy, 1949), p. 22.

[17] Edited by R. L. Johannesen, R. Strickland, and R. T. Eubanks (Louisiana State University Press, 1970), p. 53.

[18] See note 5.

[19] Cf. Harold A. Innis, note 5.

[20] Robert M. Adams, "Ideas of Ugly," in *Bad Mouth: Fugitive Papers on the Dark Side* (University of California Press, 1977), p. 94.

[21] In *Ethics and Science* (Princeton: Van Nostrand, 1964), p. v.

PART TWO

Points of View

In this section we have brought together eighteen articles and essays which, in our opinion, raise the most basic and pertinent questions regarding ethical and moral issues in mass communication. And they do so from differing points of view.

Here are represented newspaper publishers, advertising and public relations spokesmen and critics, broadcasters, television newsmen, journalists, book and magazine publishing executives, and public opinion experts. In addition, there are papers dealing with the idea of propaganda, with "public doublespeak," and TV's "failed promise."

Each of our authors identifies and discusses more than one ethical and moral concern. Some issues are acknowledged by all of the authors. Some issues seem to be of more concern in one medium than in another. Nor is there agreement about what could or should be done. Various suggestions for addressing the ethical, moral, or legal problems of the mass media are described and assessed. And scores of firsthand examples bring every key point to life.

Yet no certain solutions emerge. Perhaps this is as it should be. Before we start imposing solutions, we could gain from having a clearer and more substantial view of what the underlying questions are.

That is what, more than anything else, this set of papers can provide.

Does Mr. Jones speak for what was once referred to as the "silent majority"? You be the judge.

Certainly he takes a position. He is concerned about the ways in which our "new morality" has depreciated life in America, of which performance as mass media producer or consumer is but one symptom. Yet the mass communicators, in his view, are culpable:

> I think the time has come when the proprietors of the press, the publishers of popular magazines, the lords of television, the moguls of the screen, and the producers of the stage looked upon the social wreckage around them and faced up to their own culpability.

It is a provocative assessment. But is he right that "only the squares can save us"?

The Golden Age
of Kookery

by JENKIN LLOYD JONES*
Editor and Publisher,
The Tulsa Tribune

I would like to touch on the golden age of kookery in America and what measure of responsibility may be charged against the printed and electronic press, the motion picture and the stage.

We do have a golden age of kookery. You can examine the files of the old *Police Gazette* of the 1870's and '80's where America's gee-whiz journalism was born. You can read the dime novels of the Ned Buntline school of literature in which desperados were exposed and, in a measure, canonized in the same literary operation, if you could call it literary.

You can run through the microfilms of the Hearst and early Pulitzer press at the turn of the century when the term, "yellow journalism," was born. You can follow the pungent spoor of Bernard MacFaddenism, and the lurid love nest tales in the old Sunday supplements, and the heavy-breathing marathon-length embraces in the Theda Bara movies that brought the Hays Office into being.

And having examined all that was worst in the taste of times past I believe you will find nothing like the rain of filth in which America stands today, and nothing like the elaborate rationalizations for misbehavior which our hedonists are boldly advancing.

* At the time he delivered these remarks, Mr. Jones was also President of the Chamber of Commerce of the U.S.

I think it is the boldness of the rationalization which is the essential difference.

We have always had women who slept with anybody, but this is the first time we have had women who sleep with anybody in the interest of freedom of the spirit.

We have always had users of drugs, but this is the first time we've heard the claim that swallowing L.S.D., inhaling pot, and popping with heroin are the roads to holy revelation.

The art of thievery and looting is as old as man, but this is the first time people who clean out liquor stores have claimed kinship to the patriots who hurled the tea into Boston harbor.

All this has been described as the "New Morality." The "New Morality" is based on something else called "situational ethics." Situational ethics simply means that ethical behavior is changeable according to the situation. And by situation one means the conditions of the moment that govern the self-interest of the individual.

This is, of course, the road to social chaos, and we are well on it. We have seen our marching preachers claim that law is not to be changed by orderly process, but is simply to be defied. We have seen our drop-outs sniff at the "squares" who work, although they do not hesitate to eat sandwiches made from wheat raised by the guy who got out of bed in Nebraska at 5 a.m.

We have seen our permissive courts — and particularly the Supreme Court of the United States — strip the classic definitions of pornography down to the bone and then boil the bones.

We have watched nihilism bubble up on our campuses until the word is out that until the university is run to suit a group of activists no one may obtain an education.

At a Democratic convention we witnessed the invasion of a city by noisy carpetbaggers who had announced and even detailed in advance their plans for disrupting a lawful political assemblage, and when they met with resistance they screamed their outrage to the sympathetic clucks of sympathetic clucks.

Of more immediate interest to the American family is the growing philosophy spreading through the high school corridors that anything you can get away with is okay. A society that is based on anything you can get away with and that, at the same time, seeks to weaken laws, water down moral restraints, and generally enlarge the get-away area is heading back to the cave.

In a 1970 article in *The Intercollegiate Review*, Dr. Will Herberg said:

"To violate moral standards while at the same time acknowledging their authority is one thing; to lose all sense of the moral claim, to repudiate all moral authority is something far more serious. It is this loss of moral sense, I would suggest to you, that constitutes the real challenge in our time."

How did we get this way?

The reasons, of course, are complex. But, perhaps, for one thing we got over-worried about frustration. A frustration is something you want and can't have — at least not right now.

Sigmund Freud laid much nervous illness to the frustration factor. His researches uncovered a lot of truth. But Benjamin Spock went on from there to advise that when the baby bawled give it what it wants. There we went off the rails.

Human character is built by overcoming frustration. The boy wants a bicycle. There are two ways he can get it lawfully — shake the dough out of Dad or mow enough lawns to raise the cash. The father may properly choose to exercise his beneficence, although give-aways don't exercise the muscles of self-reliance and self-respect.

But if the boy fails to obtain the gift and chooses not to work for the prize, he has more devious alternatives. He may steal the bicycle directly, or he may break into enough cigarette machines to make the purchase. Thus, he passes into the field of anti-social behavior.

Psychiatrists, generally, seem to agree that a general characteristic of most juvenile delinquents is a low frustration-tolerance. They cannot stand to be thwarted. They cannot plan toward a desirable objective. They can only smash and grab and insulate themselves from reality by great blankets of self-justification and self-pity.

Many of these are the children of parents who remember well the privations and insecurities of the Great Depression and who have determined to give them all the "advantages." And they have been given all the advantages except an appreciation of the labor and devotion it takes to make a workable society.

Since babyhood they have heard the announcer urge them to "be the first kid on your block" with the new gizmo. All the power of advertising persuasion has been devoted to making them expect instant satisfaction.

Can we wonder too much that when they grow older and when it appears to them that Society has handed them less than a perfect world their reaction is either to drop out or burn down?

In our effort to eliminate a little healthy frustration at an age where it would build patience, tolerance, and an appreciation of the attainable, we may have condemned these kids to the worst frustration of all. Self-doubt, anger, and unease are the endemic diseases of hippiedom.

Still, the human animal has changed very little. A strong tide of wistful idealism flows beneath turbulent waves of self-indulgence.

Some time ago I had a free hour in San Francisco, so I went out to the corner of Haight and Ashbury to see the animals. There I picked up several copies of the underground press, including something called the

Berkeley Barb. And in the classified section, among all the ads of deviates, lesbians, sadists, and masochists I came across the following from a post-office box in Daly City:

"Wanted, attractive girl for uninhibited weekend fun at a beach house by member of the male gender. I'm Caucasian, clean-cut, 25 and shy. Hope you don't normally answer ads like this."

I didn't know whether this ad was funny or tragic: The eternal male making the immoral proposition to what he hopes is a fairly moral girl. But I think in a way it expresses the dichotomy of the moment — young people with considerable idealism trying to find fulfillment in sleazy ways. It isn't going to work.

There is nothing new, of course, about the New Morality. One would have to cut a lot of history classes to imagine that humankind had not attempted to find happiness in utter animalism. Or that they would not attempt to rationalize misbehavior by claiming lofty, even spiritual, motives. The temple prostitutes of Astarte 3,500 years ago expressed a philosophy which *Playboy* seems to have just rediscovered. The hashish-maddened Thugs of India went through elaborate religious rites before they set forth to rob and strangle travelers.

But none of these noble experiments produced workable societies. Nations that wallowed in corruption found commercial strength hard to achieve, for you can't build bankable credits where bribery is the norm and graft and short-weight the custom. And where moral standards were abysmal there occurred, paradoxically, an emasculation of the male, for irresponsibility produces incompetence to cope and it leads to the matriarchy which is the chief social headache of America's current ghetto societies.

Some peoples never recovered. Much of our foreign aid has sunk without a trace in social systems that cannot organize themselves for any degree of success. Other civilizations, more happily, eventually became nauseated and went through puritan renaissances, some of them carried to ridiculous extremes.

The popular view of the moralist is that of a dour bluenose who doesn't want people to have fun. There are, indeed, such people. But the best excuse for morality is a pragmatic excuse. Proper and reasonable morals produce a productive society in which the fruits of energy are protected and the seeds of creativity are watered.

Our word "morals" comes from the old Latin, *moralis,* simply meaning a way of life. And our Greek word, "ethics," is defined by Webster as the ideal end of human action.

It is a human fact that man generally operates a considerable distance below his ideals. Where his ideals are low, his behavior will be lower still. And the jam we are in today is in large measure caused by the fact that in recent years our mass communications and entertainment media have publicized deviation from our traditional moral standards to the point where impressionable youth imagines that deviation is the norm.

We have seen the mass circulation slick magazines, beautifully written and beautifully printed, produce long and alluring articles on the wonders of psychedelia. We have read long testimonials from college couples practicing what is called the "arrangement," a modern euphemism for the old-fashioned shack-up.

One national magazine not long ago ran an admiring article on three avant-guard playwrights — one described as a "master of meaningless dialogue," another as "wallowing in filth, but writing like an angel," and a third as preaching that "up might as well be down, right might as well be wrong."

We have seen the vast amount of publicity which any unmarried and defiantly cohabiting movie couple is guaranteed. There is money in blatant misbehavior.

And deviates who were once furtive are now open and in danger of becoming evangelical. The twisted have a compulsion to twist others and recruitment is most effective and most devastating among the young. Thus, tolerance for the homosexual and the lesbian does not, as many liberals imagine, mean simply sympathetic understanding for those who may be hooked on a distressing aberration. It means, in addition, increasingly effective efforts to pervert adolescents of low sophistication and malleable habits.

A man is wise to learn from his enemies. Enemies can be good teachers. And the United States has, as its most implacable and tireless enemy, the communist theoreticians of Eastern Europe and Asia. However much Moscow and Peking may battle with each other over geopolitics, they are united in the hope and belief that western civilization will destroy itself.

Some first-time visitors to Russia are amazed at the enforced puritanism of the stage and literature. They are confused because most left-wing organizations in the United States are the preachers of the utmost libertarianism and move quickly to the aid of purveyors of filth, practitioners of immorality, and inciters to riot.

But there is no confusion at all in the mind of the dedicated communist. The quickest way to destroy what you consider a rotten civilization is to make it as rotten as possible. You give aid and comfort to the worst that is in it, counting on weakness and pruriency to rot it from within. You have to chop down a healthy tree, but a rotten one is a pushover.

Television entertainment is a new phenomenon in the world, and television entertainment that must be sustained by commercial advertising is a phenomenon of a relatively few countries in which television is privately-owned.

Advertisers are attracted by head-counts and head-counts mean ratings. It is difficult to produce great literature, but easy to produce violence. Violence is action, which has a particular attraction for the young.

As a result we in America have subjected an entire generation already to an almost unrelieved diet of shoot-'em-ups. In a single afternoon a child may see 50 people pistoled, strangled, stabbed, burnt, crushed, and eliminated in even more exotic ways.

For a while, some psychiatrists expressed the hope that these vicarious murders would sublimate inner aggressions. But the water level of youthful violence has risen like a tidal bore, and it is now being generally acknowledged that there is less restraint about doing in Grandma or bludgeoning your kid companion if you are raised on a diet of electronic mayhem.

The motion picture industry, dismayed at the inroads of television, discovered that it could lure back the teenage crowd with great gobs of sex. Fortuitously, this key to solvency was discovered at the same moment the U.S. Supreme Court removed practically all restraints. With thousands of movie houses busy each evening pouring gasoline on the smoldering fires of normal, stamenate youth, the results were predictable. Why should we be surprised?

And now the movies that were designed to halt the inroads of television are beginning to appear on television. So now we have made the full circle.

But it is the stage that has sunk to the lowest depth. Consider the play "Hair." It defends itself on the grounds of realism. It is less true to life than Little Lord Fauntleroy or Rebecca of Sunnybrook Farm.

It is also a boxoffice success. It has been copied. Where in New York today can you find a theater that would inspire your formative son and daughter with a sense of heroism and self-sacrifice and human triumph? No wonder Dave Merrick, the theatrical producer, said that he left for California until the filth clouds blow over. Let's hope he doesn't die in California.

I think the time has come when the proprietors of the press, the publishers of popular magazines, the lords of television, the moguls of the screen, and the producers of the stage looked upon the social wreckage around them and faced up to their own culpability.

We should have had about enough of cluck-smack journalism, the journalism that clucks piously over social misbehavior, portrays it in all its lip-smacking detail, and waits for the circulation figures to soar.

I think it's time that the great television advertisers weighed the business of pulling sales figures up by pulling Young America down.

I think it's time that our courts consider the ancient truism that there have always been people who would do anything for a drachma, a denarius, a shilling, or a buck, and that the very guts of the law is the courage to draw a line.

I speak of these things not because I believe that prohibitions and restraints are good things in themselves. They are merely means to a desirable end. And the desirable end is a workable, orderly, creative way of life. There is no commerce in a climate of plunder. There is little love in the barnyard. There are few ideals in an animal existence. There isn't much happiness in human abasement.

What concerns me is the survival power of a great nation. Athens didn't survive the riots of the youth who followed Alcibiades. The Ptolemies rotted out. Rome passed from corruption to chaos to obliteration. China of the cumshaw and the squeeze collapsed before the marchers of Mao. The most consistent note in human history is that once-great people who have ceased to believe in their own nobility are generally the last of their line.

I think the world needs America. I think our children do. I think our traditional virtues are worth fighting for.

The world needs America, for the virtue and purpose and idealism and resolve which made her a great power for enlightenment and freedom could stand emulation in many parts of the globe.

Our children need a strong, effective, orderly society.

But only the squares can save us.

Kookery, self-indulgence, and the philosophy of damn-the-other-man are way stations on the way to Nowheresville.

I believe the time has come for decent Americans to quit apologizing for their quaintness, and to begin yelling like hell.

Mr. Newman has obviously enjoyed a more privileged perspective on the inner workings of the TV journalist than have most. Has this left him cynical?

> Will . . . [politicians] act with dignity? There isn't any great likelihood of it, because dignity is no longer generally valued.

Or unwaveringly realistic?

> In journalism, it is a mistake to believe that we are ever going to get rid entirely of fiction that masquerades as fact. Nor are we ever going to get rid entirely of the overstatement, the exaggeration, the extravagance, the embroidery, the gimmickry. We are not going to get rid of them so long as people make money from them. . . .

Is Mr. Newman against making money? "No, I am not."

In this paper, he outlines some suggestions for coping with the dilemmas in our present-day world of the media. His is a forward look with positive proposals, for "There is no point in crying for a world that can no longer be." His paper moves toward what may be the key to the whole issue of ethical media performance: The responsibility of the public. What is the public's responsibility? is the question he answers here.

The Journalist's Responsibility, and the Public's *

EDWIN NEWMAN
NBC News

I am beginning to be leery about saying anything in public. Not long ago I did a broadcast about the sixtieth birthday of the teddy bear and said that one of the attractive things about this toy was that it had not been excessively humanized. Later, a man in a state of some indignation called and accused me of saying that the teddy bear was not civilized. What the man's interest was, I never did find out.

It isn't only *what* you say; on television, it is also how you *look* when you say it. A few years ago, I appeared on a program with Walter Judd, then Republican Representative from Minnesota, and Hugh Gaitskell, then leader of the British Labor party. It was a one hour program, and I got to ask one question. That was my only contribution. The fan mail poured in, that is to say there was a letter from a Baptist clergyman in Connersville, Indiana, who accused me of smirking at Judd.

The letter went to an NBC executive, who told the clergyman that a smirk was a facial expression reflecting inner malice, and that was no part of my makeup at all. The clergyman replied that in his view, and according to the dictionary, a smirk was "an affected, silly, self-satisfied smile," and

* Adapted from a presentation at the Third Centennial Symposium, "The Responsible Individual," at the University of Denver. Though prepared some time ago, Mr. Newman feels his remarks are still pertinent.

that certainly *was* part of my makeup. It seemed wise to drop the correspondence at that point.

Incidents of this kind leave one wary. . . .

I have been asked to speak about the individual response to the flood
of information and ideas made possible by the existence of the mass
media. I have to begin, I think, by pointing out that we have mass media
first of all because we have mass, or it might be better to say masses, if one
can do that without being thought to be a Marxist.

Let's start by discussing some of the effects of the existence of masses.
This really means talking about the population explosion and the effect it
has had in the field of public affairs. It has had effects in other fields, as
well, but I will stick to public affairs, by which I really mean politics.

The most obvious effect of the population explosion on politics is that
it helps to restrict the holding of important public office to the rich. Now
that is clearly *not* the only factor at work. We have a very large country,
highly developed technologically, and devoted to advertising and public
relations. All of these things contribute to making politics expensive. But
the mere existence of so many people is also a factor — so many people to
reach, so many people to persuade. . . .

I would like to talk a bit about primaries, because they seem to me to
exemplify a good deal of what is wrong in our system, and what is becoming more wrong as time goes by. The mass media have a hand in this, by
what they do, and what they do not do.

First, there is something ridiculous about two well-known senators
pounding around the country, telling where they stand, or obscuring
where they stand, on every issue imaginable. . . . If their views and characters are not sufficiently well known to the people of this country already,
there is something seriously amiss.

More than that, when politicians embark on contests of this kind,
they look for angles. They look for things to say. That may lead to danger.
. . . In 1960, for example, the then Senator Kennedy, in response to a
challenge from Vice President Nixon, spoke of Cuba as though the problem could be solved simply by a change in administration. Three months
after taking office, Mr. Kennedy brought off the invasion at the Bay of
Pigs.

The primary as now conducted also emphasizes the irrelevant, especially as it relates to the personality, the so-called image. It should make
very little difference whether one has a firmer handshake than another, or
whether one has a brighter smile — or perhaps a more competent dentist
than the other. Nor should it matter whether one candidate eats hot dogs
and blintzes with greater zest than the other, though by the time we elect a
president, the candidates will have eaten regional dishes and the food of
the common man all over the United States.

Essentially, it *is* desirable that candidates make themselves known to the people, that they see and be seen, and that they make their views known. But we are now a nation of over 200,000,000 people. We are 3,000 miles across. The primary campaigns we have now are no longer practical. They are murderous physically and they take tremendous amounts of money. Also, the great welter of talk wearies the voter and may confuse as much as it clarifies.

Those who object to the primaries, and the endless, hit or miss, unfocused oratory that accompanies them, are under an obligation to suggest something better. There may not be anything better — as a system. There should be a better way of making the system run. That, I think, would have three parts. One is for the Congress to institute some real checks on the use of money in political campaigning. The second is for the various politicians to conduct themselves with greater dignity, responsibility, and restraint. The third is most important. It is for the people to take appropriate notice of those politicians who do so. In this, the help of the mass media of information is badly needed. In fact, it would be impossible to accomplish anything without it. If the news organizations do not act with dignity, nobody will.

Will they act with dignity? There isn't any great likelihood of it, because dignity is no longer generally valued. It may not even be generally comprehended. Not long ago, I wandered into the dog care section of a leading New York department store. There were collars shining with jewelry made of paste and glass. There were sweaters. There were coats of wool, corduroy, and imported broadtail. There were raincoats in a variety of materials, including one of simulated zebra skin tailored to fit a dachshund. There were sun glasses. There were hats.

There was also a great batch of photographs of satisfied customers, suitably inscribed. Some of them had posed for what amounted to formal portraits, suitable for framing and hanging in the kennel alongside portraits of distinguished ancestors.

Nor was that all. The canine care counter had stainless steel bowls for dogs' food, and china bowls bearing the slogan, "Good appetite," in French, misspelled. It had scented soap that made a bubble bath and was called, "Faithfully yours." There was a dog's equivalent of a baby book — the puppy book, in which to paste his photographs, and record his measurements, the tricks he learned, and the bright sayings he barked.

For people to conduct themselves in that way with dogs is not dignified. It is is not even dignified for the dogs. . . .

There is no point in crying for a world that can no longer be. These trends are irreversible; but we should be thinking about how to offset some of the *political* advantages of wealth. I believe that radio and television can play a large part in that. That is to say, they can give politicians large audiences, local, regional and national, and this can be useful, provided that some sort of equality of access to them is worked out.

There are objections to that, and they are well known. Television puts a premium on quickness, on a ready smile, on a kind of charm (I hear somebody asking— How did Newman get on?), and on an argument that makes a mass appeal. But television and radio did not create the conditions in which those attributes count. We have a mass market because we have a mass. It was inevitable, and natural, that the methods of mass advertising and publicity and selling be adapted to politics.

It hardly needs to be said that, in these circumstances, the quality of political argument may suffer. Here again, there is no point in moaning for the past. We have to devise ways of bringing sophistication and subtlety to political argument in the circumstances as they are. I believe that radio and television have a part to play in this, partly by being somewhat more jaundiced than they often are.

The population explosion has given a new content to politics. . . . We have reached the point where contraception has become a political issue in Chicago; the dissemination of birth control information has in Connecticut and Massachusetts; and the use of public funds for sterilization has in Virginia. A bill was introduced in the Mississippi legislature in 1964 providing for voluntary sterilization of charity patients after they had had two children. It did not get out of committee, and in Mississippi, it probably had a racial angle attached to it, but that does not affect the point, which is the sort of thing that politics now deals with.

The issue of relief, welfare, whatever you choose to call it, helps to create a group that is set off from the rest of the community and which often remains cut off, living on relief.

I do not want to pursue this point in detail, but it is obvious that keeping people on relief will damage them permanently. They may begin by resenting the circumstances that put them on relief, and by feeling ashamed of having to accept the help, and they will finish by accepting the payments as their rights, by using political means to get them, and by corrupting the system under which they get the payments.

Millions are poured out in relief payments, in a self-perpetuating process. We face the prospect that this will get worse, because of the great number of poor people being born and not being educated. . . . The population explosion is coming in part among those groups least well equipped to get on in the world, and to get the jobs that are going.

Again, you cannot have a population explosion without it affecting the pattern of the population. The population of the United States is growing older, which is to say, a larger percentage of the population is aged sixty-five and over. This creates pressure groups, one of which we have not had before, that being the pressure group of the aged.

All of these things combine to create colonies of old people, concentrated in states where retirement is relatively inexpensive and where the climate is kind. This means, first of all, California, Arizona, and Florida. Unless our old people are reasonably well taken care of, it could lead to antagonisms that express themselves politically. With old people clustered together, they might be able to make their votes count very heavily in a few states and come to wield disproportionate power.

Something else goes into the content of politics because of the population explosion — questions of traffic, density, housing, urban rot, and the like. Education also becomes a more pressing political question, and because education does, so does religion, since it intrudes on the question whether and how far the federal government is to subsidize schools. . . .

Theodore Sorenson, who was perhaps Mr. Kennedy's closest adviser, said at Columbia University: "While it should not be impossible to find an equitable constitutional formula to settle the church-school aid problem, it is difficult for the formula to be suggested by the nation's first Catholic president." (Mr. Kennedy was not the country's first Catholic president. He was the country's first president who was a Catholic. There is a profound difference. Mr. Kennedy was not a Catholic president any more than Harry Truman, say, was a Baptist president.) . . .

The plain meaning of Sorenson's words was that because Mr. Kennedy was a Catholic, he was unable to deal with one of the liveliest issues of our time. That was extremely unfortunate. We cannot have presidents who disqualify themselves from acting, as judges do, because they have an interest in the case. We expect them to have an interest in the case. They are presumed to have such an interest. That is why they are in politics in the first place.

To use a parallel, President Kennedy did not steer clear of economic issues — taxes, for example, or deficit spending — because he had money. He did not tell us that he would say nothing about racial matters because he was a member of a race . . .

As our recent presidents go, Mr. Kennedy was aware of the problems and issues before the nation far more than most, and yet he evaded this particular issue. My point is that these new issues are being forced upon us with tremendous speed, almost without our realizing it, because of the rate at which the population is growing, and the rate at which people are gathering in cities. The longer we put off dealing with them, the worse they are going to be.

I was in England not long ago, to push on, and I saw the argument put forward that every effort should be made to preserve the *railways,* and not to cut them down, as the present British government is doing. The argument came from Jacquetta Hawkes, who is an archaeologist and the wife of the writer, J. B. Priestley. Miss Hawkes said that life grows more impersonal all the time, but the railways are civilized and pleasant, and an antidote to this impersonalness. The government is asked to make a political decision to save the railways not because of their value to the economy, but because of their contribution to the quality of life. That is what I mean by the new content of politics.

I would also like to quote Gertrude Stein. She is best known for her incontrovertible statement, "A rose is a rose is a rose." Lately, she has begun to be quoted for a remark she made about the city of Oakland, California. "When you get there," Miss Stein said, "there is no there, there."

What Gertrude Stein meant was not complimentary to Oakland. She was saying that it did not do what a city should; it did not excite, or attract, or inspire. I have never been in Oakland, so I do not know whether the comment was justified, but Miss Stein's remark is quoted with approval in a book about what might be called the urban crisis. It is called *Community and Privacy,* and it is by Serge Chermayeff, a professor at Yale, and Christopher Alexander, an architect. As the title suggests, it is about the accelerating disappearance of privacy from our lives.

Chermayeff and Alexander describe privacy as "That marvelous compound of withdrawal, self-reliance, solitude, quiet, contemplation and concentration." They insist that only through the restored opportunity for first hand experience that privacy gives can health and sanity be brought back to our world. If you accept this, it follows that some means must be found of restoring privacy — and drama and dignity — to our cities, because that is where the great majority of us live, and where an even greater proportion of us will be living in the future.

However, so Chermayeff and Alexander write, our cities are obsolete and out of date, and they have also surrendered to two invaders, traffic and noise. Two examples: first, on traffic: in downtown Los Angeles, about 66% of all available land is devoted to the automobile. Second, on noise: in some crowded offices, the acoustic experts have given up trying to eliminate or isolate the noises that business gives rise to. Instead, they are introducing artificial background noises to drown the other noises out.

All of this is making privacy a political question or, more precisely, it is making the lack of privacy something that requires a political solution, if it is to be solved at all. Sometimes, the issue is presented badly, as when recorded advertisements are placed in the streetcars of Washington, D.C., or in Grand Central Terminal in New York. More often, however, privacy disappears without our realizing it. It disappears not merely because there are more people — which means less space for each of us — but because the existence of more and more people creates a climate in which privacy seems less important, less natural, less to be expected and insisted on. There is, in other words, a change in the quality of life which, once set in train, becomes almost impossible to reverse.

For example, you never get in a taxi any more in which the driver is set off from the passengers, although that used to be the normal thing in the United States, and still is in England. You are subjected to the driver's radio, to his opinions, if he cares to make them known, and to his cigar. He is also denied privacy from you. But this is taken for granted, so that it is now impossible to have a private conversation in a taxi. . . .

Solitude cannot disappear without affecting people's outlooks. I believe that its disappearance has a vulgarizing effect, and that unorthodoxy becomes more difficult . . .

Someday, somebody will propose that nobody on foot be allowed to enter the center of New York, so that there need be no sidewalks at all. Eventually, automobiles will be produced that dispense with human drivers. They will cruise continuously around the city's center, and there will be no people there at all — only cars and highways. That is the way we are headed. In the meantime, civilization has reached the point where some people are willing to pay to go to a place with nothing to do but listen to the quiet . . .

We are often told that a continued population growth is a guarantee of continued prosperity. That is a popular line with stockbrokers. The argument is that business and the economy will continue to grow because the population is expanding, and needs are created that must be met.

In February, 1957, the census clock in the lobby of the Commerce Department in Washington showed 170,000,000. Secretary of Commerce Sinclair Weeks, a Republican, said: "I am happy to welcome this vast throng of new customers for America's goods and services. They help insure a rising standard of living and reflect our prosperous times."

In December, 1961, the census clock hit 185,000,000. Secretary of Commerce Luther Hodges, a Democrat, said that the growth of five million in a year "gives some idea of the future needs of the country from the economic standpoint."

Unfortunately, it doesn't work that way. To begin with, the population does not grow at the same rate among all segments. Every survey made suggests that the practice of birth control increases as education increases, so that there is a much higher proportion of women with a college education practicing birth control than women with a grade school education. Every survey suggests that it is also an economic matter — the *higher income* families are much more likely to practice birth control. They are also more likely to use it effectively.

Population therefore tends to grow most explosively among those who are poorer. That means those who are least educated, and in this country it also means those who are most discriminated against and therefore least able to take care of their children. These children will therefore get less education than others, they will grow up with disadvantages that others do not have, and they consequently will not create an *enforcible* demand for goods. They may want the goods and services, but they will not be in a position to pay for them. They will therefore not help the economy, and they will not act as a guarantee of prosperity. They may *hurt* the economy, and they will have a debasing effect on the community that in turn must affect our political life.

It is true that people on relief, and we have millions on relief, do help the economy in a limited way. If they were not on relief, if they had nothing, they would create no demand at all. Relief and other forms of welfare payments, unemployment compensation, sick pay, old age pensions — all of these things are now well understood. They help to keep purchasing power up. If recessions come, it is generally agreed that these built-in defenses keep them from being worse — but they do no more than that.

On the other hand, having large numbers of people on relief tends to divide the community; by running counter to the process of the survival of the fittest, it keeps in being the people who cannot take care of themselves; and it burdens the economy with millions of unproductive hands. A growing population is therefore not necessarily an economic blessing. It may be an economic curse because it consumes funds that might better be invested in other things and in more creative ways.

In our country, as I have said, these effects are exaggerated by being coupled with the practice of discrimination by color, so that the population explosion has come to a disproportionate degree among people who are to varying degrees alienated from the mainstream of American life. Great wells of resentment are being stored up.

There is, so far, only the beginning of an understanding of the political consequences of these developments. It is perfectly predictable that they will be the stuff of politics of the future.

If you are ever tempted to believe that rapid population growth is a guarantee of prosperity, take a ride some day on a New York bus, and look at the advertising signs. There is first the charity bus. On a bus I rode recently, there were signs asking for contributions to the Legal Aid Society, which provides lawyers for people who cannot otherwise afford them; for the Visiting Nurse Service, which sends nurses to families in the poorer sections of town; for the Greater New York Fund, which covers more than a hundred charities; for the Boys Clubs of America; for the Catholic Youth Organization. There was a sign that said, "Give to the college of your choice," apparently to keep you from giving to the college of somebody else's choice. There was one for the Young Men's Christian Association, and one for the Federation of Jewish Charities.

All of these are worthy organizations. I do not mean to say anything against them. Nor do I mean to say anything against charity itself, which is after all one of the noblest of impulses. Still, that makes ten separate appeals, and as charity buses go, this one had a rather low count. You wonder why so many people need charity in the greatest city in the richest country in the world.

There is another sort of bus — the illness bus, on which contributions are solicited for research into various diseases. There are appeals for help in fighting cancer, heart disease, multiple sclerosis, cerebral palsy, hemophilia, mental retardation, mental illness, epilepsy, among others. Riding in an illness bus may give you the idea that New York is one vast hospital or sanitarium. Did you ever see the sign that says, "One in ten New Yorkers is mentally ill and needs help"? That means there is one chance in ten that somebody mentally ill and in need of help will turn out to be driving the bus.

I think I have said enough about our having mass media because we have masses, and enough about some of the problems created by the existence of those masses. It is the responsibility of the citizen at least to understand what the problems are, and it is the responsibility of the mass media to help him to do that. All right. But how do we go about it?

Let me begin by telling a story that came, about six weeks ago, from Grottarosa, in Italy. It was about the finding of a mummy, more than twenty centuries old. The stories said it was the mummy of a beautiful woman. Naturally. They did not say how anybody knew, since there are no generally accepted standards of beauty for mummies twenty centuries old, but that is what they said.

A few days later, when experts had finished examining the mummy, it was stated to be that of an eight year old girl. With rickets.

That is not in itself a significant story, but it is an illustrative one. It illustrates how much the reader, the citizen, must be on his guard.

In journalism, it is a mistake to believe that we are ever going to get rid entirely of fiction that masquerades as fact. Nor are we ever going to get rid entirely of the overstatement, the exaggeration, the extravagance, the embroidery, the gimmickry. We are not going to get rid of them so long as people make money from them, and we remain a money-making society. (I don't mean to suggest that there are no other reasons that people sometimes avoid the strict truth, but they are not immediately relevant.) In short, overstatement and exaggeration and the rest are a source of profit, and that is not going to be cast aside.

Well then, you will say to me, are you against making money? No, I am not. Are you against the profit system, then? No, I am not. I work for a corporation whose continued existence depends on profit. What am I saying, then?

I am saying that it is necessary to examine things far more closely than we do. There are people who have an interest in what you believe and what I believe. When we believe certain things, it may be advantageous to them. It may or may not be advantageous to us, but the essential thing for us is to understand that much of the information that comes our way is extremely unlikely to have come from the blue. It was shaped and formed; it may even have been invented. We must therefore be more critical. We must be less ready to believe. We must be especially suspicious of slogans. We should try to defend the integrity of the language. Nothing is more important than that last, for nothing is more important than that people should express themselves precisely. You needn't think for more than a minute or two to compile a list of words that have lost their meanings through misuse or excessive use. "Fantastic" is one. "Wild" is another. "Controversial" is another. They have all become useless.

Words alone can accomplish miracles. Most people in this country don't like to buy anything that is foreign. However, they very much like to have imports.

The problem of preserving the language is not the sort of problem that is going to be solved by some foundation setting aside millions of dollars to deal with it. It can only be solved by people who are not afraid to buck the trend and who start with the assumption that a large part of what is said and written is either partisan or inaccurate . . .

Obviously, it is terribly difficult for the individual who does his job, goes home at night, and has all the ordinary tasks that make up living, to try to find out what is going on in the city, the state, the nation, and the world. He cannot hope to keep up. The principal burden therefore falls on those of us who supply the ordinary individual with the information he uses. We have the great responsibility.

In practical terms, it has always seemed to me that the best thing the individual can do is to get to know, extremely well, a few people or organizations on which he depends for his news. If you are in the habit of reading *Time* magazine, let us say, you should familiarize yourself with its idiosyncrasies. You should try to find out what its prejudices and blind spots are.

If you read the *New York Times*, for example, you should know that the *Times* is extremely sensitive to anything that appears to mock royalty or be unfriendly to it. I don't know why it is, but it is, and you have to make allowances for that in any *Times* story about royalty.

You must also understand that news is a competitive business, and one important way in which that competition makes itself felt is in leads, which is to say in the first sentence of a news story: the who, what, when, where. The theory of the lead is that it sums up the entire story and that somebody in a hurry could read it and nothing else in the story and still have the essential facts.

Fair enough, but the lead is also the thing that hooks the reader, piques his curiosity. This is especially important in competition between the wire services, Associated Press and United Press International. I speak with some knowledge here; I used to be a wire service reporter in Washington, and the competition was direct and hard. So — it is always wise to read down into a story, to see whether the lead is supported by facts cited below. Fairly often, it isn't.

There is something else that disfigures our journalism. We are far too sensitive as Americans, by which I mean we are looking for insults and affronts all over the place. It really is not necessary to look for them; they will come, in large volume and considerable variety, of their own accord. But there is a tendency to see anti-American angles in things that are not anti-American at all. That is to say, they may not be welcome to us, but that was not the reason for which they were committed, and that was not the object their perpetrator had in mind.

In this connection, it would help us to try to see ourselves as others see us. . .

We tell the French and the British to sink their differences, which happen to be profound, when we cannot achieve unity among our own people, when millions of Americans are held in an inferior position by other Americans because of their color. Imagine then how we look when we tell other people what to do, and tell them not on the basis of what we are but on the basis of what we say we are. . . . .

It was interesting to watch the way that President Kennedy was treated. Early in 1963, it became fashionable to write about his shortcomings. His so-called grand design for partnership between the United States and Western Europe was not prospering; the country was not moving again, certainly when measured by unemployment; South Vietnam was beginning to seem an insoluble problem; Cuba was still with us; the Alliance for Progress was foundering, and so on.

We were, therefore, treated to long analyses of the situation, boiling down to the earnest statement that the President's leadership had not been what it should have been. This was usually presented in tones of pained surprise.

There was one thing wrong with most of those articles. They spoke of disappointment with the President's performance, but the disappointment arose from self-deception. The President came into power on the slimmest of majorities. He came in with little personal standing, the result of having had no particular accomplishments in government. His youthfulness was an advantage in some ways, but youth does not necessarily lend weight to presidential pronouncements. He also entered with no well-defined program, especially in economic matters, where he began as a budget balancer and became a deficit spender.

It should also have been obvious from the outset that he would have the same problems with Congress and with this country's allies that other Presidents have had. Congress does not roll over and play dead because of articles implying that a President is a political genius, especially when he isn't. As for allies, as far as they can, they pursue their own interests.

In the self-deception that went on early in the Kennedy administration, the President himself shared. That was evident in the Bay of Pigs Invasion, which he embarked on in a great burst of confidence, and which came close to shattering his confidence forever.

I am saying, in other words, that somewhat more realism and independence among news organizations in the beginning could have saved much disillusionment and disappointment later on.

All of this is tied in with the question of news management, and with the performance of the news business. The Kennedy administration was accused many times of managing the news, and it did do it, in South Vietnam, among other places. The Kennedy administration was a peculiarly self-conscious one — terribly concerned about how it would look in the history books, and how it was presented in the press and on the air. The President himself, in his speeches, always sounded as though he were writing sentences that would fit on the pedestals of statues.

That, in any case, was his business, and all governments try to manage the news. They can't help it. However, the foolish and uncritical articles, and radio and television programs, about the President before he took office and shortly after were fine examples of news management by the news business itself.

It seems to me that news organizations, in dealing with governments, must cultivate a critical sense, a feeling of suspicion. We want to believe that our government tells us the truth. We should not assume that it doesn't. We should assume, however, that in the nature of things, its view of what is important, its view of what the public should know, its version of the truth, will not always accord with ours.

News organizations do not always cultivate that point of view. There are too many stories that come out of Washington attributed to high officials who are not named. Nobody is responsible, therefore, for what is said. The practice of planting stories without being quoted has become a game to officials in Washington. It has the same appeal as secret societies with mystic rites and passwords. It gives these officials the feeling that they are on the inside, and everybody else is on the outside. Reporters generally go along with it without protest. They enjoy the feeling that they are on the inside, too. The system is ever-expanding. . . .

A certain man recently elevated to very high office in Washington was heard to say to reporters, "You treat me right and I'll treat you right." It is not the reporter's job to treat anybody right, or to treat anybody wrong. His job is to give the news.

In this matter of relations between the news business and governments, it seems to me that some of the most sensible comments have come from Robert Manning, a former assistant secretary of state who had a long and successful career in journalism before entering government service. Manning told a Congressional committee that there is a built-in conflict between the government and news organizations. The government must sometimes conduct its business in privacy. The public has a right to know what lies behind government policy. The plain meaning of Manning's remarks is that there are times when these two needs cannot be reconciled, and no amount of argument or soul-searching will reconcile them.

Let us push a step further. There are times when the government wants to keep things quiet. If the newspeople catch on to what the government is doing, they must consult their own consciences about publishing. What about a different situation — when the government is deliberately misinforming the public? This happened in the Bay of Pigs Invasion in April, 1961, when word was leaked, for example, that landings had taken place in four different parts of Cuba and were going forward. The government agencies involved no doubt thought they had good reasons for putting out that misinformation. The news organizations had to rely on the government, at least at the beginning. The essential thing, however, was to make clear, as soon as possible, where the misinformation came from. Then, if the public has been misled and objects, it knows where to place the blame.

It also seems that the news industry should have less fear of being managed by the government. If news organizations are deliberately misinformed, if they are unfairly used, that is *news* and they have the capacity, and duty, to tell the public about it. It is a tremendous power that they hold, and they should be able to protect themselves.

I suppose that what I am saying finally is, be skeptical. That may seem to run counter to other bits of aphoristic advice it is easy to get, such as have faith, but in a way, they do not cancel each other out. Be skeptical, and have faith that skepticalness is the advisable course.

I could say be serious-minded, but that would really be excessively optimistic, in view of a recent study which showed that a hundred million Americans regularly read the comic strips, and that they are the most widely read part of the newspapers. Only one paper in the country dares to do without them, that being the *New York Times*. The peak age for reading the comics is thirty to thirty-nine and, while reading them tails off as people get older, that may only reflect the fact that people read less as they age, and the comics suffer with all the rest.

There is nothing to suggest that reading the comics is confined to the uneducated and unintelligent. If having gone to college may be taken as a sign of education, those who are educated read them as much as those who are not.

I feel justified in talking about the comics at some length because they seem to me to typify the need for the skeptical attitude. The name "comics" itself, or the alternative, "funnies," has always seemed to me to be something of a come-on. It inclines people toward a favorable view of what they are about to read, whereas a great many of the so-called comics are not comic or funny at all, even those that are meant to be. A little realism about them might knock off a lot of readers, and that would be an encouraging sign.

I don't want to end by talking about comic strips. I don't want to end by saying that if you want to know what is going on in the world, watch

Edwin Newman regularly. If you do want to know what is going on, you have to work at it. Even then, there will be vast amounts you will not know, you will be fooled some of the time, and you will certainly be wrong some of the time. The main thing is to avoid putting slogans where thought should be. That is the responsibility of the public, and it is even more the responsibility of those of us in the news business to help the public do it.

Might we not expect that the press as a social institution will not only engage in a critical analysis of the social environment, but will also undergo periods of intense criticism itself, either from within or from any of a number of outside sources? This is neither a new nor a unique development of the American mass communication scene. What we are beginning to realize, however, is that, to be effective and useful, criticism must become part of a larger, ongoing dialogue among all parts of a society.

In his evaluation of press critics, Mr. Clark acknowledges the need to get into conversation with those who would attack the press, to the extent that it is seriously attempting to deal with the complexities of society. This means willingness to listen and provides a first condition for the establishment of a dialogue.

Mr. Clark describes, at least implicitly, the inadequate and incorrect assumptions on which relationships between the changing moods of American society and the activities of the press are based. Can the fundamental changes American society has undergone in the last decades and which have led to a loss of consensus, for instance, be traced to the effectiveness of press performance alone? On the other hand, has the press made an effort to study and explain the roots and reasons for this lack or loss of consensus? Is it enough to say, for example, that the function of the press is to "amplify the university's critical mood and style"? And what if this results in a crisis of public confidence? Do the media bear any responsibility for the social consequences of fulfilling their presumed function? And, at the outset, who is to have the say as to what the functions of the media in society are to be?

Max Weber once said, "Not everybody realizes that a really good journalistic accomplishment requires at least as much genius as any scholarly accomplishment, especially because of the necessity of producing at once and 'on order,' and because of the necessity of being effective. . . ." *
Are journalists, therefore, to be seen merely as transmitters of news? Don't they share *with their audiences* the process of developing insights and offering directions for society? To the extent it were successful in this, therefore, the press would encourage intellectual growth and stimulate the ability to be critical and to accept criticism; and it would thereby succeed in combining the presentation of facts with the teaching of methods of thinking. How would you evaluate the press on these criteria?

A responsible press must be a responsive press, that is, responsive to its critics as well as responsive to the issues of the day and to the demands of its readers. A responsible press cannot ignore the importance of a day's events; however, it must not underestimate its role as an interpreter of these events and as a social and intellectual leader in society.

* Max Weber, Politics as a Vocation (1921) (from H. H. Gerth and C. Wright Mills, *From Max Weber: Essays in Sociology,* New York: Oxford U. Press, 1969, paperback).

Should journalists, therefore, be qualified to describe and analyze the problems of American society? And should journalists be able to predict the social, political, and economic conditions of the future and, if necessary, suggest measures that may help us prevent major disasters *before* we read about them in the newspapers?

Indeed, as Mr. Clark suggests, are their competencies and their responsibilities separable?

The Press and Its Critics *

by PETER B. CLARK

President and Publisher
The Evening News Association
Detroit

We are enduring another of those recurrent periods in American history in which the press is blamed for many national ills. We of the press will survive the period. The interesting question is, in what condition and form will the nation survive?

These remarks will suggest that the most thoughtful of the current press critics are less angry at the press than concerned for the nation. Instead of reacting to our critics with anger, we might help them and ourselves by engaging them in conversation about one of the more curious facts of national life. In recent years, most major American institutions have been intensely criticized by Americans. The press is only one among many targets of this criticism. Our time may be remembered as the era of the social critic.

I

Some of us like to say that the public resents the press just because we have brought it bad news, especially in the dismal decade of the 60's. There is a germ of truth in this explanation, but while it may be soothing

* Based on a talk originally presented to a group of Detroit reporters and writers.

for us to believe in it, there is little we can do about the "bearers of bad tidings" theory. Those few who criticize us for the facts we report fail to understand the times in which we live and the functions of the press. Unfortunately, we have little basis for discussion with such people.

We are experienced enough not to be surprised when some interest we have challenged hits back at us. Nor should we be surprised when politicians take us on. The American politicians' job is to transmute public dissatisfactions into workable political majorities. What should surprise us is that there was so much dissatisfaction with which the politicians could work.

The most thoughtful criticisms have to do with the values expressed in the press and with the behavior such values may encourage. The thoughtful criticisms may be found at progressively deeper levels of subtlety, but they are linked by a common theme: words and ideas have consequences in behavior. Thus, our critics say to us, the press is partly responsible for the behavior of the total society.

Let us scan what the thoughtful critics say and consider some bases for conversation with them.

Some object to the appearance that we approve of the "bad" events we report. It is not easy to dismiss this charge, especially when various publics differ so widely about which events are good and which bad. At a time, for example, when a significant portion of the public resists change, all of the press is likely to suffer criticism on behalf of that part of our profession which seeks rapid change. Explicit discussion of all of the values involved might help.

Some critics accuse us of fomenting the "bad" events we report. While there may be some unavoidable feedback effect between reporting extreme behavior and encouraging additional extreme behavior, the criticism can be met with facts and with journalistic restraint.

Some critics make a more sophisticated comment: The press has led parts of the public to expect too much good or to be prepared for too little bad. By overplaying the prospects of good effects which might result from, for example, the New Frontier, the civil rights movement of 1961–64, the War on Poverty, or ending the Vietnam War, hopes and expectations were aroused which, almost in the nature of the cases, could not be satisfied in a short time. These soured expectations have, especially among some blacks and students, turned to resentment.

The obverse criticism is that we failed to prepare the public for continuing difficulties, especially in respect to race relations, national security questions, and foreign affairs. For example, by overplaying criticisms of the military and underplaying foreign threats to American interests (an old story which currently excites little interest) the press and others have for several years led the public to believe that a new era of peaceful international relations had dawned, when in fact the old era may still linger on. Cynicism results, directed either at the government or at the press.

While complex, these criticisms can be answered with the skills with which good journalists are best equipped: careful reporting and honest analysis.

But the most serious criticisms are much more difficult to treat, for they are directed as much at the condition of the society as at our profession.

II

Millions of well-intentioned and informed people sense that in the 60's and early 70's something fundamental had gone out of American life. The public beliefs which held the country together, and helped to carry us through World War II and the 1940's and 50's, no longer always command assent. The national consensus which maintained hope, confidence, and unity has been gravely injured. No new substantive consensus has yet arisen to flesh out the almost bare bones of Constitutional governmental procedures. A feeling exists of unease, perhaps of national crisis. Many thoughtful people place part of the blame upon the press.

It is impossible briefly to state the substance of the damaged consensus. We may remind ourselves of its flavor by stating some propositions with which most thoughtful people probably would have agreed in, say, 1955, but which are not widely accepted today:

1) The American political system takes account of all legitimate grievances, encourages moderation and restraint, and consistently produces compromise accommodations which all interested groups accept as workable approximations of justice;

2) Most Americans accept middle-class values as proper guides to behavior and aspiration; their children will emulate these standards;

3) Our college and university system prepares young people for useful functions in our social and economic system and transmits accumulated experience and wisdom to succeeding generations;

4) The United States has a bi-partisan foreign policy on the fundamental premises of which all major political leaders agree;

5) The American people rally behind their government and armed forces in times of military activity;

6) A basic constituent of the good life is constantly increasing production and distribution of goods and services — and our economic system provides this constituent;

7) The market mechanism of commodity pricing and distribution generally provides the most effective method of consumer satisfaction and protection;

8) Our system of labor-management relations produces a workable approximation of economic fairness while permitting non-inflationary growth;

9) Race relations in the United States are slowly but steadily improving; the minorities' standards of living, and their attitudes about their prospects are steadily getting better.

To repeat, most thoughtful Americans probably would have accepted these somewhat nostalgic propositions in 1955. How many would today? Every week, or every day, our own pages report people who express the very opposite of each proposition.

This simplified statement of some elements of our damaged consensus may convey the seriousness of the problem and some idea why so many Americans feel uneasy. If the tacit agreements and faiths which permitted a diverse society to hold itself together no longer command respect, what will?

What difference does it make if the consensus — which evolved in the 1930's and endured through the 1950's — has been damaged? Only future historians will know. It will have caused no more than intense concern *if* external and internal circumstances allow the country sufficient time to pull itself together again. But the broken consensus at least makes it exceedingly difficult to maintain an effective foreign policy. At worst, it will remind us of the Weimar Republic or of the period preceding our own Civil War.

III

Who killed the consensus? Did the press kill it?

In one sense the answer is, the press certainly did not kill it. Events killed it, increasing social cleavages killed it, growing disagreements about basic values killed it. Vietnam, riots, campus unrest — Lee Harvey Oswald, Mario Savio, Rap Brown, William Fulbright, Eugene McCarthy, or Lyndon Johnson or Richard Nixon are each said by some to have killed the consensus.

But let us ask the question again and more insistently.

Let us reflect upon the biggest stories of the 60's, upon the continuing journalistic themes and fashions since 1960. Many have been themes of sweeping social criticism. They have cut deeply, not just into "The Establishment" (whatever that may be), but into established beliefs and convictions.

Can you recall a decade in which so much news was made by critics or was about criticism? The New Frontier opened with systematic criticism of alleged pre-existing complacency. The civil rights movement, the War on Poverty, the anti-Vietnam War movement, the campus disturbances, the social commentary following the urban riots, the challenge to our entire military apparatus: each was intensely critical. College and university professors made news with criticisms of all sorts; their students emulated them (and vice-versa). Even the later news themes, "environmentalism" and "consumerism," struck sparks because they criticized values, assumptions, and organizations.

The press has devoted great attention to the critics and to what they have said. We have lent weight to, and bestowed a certain legitimacy upon, a variety of criticisms by giving them wide and frequent exposure. In effect, the press has amplified the university's critical mood and style and aimed it at the total society. The net result has been an unprecedented barrage of challenges to government agencies, public policies, private relationships, long-established understandings, values, beliefs, and faiths. While no one can prove it, the cumulative effect seems to have been to erode public confidence in them all.

We of the press may say, don't blame the press, that was the nature of the decade. Criticism was where the news was. We don't make the news; we just report it.

Entirely correct. But it is just here that the going gets rougher.

It is here that the thoughtful critics of the press meet the thoughtful members of the press on about equal terms.

If the treatment of news in a free society runs a significant risk of damaging the consensual bonds which hold the society together, some sort of moral dilemma is created.

If it is true that one may never know where a society's breaking point is until it is reached, some sort of moral dilemma is created.

This is what the most thoughtful critics of the press seem to be trying to say. They do not deny the difficult nature of the decade. They seem to say, an exceptionally difficult time requires exceptionally thoughtful treatment by the press.

IV

What can the press do?

The press certainly cannot attempt to create and impose a new national consensus. Some major communications media seem to share the critical viewpoint of the universities. But while critics can damage public agreement, only political leadership can create it. Even if the enormous opinion-forming influence of major media and university faculties were combined in an attempt to impose a new consensus, the effort would surely and deservedly fail. The press is already questioned for the apparent homogeniety of its social and political value judgments. It would be morally repugnant if the press were to attempt to propagandize any single viewpoint to a free society whose avowed strength is philosophical pluralism.

But thinking about the idea of national consensus might stimulate the press to reconsider the question: What was so wrong with the old consensus? Are we certain the critics did the right thing when in piecemeal fashion they eroded confidence in it? Are we certain that its elements were so untrue or so unworthy as to be valueless? Are we sure that faith in the elements of the old consensus could not be and does not deserve to be repaired?

Now the press is criticized for giving the critic too much uncritical attention. It is criticized for spending too much time transmitting to everyone one man's criticism of another. There is a certain merit in these charges, in my opinion.

Yet we seem to be living in the time of the critic. Perhaps a time of intense social criticism calls for special press investigation of the phenomenon of criticism itself. And perhaps we would improve the level of public understanding, and better serve ourselves, if we always struggle to report the total context in which criticism occurs as thoroughly as we report its substance.

1) Do we put the criticism in perspective? How important is it? What moral weight does it deserve? Do we understand the history of the problem at issue and, hence, the history of the criticism?

2) Do we put the critic in perspective? What are his credentials, his record for accuracy in the public interest — or in the national interest? Do we sometimes allow the critic immunity from criticism? Why?

3) Do we analyze the consequences of the alternative courses of action implied by the criticism? The critic usually recommends or implies that "something different" be done. Do we fully explore its direct effects, its possible unintended side-effects, its costs (in the broadest sense of that word)?

4) Do we take account of the inherent advantages a critic may enjoy? A critic can shift tactics or even shift targets; a defender is confined to a fixed position which he must hold. Moreover, the defender typically receives less, and later, news attention than the critic.

5) Do we consider the cumulative effect upon public attitudes of chipping away one more element of public belief? Are we certain that the news value or moral worth of a criticism outweighs the continuing erosion of faith in a time of little faith?

Perhaps the recent wave of criticism of our profession can do us an unintended service. The first-hand experience of being criticized may help us to see better the damaging consequences of sweeping criticisms which are not placed in perspective. Newsmen are probably the best equipped to place all social criticism in balanced, experienced, mature perspective. In that essential effort our best tools remain those we have always relied upon: accuracy, completeness, and honesty.

Mr. Ashmore traces recent developments in journalism and comes to the conclusion that there is a need to define journalists in terms of the position they take vis-à-vis the events they report. Responsible journalism must be assessed in the context of whatever substantive contributions are made through the press to the public debate and to providing answers to the complexities of life in contemporary society.

This is a demand for advocacy, for taking a critical position on the issues of the day. There are two problems with this: one, the kind of individual who is capable not only of intelligent criticism of his environment, but also of his own activities, is rare in this society and thus also among journalists. And, second, the forces responsible for the shaping of the new generation fail in the attempt to inspire men and women to become competent critics of their social and political environments if they do not avoid the coziness of conformity and the ease of majority rule.

The events of the 60's demonstrated that it was easy and perhaps even comfortable to join in protest against violence as long as there was a "cause." It became more difficult and, in the end, impossible to sustain that protest movement partly because the issues became more complex, and partly because the movement had lived on emotional reactions to intolerant situations rather than on an understanding of the political activities involved. A generation that had known the importance of the role of the critic and heretic in a democratic society as a driving force for changing that society might have survived and continued to raise its voice. But few survived.

Journalists were no exception in this case. The advocacy of anti-government actions to bring about social and political changes was often based on sympathy with the causes of the protest movement rather than on the belief that the press has an obligation to provide alternatives to ideas and movements championed by the government *or by any other group in a society*. But can such a position be maintained if self-criticism and review of the activities of the press are not a part of the ongoing process of examination? How critical can the media be of their own actions outside of an ongoing dialogue with those they purport to serve?

As Mr. Ashmore says, there is a challenge here for journalism and mass communication programs in universities to assume leadership in the education of young men and women who have chosen a career in communication. By stressing the intellectual and social history of the professional communicator as well as emphasizing the importance of self-discovery, social relationships, and the power of criticism and self-criticism in the process of learning, such programs could help focus attention on those theoretical and practical issues that seem most important to the understanding of the role and function of modern journalism.

Journalism has moved beyond the point of serving as a transmission belt for news and entertainment. It is — theoretically, at least — the most powerful instrument for the education of society. Can journalists fulfill their responsibilities short of providing intellectual leadership in discussions of the future of mankind?

Journalism: the State of the Art

HARRY S. ASHMORE,

President, Center for the Study of Democratic Institutions

Eric Sevareid once characterized this as the age of journalism, and by most of the ordinary tests he may be right. When he and I were breaking in a generation ago, our contemporaries' main concerns were lack of job security, low wages, barely tolerable working conditions, and negligible social and intellectual status. On all these counts the passage of thirty years has seen a virtually complete transformation.

By contract or precept, the Newspaper Guild and the broadcast unions have established grievance procedures to protect the rank and file against the kind of captious dismissal that long provided grist for newsroom raconteurs. In the executive suites, where the individual stakes are higher, the power struggle goes on as before, and a prudent editor still works with his hat on. But if he has no certain hold on any given job, he has fair assurance of continuing his career; the shifting balance of newspaper, magazine, and broadcast journalism has not diminished the number of front-line practitioners, and this total is more than doubled by the still proliferating mass of journalists who employ their skills in some form of public relations.

As to pay, the more prominent among the reporters and commentators have attained show-business celebrity and incomes to match. When Martha Mitchell called up my old alma mater, *The Arkansas Gazette,* to suggest the crucifixion of Senator Fulbright, an innocent bystander got hoist onto the cross and it was revealed that the news director of an *educational* television station had been drawing down $50,000 a year. In Los Angeles the six *local* TV anchormen enjoy salaries ranging from $60,000 to $300,000. Proceeding upward from these benchmarks to the misty heights of income available to top hands on *network* TV, we find Chet Huntley announcing that when he retires from NBC News he plans to buy Montana.

While an ordinary journalist still can't expect to earn as much as a plumber, he has attained the income bracket of a college professor — and like his academic contemporaries he enjoys emoluments, including side income and expense account travel and maintenance. If he works in anything approximating a metropolitan market his office is certain to be turned out with all the plastic comforts of a savings and loan headquarters. The old lobster trick is no more than a sentimental memory; these days nothing less than a grade-A assassination is covered after 8 p.m., and the riots and assorted confrontations which provide most of the news are carefully timed for the maximum convenience of reporters and cameramen. On weekends the newsrooms of the nation are occupied only by the most junior copy boys, which is probably just as well since Sunday newscasts and Monday morning newspapers are primarily repositories for handouts from accommodating public relations men.

Whether or not it is actually so, journalists are widely assumed to exert profound influence on public affairs. Collectively they have the power to confer celebrity or notoriety, or to withhold them, and their more ambitious fellow-citizens have never scrupled between the two. (Just spell the name right, boys. . . .) So journalists are courted, and condemned, as never before. . . . In this onslaught mere newsmen have been called by name and established as co-equals with leading university presidents, Supreme Court justices, prominent philanthropists, and even their own publishers. This represents a considerable climb on the prestige scale over the days when they received such treatment only from Southern governors and lone Senatorial demagogues.

By all the material standards, then, the contemporary journalist has arrived. His personal compensation, in money and prestige, at least equals that of any other professional with whom he would willingly compare himself. The shakedown in the print media brought on by the advent of television appears to be about over, and as a whole the institutional base of journalism is highly profitable and technologically innovative — providing marvelous new resources for reaching a virtually universal audience.

Yet it appears that there is as much discontent in the profession as there ever has been. My palate was hopelessly corrupted in my early youth and I still have a weakness for the splendid drinks and dreadful food served in press clubs and those saloons that function as adjuncts to newspaper offices. I find these resorts filled with a general unease. It is a mark of the great sea change that this appears to stem less from the personal circumstances of practicing journalists than it does from an increasingly painful awareness of the implications of the subject assigned for our discussion — the ethical and moral issues in mass communication.

I do not believe anyone can seriously argue that these issues are not urgent. They have been raised in both institutional and individual terms by the dislocations that have destroyed the last vestige of domestic tranquilty in the United States, and have led sober men to consider the possibility that we may have entered upon the final decline of Western civilization.

In these circumstances the communications media inevitably have come under attack. They are, first of all, conspicuous among those institutions the dissidents lump together as The Establishment — so they are prime targets for the radical Left, and they also receive a large share of the retaliatory salvos fired by the radical Right. When politics is polarized, as is increasingly the case in the United States, the mass media are necessarily exposed to such cross-fire; by their nature they are positioned on the middle ground.

The media may complain that they are misunderstood, but they cannot plead that they have been mis-identified. Formally or informally, journalistic institutions are organs of The Establishment; in a Communist country it is their function to defend and propagate the official faith; in a capitalist society they enjoy guarantees against state control and are expected to perform a critical role, but their economic dependence upon the prevailing system establishes fixed limits to the range of dissent. The media can be stringently reformist, and in my view they must be if they and the society are to survive. But they cannot be revolutionary; they are irrevocably bound into the system and it is nonsense to urge, or charge, that they support those who are bent upon bringing the system down. Those who practice kamikaze journalism must do so outside the institutional base, waiving its privileges and immunities along with its essential sources of support.

The media, then, are properly subject to the general indictment that has brought on some blind reaction, and perhaps as much agonizing reappraisal, among all the major institutions of our society — the executive and parliamentary agencies of government, the courts, the church, the university, the market system, political parties, even the family. A generation is rising which regards none of these as sacrosanct, or even worthy of respect, and I believe it is a matter of the first importance that the media not be diverted from consideration of the profound implications of that condition by the excesses of their detractors.

The record so far is not encouraging. There is some truth in the contention of the media's apologists that the press traditionally suffers unpopularity when it adequately performs its function; if it accurately mirrors the horrors and depredations of contemporary society it may be greeted with the combination of disbelief and wrath commonly accorded the bearer of bad tidings. But this, surely, is a minor aspect of the credibility gap that now separates the media from the disaffected young, the racial minorities, virtually the whole of the intellectual community, *and* the "silent majority."

The arguments most commonly offered in defense of the media have a wistful, old-fashioned air — as though we were still concerned with protecting John Peter Zenger against the king's bailiffs. The fact is that public affairs journalism, which once dominated the mass media and justified their privileged constitutional status, now rides piggyback on a massive popular entertainment enterprise which never entered Thomas Jefferson's imagination, and doubtless would have deeply offended him if it had. The size, and the character, of the institutions that embrace and sustain contemporary journalism have been so altered in the middle years of this century that they clearly raise issues beyond the ken of the Eighteenth Century establishmentarians who drafted the Bill of Rights.

Maury Green, a perceptive veteran of CBS newscasting who now views the scene as a professor of journalism in Los Angeles, has written:

> TV news *is* entertainment, no matter how much TV newsmen protest that it isn't. Dr. Frank Stanton, the president of CBS, doesn't like his employes to call newscasts "shows." But they are "shown" aren't they? They even need to be put together somewhat like a variety entertainment show, except for content. If they aren't good shows, or they don't keep you entertained, you don't watch. You change channels. That's show biz. And the "cult of personality," which all the critics deplore, that's show business too. Even David Brinkley, who makes his living by it, deplores it. But TV news couldn't get away from the cult of personality if it tried, which it is not likely to.

Years ago Walter Lippmann wrote that it is the function of journalism to present a picture of the world upon which men can act. That picture now reaches most of the people as part of a package of broadcast images designed primarily for the senses and only incidentally for the mind. There is evidently a connection between this new aspect of mass communication and the fact that many of the young no longer draw a clear line between reality and romantic fancy — or at least no longer locate it according to the norms of their elders.

Thus the American society finds itself quite literally confronted by the first generation weaned on television — a generation subjected from earliest imprinting to a torrent of fantasy and violence in which dramatic conflict is neatly resolved by the good-and-evil simplicities of a medieval morality play. We may hope that from their secondary position the print media can provide the offsetting antidote of perspective, but there is not much evidence that they are doing so. The distinguished poet and wordsmith, Karl Shapiro, who teaches at California and regularly lectures on major campuses, warned in a recent issue of the *Library Journal* that "this generation cannot and does not read. I am speaking of university students in what are supposed to be our best universities. Their illiteracy is staggering."

"We are experiencing a literacy breakdown which is unlike anything I know of in the history of letters," Shapiro wrote. "It is something new and something to be reckoned with. We have reached the level of mindlessness at which students and the literate public can no longer distinguish between poetry and gibberish.

"Arrogance and ignorance always go hand in hand and now we are having both shoved at us from all sides. The greed and cynicism of even the best publishers appalls me; the wild exploitation of primitivism by the media has rendered us insensible and made us a prey to every disease of esthetic decadence which the lower reaches of the imagination can concoct."

This poetic indictment rightly goes beyond the presumed deficiencies of journalism, and deals with the total cultural impact of the media; if broadcasting is the principal villain, the print media are not absolved, nor should they be. Yet such self-criticism as the media indulge in usually comes down to a dubious tossing of stones between the glass houses in which publishers and broadcasters count up their profits. In rebuttal to outside critics the media barons usually fall back upon their records in public affairs journalism as the first line of defense — and I am happy to concede that at its best it is quite distinguished, and as a whole it is much better than it used to be. But this does not mean that journalism as it is being practiced is anything like as good as it ought to be, and could be. In their manic defensiveness the apologists run the First Amendment up the Madison Avenue flagpole on behalf of practices that range from irrelevant to scurrilous.

It has always seemed to me particularly ludicrous that men who pride themselves on their skill at deflating the pompous in all other walks of life should behave like so many Colonel Blimps when their own interest is challenged. Former FCC commissioner Nicholas Johnson once wrote that the broadcasting industry's hyperthyroid concern over possible governmental censorship struck him as hypocritical in view of industry practices of self-censorship stemming from timidity and economic self-interest. Richard S. Salant, as CBS News President, promptly erupted:

"Corporate management at CBS has scrupulously observed that vital doctrine of separation of powers without which honest journalism cannot thrive . . . No topic has ever been selected or omitted, and no treatment has ever been affected, by the imagined or express wish of an advertiser . . . I — and, to the best of my knowledge, my associates at CBS News — have never avoided a topic or altered treatment to protect, or to avoid displeasing, corporate management or any advertiser."

This may very well be literally true — that no direct intervention by an advertiser in a news policy decision has ever taken place at CBS. But this hardly extends to general considerations of economic self-interest of the network, which depends entirely upon income from advertisers. These permeate the atmosphere of every TV newsroom, as one of Mr. Salant's predecessors, Fred Friendly, testified when he resigned in protest after CBS refused to schedule the live broadcast of the Senate's critical Vietnam hearings because it would replace heavily sponsored re-runs of "I Love Lucy." Moreover, Mr. Salant's stirring defense was circulated by the National Association of Broadcasters on behalf of all those covered by implication — and this company includes a large number of individual station owners whose record for rampant commercialization at the expense of the public interest would leave former Commissioner Johnson guilty of gross understatement.

When they gathered in New York some years ago for one of their spring rites, the newspaper publishers were warned of one predictable consequence of this kind of butt-headed, self-serving and wholly unconvincing response to legitimate public concern over the performance of the media. Then-President Kingman Brewster of Yale identified as a main source of exacerbation among the students their conviction that most of the matters that concern them are "ducked, glossed over, or ruled out of debate."

"These are not rhetorical questions," he continued. "They are real ones. Their reality is more convincing because the students who ask them don't pretend to have the answers. Most students are smart enough to know that there are no easy answers, but they would like their elders to admit that the questions are real . . . If they lose confidence in the rule of law, if they lose confidence in the integrity of learning, if they lose confidence in the freedom of the press and of opinion, then we will have lost them. . . ."

I wish I were more optimistic about the ability of the institutions of journalism to respond to Brewster's call to action. Their comparatively recent stability and affluence have provided the means to do the job expected of them — the money and the machinery and the journalistic manpower — but in the process of attaining material success they have become corporate bureaucracies that display little capacity for adjusting to the demands of the times.

There is a conspicuous symptom of intellectual bankruptcy in the media's massive redundancy. In print and on the air the reporters and commentators march in lockstep as they overblow every new issue as it arises, treat the most complex matters in terms of personality cult, and then anesthetize the public with over-exposure so that the editors and news directors must come up with a new sensation if they are to hold the circulation and the ratings. Thus we have been galloped from race to poverty to Vietnam to drugs to sex to ecology — a process that stultifies the possibilities of effective political action by rapidly making each issue one with yesterday's newspaper and last week's documentary film.

Before there can be institutional change there must be an admission that it is in order, coupled with recognition that the owners and managers of the media have no capacity for effective self-criticism and internal reform. They are not unique in this. Other obviously moribund institutions in our society — for example, the Congress, the State Department, the Pentagon, and the American Medical Association — find it impossible to effect fundamental shifts in policy because to do so would require the men in charge to admit that they have been fundamentally wrong. This does not come easy, and it almost never comes voluntarily. . . .

Proposals for external criticism assume that institutional change will come from the top down, consciously brought about by owners and managers who recognize the necessity of protecting their independence from government intervention by responding intelligently to serious public criticism of their manifest shortcomings. We might also give serious attention to the possibilities of concurrent action from the bottom up. This, presumably, would flow from the exercise of the individual moral and ethical responsibilities that rest upon journalists practicing in the vastly changed milieu of present day communications.

All journalists, I think, cling to some ideal of autonomy. It is this, as well as the compulsions of ego, that prompts us to resist the copyreaders who challenge our facts and seek to change our style, and fight with editors who impose limitations of policy. But we must recognize that in the contemporary communications complex there simply is no possibility of attaining the modern equivalent of what Marse Henry Watterson of the Louisville *Courier Journal* once defined as the minimum requirements of journalistic independence: great wisdom, great courage, great energy, and fifty-one per cent of the newspaper's stock.

For better or worse, group journalism is the order of the day. Only a small, and I suspect diminishing, proportion of news or commentary originates in one man's idea, executed by him alone, presented in his own words, in the context of his choosing. This is manifestly impossible in the case of TV, which now transmits an estimated eighty per cent of the news received by the American public. An hour TV news show contains fewer words than a single newspaper page. The main impact is visual, and this is provided by cameramen, directors, and film editors who, of necessity, work outside the control of the man who wrote the script — who may, or may not, be the man who presents the words on the air.

Bob Abernethy, the intelligent and dedicated senior commentator on the late-afternoon news operation at NBC's Los Angeles station, has provided some arithmetic to demonstrate how this works in practice. Five days a week Abernethy presided over a two-hour stretch of news, coming on before and after the old Huntley-Brinkley show. More than a hundred people, including thirteen camera crews, work at putting together the daily Abernethy report. The commentator's contract gives him considerable editorial authority; he can personally cover any story he chooses, change the wording of any script presented to him, and veto copy and visual material. In practice he is able to effectively exercise those options only rarely.

The pressures of time and the size and diversity of his supporting operation deny Abernethy any real supervision of those who put together the picture of the world that goes on the air bearing the imprimatur of his own reassuring image. Devoting all his time and energy to the effort, he found that in the end he could bring under his personal control only an average of seven minutes out of the total of one hundred twenty minutes on the air (less commercials).

Under these not untypical circumstances it may seem absurd even to raise the old question as to whether journalism might be truly constituted as a profession. The self-employment that has made professional status possible for doctors, lawyers, and some other specialists is clearly out of the question for the journalist. He had got to work for somebody, not only to earn a living but to obtain access to the tools of his trade. Information is not news until it is printed or broadcast, and no one manages that alone.

Yet I find myself wondering if the amorphous quality of the new corporate management of communication may not provide an opportunity for professionalization at the working level. The old-time, highly individual proprietors rejected the notion on the ground that responsibility for the editorial product was indivisible, and must rest ultimately with ownership. But there is not any longer much connection between ownership and management in communications, and the diffusion of responsibility is a leading characteristic of bureaucracy everywhere. I often amuse myself by visualizing an outraged citizen arriving with a horsewhip to seek satisfaction for a public insult perpetrated by NBC. I see him as a kind of Flying Dutchman of the RCA Building, passing in perpetuity from vice-president to vice-president to executive committee to review board in his search for the man ultimately responsible for traducing him.

A challenge to professionalize journalism was offered before the National Press Club a few years ago by Dr. Walter Menninger, the psychiatrist who served on the National Commission on the Causes of Crime and Violence. That experience, he said, had given him a new concern over the public responsibilities of those who report and interpret the news — which he clearly feels are not being adequately discharged. Freedom of the press, he pointed out, is the only guarantee in the Bill of Rights which cannot be exercised by the individual citizen; it must be discharged by journalists presumably acting in the public interest. Dr. Menninger concluded:

"In other professions with a public trust — medicine, law, education — laws for licensure and certification assure the public that the practitioner has fulfilled minimum standards, met certain requirements for training, and demonstrated competence in the profession. The public is entitled to similar safeguards in the quality of the practitioners of this most important cornerstone of our democratic society, the news media."

The mention of licensing produced predictable bellows of outrage against the intervention of a meddling outsider, but in a later speech recounting his experience in Washington, Dr. Menninger pointed out that the matter had been before the professional journalism society, Sigma Delta Chi, for at least four years. As recently as 1966, a professional development committee reported to the fraternity's annual convention that its considerations necessarily must involve "adequate training for the profession and enforcement of its code of ethics." However, the convention did not agree with its committee's conclusion that the time was "long overdue for the profession of journalism to establish its minimum standards, announce them to the public, and begin enforcing them."

To even consider the possibilities of professionalization it is, I think, necessary to begin with a more satisfactory and comprehensive definition of journalism than any in common usage. Webster tells us a journalist is "a writer who aims or is felt to aim chiefly at a mass audience or strives for immediate popular appeal in his writings." There is, I would contend, a good deal more to it than that. It has been my observation that the public tends to expect too much from the media and, in frustration, to settle for too little. It might, then, be useful to establish what the journalist is not.

He is not a scientist, social or otherwise. The pressures of time and space rarely permit him to begin his examination of the phenomena he records with a hypothesis; the data he collects are transient and fragmentary; the conclusions with which he ends his endeavor are tentative. His mission is to present the facts as they are available, but he has no reason to confuse their sum with the truth.

He is not an artist. He has no claim to poetic license, and it is fatal to his enterprise if he attempts to employ his imagination to construct a larger view than the facts at hand will support.

He is not a polemicist. The limit of argumentation for the journalist is advocacy, and this he must undertake with a decent respect for the opinions of mankind. He has to assume that he has not yet arrived at the ultimate truth, that his adversary has a right to challenge his opinion, and that he has an obligation to treat the challenge seriously. His most resounding pronouncement must be studded with qualifiers, for it is a requirement of his calling that he put his view on record before all the returns are in — often before he has himself had the advantage of detached reflection upon what he has seen and heard and thinks he knows. Elemental honesty requires that he be long on tolerance and short on moral certitude.

Some of the most severe of these limitations result simply from the pressure of time; the scholar or the artist pursues his goal until by internal tests and the judgment of his peers he is convinced he has achieved it, or should abandon the quest; the journalist has no control over the matters that occupy him, and he lives by deadlines as arbitrary as the clock on the wall.

There are also limitations of temperament. It takes a special kind of literary discipline to accept what Robert Kirsch, the Los Angeles *Times* critic, terms the first lesson of reporting: "Often the best that can be done is a kind of evocation, rendering experience into words, and relying on one's total stance to bring some perspective and judgment into the piece." And, I would add, it takes a special kind of integrity to hold to standards of honesty and fairness when pressures are so great, time is so short, and so many shortcuts and unassailable alibis are available to those who want to shade the news to promote an advantage or nurture a prejudice.

There is currently a renewal of the old argument about objectivity — with most of the practitioners rightly holding that in journalism there is no such thing as the allegedly value-free judgments some social scientists insist are the basis of their work. The journalist who attempts to do no more than simply record what he and others saw and heard at the site of the news will not only have an unreadable report but a hopelessly imcomplete one; selecting and ordering the available facts and placing them in context is a subjective process, and if he is dealing with any human event that really matters his own values will color his judgment. If he functions at the level of analytic reporting — and in my view nothing less is worth bothering with — he must find himself operating in the manner described by John Fischer as that adopted by his predecessors in *Harper's* "Easy Chair" over the last one hundred years:

"No sensible reader, it seems to me, will be interested in a writer's opinion on any subject unless he knows the facts on which it is based and the line of reasoning by which the judgment is reached . . . [This] calls for something more than responsible reporting. It requires taking a position. It is not enough for a writer to say 'There is a bunch of facts. Make what you can out of them.' He is obligated to go a step further and say, 'I have examined these facts as best I can, discussed them with other knowledgeable people, and arranged them in some kind of order. Here, then, is a conclusion which common sense might draw from them, and a course of action which a reasonable man might follow.' "

I would say that this is a fair definition of what I believe journalism to be about. It extends into advocacy, but it stops short of action. As Fischer says, the analytic reporter will not measure his utility by the number of readers who forthwith adopt the course he recommends: "The real function of such analytic reporting is to help readers arrive at conclusions of their own."

It will be noted that I have drawn my examples from the print media.

This is not only evidence of my ingrained Gutenberg prejudices, but admission that I do not really know how these practices can be translated into usage by the majority medium. What we know about the impact of television news — and we don't know nearly enough — indicates that it has an intensely personal quality unlike anything journalists have encountered before. Maury Green has reported the findings of Albert Mehrabian, a UCLA psychologist, whose controlled research indicates that of the total message transmitted by a TV newsman only seven per cent is in words. Green draws these inferences from Mehrabian's research:

"All the rest — 93 per cent — is conveyed by the newscaster's personality: 38 per cent by vocal intonation and inflection and 55 per cent by facial expression and physical posture . . . Watching TV news, in other words, is in no sense a reasoning process like reading a newspaper. The medium really *is* the massage, and the newsman is the masseur. The content may be the same as the content of a newspaper story, but you receive it in the subconscious. And you react atavistically. . . .

"TV conveys information in exactly the same way it is conveyed when two people talk to one another. The trouble is we don't understand that either. The difference is that with TV one may talk to millions person to person, and the millions can't talk back. They can only react."

Even with a heavy discount for the tentative nature of Mehrabian's research and Green's interpretation, this condition must be seen as posing grave new problems for those concerned with the ethics of mass communication. But if it can be said to make professionalization more difficult, it also makes it more urgent. For what it really means is that, while the complex supporting organization required to put the TV journalist in touch with his audience is beyond his own control, he is himself functioning at a point beyond the reach of the backstage executives who theoretically are responsible for the end product of all this effort. This leaves the viewer to a large extent dependent upon the conscience of the man who casts the image on his picture tube. Yet the commentator who enters his living room with the manner of a confidant may well have been chosen for charm rather than perspicacity. Surely all those in the communications business, and all those who depend upon them for their view of the great world, need assurance that this performance is being judged by some standard other than audience rating.

It seems to me, finally, that these are matters that should be of special concern to those who are just now entering upon the practice of journalism. The life-style of this new generation is rebellion, the casting out of old values, the breaking of icons. The revolt of the young has been characterized by the cult of the sensory, pushed to the extreme of denouncing the rational as irrelevant. Yet in many ways it is the most conformist generation we have yet seen; it declares the wisdom and morality of the elders open to challenge, as they should be, but applies no similar test to the leaders of the young; so long as the vibes are good a substantial number of students are willing to blindly follow the most extreme among them down the dead-end paths of violence, while the rest stand intimidated and silent.

If journalism is to survive — and I cannot imagine that a civilized community can exist without the near-focus perspective it alone provides — it will require practitioners with 360-degree skepticism, men and women willing to challenge their own peers, question any proposition offered on faith, and endure the peculiar loneliness that comes of marching alongside a movement and not being of it. In the stormy time ahead professionalism may prove to be an absolute essential to provide the journalist with a standard to cling to as the waves of dissent break around him.

Kingman Brewster properly challenged the elders of the journalistic tribe when he told them that survival of traditional American culture depends upon two circumstances still under their control:

"First, whether or not the younger generations feel that the critic, the skeptic, the heretic, are still welcome, even honored and respected in the United States.

"Second, whether or not they feel that the channels of communication, persuasion, and change are truly open, as the Bill of Rights intended they should be."

It seems to me those questions apply with equal force to the other side of the generation gap — to the internal circumstances of the youth movement itself. That movement, I suggest, stands in urgent need of scrutiny by young journalists who have the skill and the stamina to apply a cool, clear, professional eye.

Mr. Vanocur's plea here is a poignant one, coming as it did when he resigned from NBC a few years ago.

"I am still searching, still groping," he writes, "for I fear there is something about television itself which defies those of us who hoped to use it as a means of enlightenment."

And, later, "Illusion, of course, is for the most part much easier to live with than reality."

So what does he propose? For one, that prevailing attitudes — such as that of the media toward the government — will have to change. But is the capacity for change there?

He is not optimistic. But his view of the problems presented here may help the rest of us to see what those problems and obstacles are . . . should we be really curious.

Mr. Vanocur believes that viewers of television "will accept a good deal better than we are now giving them." Will they — we — in fact?

In any event, "What Americans really want," Mr. Vanocur suggests, "is some approximation of reality upon which they can take such action as they may deem necessary."

But how is the viewer to discriminate honesty from advocacy? Will there not always be those who would subvert *any* ethical standard for their own purposes?

TV's Failed Promise*

SANDER VANOCUR
ABC News

When it was announced that I had resigned from NBC, Harry Ashmore called and asked me to set down my thoughts on leaving electronic journalism. I delayed for the longest possible time, hoping for some divine revelation. None came. What I finally had to face when I sat down before the empty sheet in the typewriter was the realization that for the past fifteen years — just about the whole of the age of television — I had been living in a kind of fantasy world, clinging with increasing desperation to belief in the proposition that television could enlighten mankind. I labored in the vineyard dutifully, and until recently, fairly successfully, under the impression that the wine was good, some years better than others, but not bad overall. If my work place was not to be confused with that of the Lord, I was, at least, providing a decent libation for His flock.

But now the fruit had turned sour. It had been going bad for some time and I should have seen much earlier that no amount of effort on my part could improve the vines. The soil was too rocky, the sun had ceased to shine, and, to run the metaphor fully into the ground, the bloom was off the grape.

My task would be less difficult if I could assign blame. But I cannot.

* Reprinted from the *Center Magazine* (Vol. 4, No. 6), December 1971, by permission of the author and the publisher. At the time he prepared this, Mr. Vanocur was with the National Public Affairs Center for Television.

There are no villains, but neither are there any heroes. Television exists, therefore it is. In the nature of my calling I have thought of it in terms of public information, and I have been concerned with its function. The last time we discussed those matters at the Center Nick Williams of the *Los Angeles Times* sardonically defined the task of journalism as educating the elite and pacifying the masses. In television, I fear, we have done neither; the elite is evidently still uneducated in important respects, and the masses are far from pacific.

I am still searching, still groping, for I fear there is something about television itself which defies those of us who hoped to use it as a means of enlightenment, as a means of providing the citizens of a democracy with the kind of information that permits them to act wisely upon the choices that life and their leaders offer (or deny) them.

This is particularly frustrating to me, since, essentially, I am a child of television news. My newspaper career, on the *Manchester Guardian* and *The New York Times,* was brief. I found myself before the age of thirty, quickly and successfully adapting my intellect, senses, and skills to transmiting events through the new visual medium. One of the pleasures of doing this back in the nineteen-fifties was that there were not many rules. Milton Berle summed it up when he told Dave Garroway that in the early days of television entertainment you could do almost anything you wanted to and no one could complain because no one knew what you could or couldn't do.

So we tried everything. And we showed everything. The process grew and grew until we have now reached the moment when our viewers, after being served war with their cocktails, and having shared their children's learning experience while watching close-ups of political assassination, can look up from their newspapers and say with some weariness, "Christ, not another close-up of the moon." Television news programming has made us all, on both sides of the tube, spectacle-weary, sensation-weary, information-weary. Our senses have become numbed, our imaginations have been made obsolete. About the only fantasy a person can enjoy these days in private is a sexual one, and when the new videotape cassettes swing into full production they will not only empty the movie houses on Forty-Second Street, they will also very likely deprive us of this last remaining bastion of non-literalness.

But is television all that literal? Or has some gigantic shell game been perpetrated upon us? Do we think we are seeing all there is to see when in fact we are seeing less than meets the eye? Instead of seeing more of the world than we can bear, are we actually being underwhelmed?

A rerun of those musings was prompted one Sunday morning, shortly after I had left NBC, when I read an article by Anthony Lukas in *The New York Times*. It expressed his regret that men like Mel Allen and Red Barber were no longer broadcasting radio accounts of baseball games. He made this point, which I think applies no less to television news:

"Most important, radio fed the listener's fantasy, and baseball is a game that lives on fantasy. Radio was often an art form because it left space for the listener to fill with his own secret musings. But television leaves no such space. It is explicit and literal, filling the event entirely and squeezing out the intimations which might give it another dimension. At one and the same time, it tells us too much about the game, and too little."

The passage reminded me of Willie Morris's story about a regional baseball tournament in his hometown of Yazoo, Mississippi. When rain delayed the game for several hours, Willie, a player of some renown in those parts, was drafted to do "color" for the local radio station until play could be resumed. The break lasted about four hours, during which Willie interviewed the home team, the visiting team, spectators in the stands, the concessionaires, the groundkeeper, and the local sheriff. Finally, he stuck the mike in front of his coach, Chewing Gum Smith, and asked, "Chewing Gum, who do you reckon is the best player in this tournament?" Chewing Gum reflected for a moment and replied, "Why, Willie, I guess you are." Morris, taken aback, but only slightly, pressed the mike closer and said sweetly, "Chewing Gum, could you go into a little more detail?"

The problem I found myself facing more and more in television news was that I wanted to go into "a little more detail." But at the same time, due to the inherent limitations of the medium, plus those imposed by what the conventional wisdom of journalism deems important, I found that all of us were doing to the news what Lukas claims television has done to baseball, telling too much, yet too little.

*   *   *

Let us not be unduly romantic about journalism. In newspapers as well as on radio and television, the public has been getting what has come to be known as snippet journalism. One can be loose with generalizations, and no doubt I will be here, but it seems to me that television may bear a special responsibility in this regard. We seem to have, in ways I do not pretend to understand, reduced the attention span of human beings. (Immediately a conflicting thought presents itself: perhaps we have not actually reduced the attention span, but proceed on the assumption that we have, thereby involving ourselves in some kind of process that distorts our own views no less than those of the viewers.)

For years we in television news have acted on the principle that no single story, whether related without visual backup or presented by means of film plus narration, can average more than two or three minutes at the most on the big evening network programs. But how do we know this? How can we be so certain? My instinct is to say that we can go on longer on subjects that really matter — or we could if we could reach some kind of agreement on what really matters and stop using our time and resources to cover pseudo events. But I am not totally certain of this. The nagging thought continues to cross and recross my mind that there is something chemical, biological, optical — you can supply your own term — about what comes out of that box that somehow, in ways I have tried but failed to understand, changes the very nature of that which is being transmitted.

In going through my files recently I came across a speech Newton Minow made in 1962, when he was chairman of the Federal Communications Commission, dealing for the most part with the subject of international communications. Addressing the International Radio and Television Society, Minow quoted the late Edward R. Murrow who had said on one occasion:

"A communications system is totally neutral. It has no conscience, no principle, no morality. It has only a history. It will broadcast filth or inspiration with equal facility. It will speak the truth as loudly as it will speak falsehood. It is, in sum, no more nor less than the men and women who use it."

Now, in my judgment, you could take those of us who came after Ed Murrow, wrap us all together, and still not have in the sum a collection of individuals who used radio and television to more purpose than did Ed Murrow during his twenty years of service. But in the end he was done in by the communications system he once believed to be totally neutral. A case can be made that television's most distinguished journalist was shoved into eclipse by the men who run CBS, and no doubt the case would be accurate and persuasive. But it would not be complete.

Murrow's rise to fame and more importantly his rise to influence went hand in hand with the rise of the new means of communications: broadcast journalism, first on radio, then television. When he said on radio, "This is London," by God, man and boy, the listener felt he was part of history in the making. When Murrow and Fred Friendly put on the first "See It Now" program and it opened with a live shot of the Atlantic followed immediately by a live shot of the Pacific, again the viewer felt he was part of history in the making. But today when we have all been to the moon over and over again, what does television do for an encore? A communications system that rapidly reduces everything to the commonplace is not, in my judgment, "totally neutral."

So I continue to wonder whether there is not something about the transmission of observed experience as it comes through the box that embodies distortion within the experience itself — distortion arising from the fact that television may somehow erase the realization that there are usually several truths surrounding persons and events. If this is so, then we are all like characters in a Pirandello play: we may confuse illusion with reality simply because the confusion itself is built into the human condition.

Because the world contains so many truths and so many lies, so many realities, so many illusions, television, when it is *programmed,* tends to aim at simplification. This may and often does result from the conscious decision of the people who produce what goes out on the air to reduce complexity as far as possible. On a subconscious level, however, this doubtless reflects their view that simplification provides the only means by which the information they purvey can be absorbed and retained by the viewers. When this technique has been utilized year after year for two decades, it tends to be accepted as standard operating procedure both by those who put the news on the air and those who receive it. Television viewing is not like watching a magician, a situation in which the performer knows that what he is doing is illusion, and the people watching him know it too. It seems to me to be evident that a steady diet of television has caused those of us who put on the news to share with those who watch a common tendency to confuse reality and illusion.

*   *   *

Illusion, of course, is for the most part much easier to live with than reality. Illusion poses no special demands; it is based to a great extent on what Coleridge called the "willing suspension of disbelief." Dealing with reality, at least on the part of journalists, may demand the continuous intensification of disbelief, a sustained skepticism that may strain the limits of the system within which we work. Disbelief is jarring to illusion; it gets you into trouble; if you push too hard too often, you will find yourself odd man out.

I found myself in this position over Vietnam starting about 1964. Reviewing my opposition to the war, which intensified when I visited Vietnam twice in 1965, I wish now that I had been as outspoken on the air as I was in private with friends. I can see now that I made a strategic error. I practiced tactical dissent, saying just enough in those early years to register my disagreement with United States policy but never enough to force NBC to a position where the network would have to say, "Tone down your views or get out." That, at least, would have been an issue worth fighting about. But I had involved myself in a more subtle process. Once you opt for the tactical approach, responding to well-meaning friends, colleagues, and viewers who keep saying, "Don't go too far, if they bounce *you* off the air, there will be no one left to register opposition," then your reasoning tends to center around tactics, not fundamentals.

Believing you understand just how far you can bend the system you find yourself fighting not for what you believe in but for what you think you can get away with. It is a process I often suspected Undersecretary of State George Ball employed in his choreographed dissent within the Johnson Administration over Vietnam. The point was made by Leslie Gelb, who directed the studies made famous as the Pentagon Papers, in an article in *Life* when he picked up something Ball once said in a television interview, "What I was proposing was something which I thought had a fair chance of being persuasive . . . If I had said let's pull out everything or do something of this kind, I obviously wouldn't have been persuasive at all. They'd have said the man's mad."

The kind of self-limiting factor that prevails in government is not different from that which prevails at the networks. In either case, if you play the tactical game and smooth over the fundamental issue you can buy time, but you wind up losing in the end. Perhaps such failure is built into both systems. More and more I see a parallel between government and network journalism: both concentrate their primary communication effort on purveying to the public illusion passing as reality.

Take the whole question of objectivity, the balancing of opposing views. The President of the United States holds a televised news conference or makes a speech about the economy, or whatever, and the networks follow with what has been styled as "instant analysis." There is, as anyone who has ever watched the proceedings can testify, precious little analysis, instant or otherwise; all of us sitting around the horseshoe obviously are compelled by the prevailing tendency to take it easy on the President. Later, if the issue is of sufficient moment, the networks will present a special on the subject, always being careful to "balance" the established version against the dissenting view.

This increasingly has troubled me for the subject matter is by definition already out of balance. The President, with the enormous propaganda advantage that any incumbent enjoys, has already dominated on his own terms the television screens and the front pages of newspapers. The only thing, in my judgment, which can be done in the name of fairness is to provide real equal time to dissenting views. And even this will not fully redress the fundamental inequality of treatment.

This fallacy was brought home to me sharply by NBC's response toward the President's economic statements and to the issues raised by Daniel Ellsberg. In the first instance, NBC, somewhat after the fact, decided to put on two programs, each of half-hour duration, at 7:30 p.m. on successive nights. I watched the first which consisted of my colleague John Chancellor asking questions of Administration officials on how the wage-price freeze would work. The following morning I happened to run into one of the network officials who managed these specials and asked him if that night they were going to put on dissenting voices like George Meany or Leonard Woodcock. He expressed surprise at my question and told me that more Administration officials would appear on the second program because the purpose of the series was to explain how the wage-price freeze would work. I was stunned. Here, a major network first presents the President in prime time then follows up with two programs devoted solely to elaboration on what he has proposed. I later learned that the president of NBC News had made it clear to Chancellor that his role was to ask questions, not to dispute or debate the efficacy of the measures the President set forth.

The Ellsberg matter was even more depressing to me personally. When Ellsberg went into seclusion following the publication of the Pentagon Papers, CBS managed to get an interview with him which appeared in part of the Walter Cronkite Evening News and which later that night was expanded to a half-hour program. I complained bitterly to a vice-president of NBC News that we should have made an effort to get to Ellsberg. I further stated my judgment that CBS's exclusive on Ellsberg did not result wholly from journalistic enterprise but was a product of the view of the peace movement, that CBS had been fairer in its reporting of the Vietnam war and the opposition to it than we had been. The executive disagreed. His basic point of view was reflected in his suggestion that CBS got the interview because its nightly news program ranked higher in the ratings than ours did.

A week later, I had a call from a young man in the peace movement who asked if NBC would like to put Ellsberg on the air. He specifically offered to make him available for a half-hour interview during prime time, in which Ellsberg would expand on the reasons why he had done what he had done. I took the proposal to Reuven Frank, president of NBC News, who found every reason under the sun why NBC should not give Ellsberg the time. I gave up in disgust and tuned in a few mornings later to see Ellsberg being given about twelve minutes on NBC's "Today" show, much in the same manner that Meany and Woodcock later appeared to register their opposition to the President's economic program. To compound the matter, NBC fell all over itself to give Dean Rusk an *hour* in prime time to give his views on the Pentagon Papers.

*   *   *

These incidents drove home to me how much a part of the selling process of governmental propaganda our broadcasts have become. (I am confining myself primarily to network television because it is what I know best, but when the score is added up by future historians I doubt very much that the printed press is going to come out much better.)

I do not see how we can allow this process to continue. We are playing with a stacked deck, and it is stacked not only against the practitioners but against the public. If we accept the premise that we exist to help people deal with reality, not to compound illusion, then we simply are going to have to find new techniques for dealing with the flow of news and information.

There are those who argue that it cannot be otherwise in a medium licensed by the government. I think this is a cop-out. What the argument avoids is an examination of the willingness of those who run the networks to be used, a consideration of how satisfying they find it to be part and parcel of established authority. I do not recall many incidents of rape, but seduction is rampant in the industry.

I believe this prevailing attitude to be a far more profound factor in shaping network practice than advertising-sponsor influence. It flows from a basic misinterpretation of what our role should be. The prevailing view is that we must not stick our necks out: we are, after all, guests in people's living rooms. Anyone who day after day is boldly insisting or even gently implying that the government is, at worst, lying, at best, incompetent, according to the conventional wisdom is bound to wear out his welcome not only with those who watch him but with those who are his sources.

To take the second point first, the people who are supposed to be our sources are damned well going to tell us what they want us to pass on to the American people. They are not giving us information because they are fond either of us or the truth. As to the first point, our obligation to the public is not to be pleasant and reassuring but to be as honest as we know how, whatever discomfort that entails us or our viewers — which these days is likely to be a good deal.

There is no evidence, outside a few high-sounding speeches, that the men who run the networks accept the notion that they run an organization that has a duty to rock the boat. On the contrary they are devoted to the principle Sam Rayburn used to enunciate to all freshmen members of the House, "To get along, go along."

I submit that this policy is no longer sufficient. Even if it is true that it conforms to what the American people think they want, it is not what the country needs. Being essentially a decent people and usually ahead of their leaders, what Americans really want, I would suppose, is some approximation of reality upon which they can take such action as they may deem necessary.

In my naïveté I clung for a long time to the hope that broadcast journalism could provide an umbrella broad enough to accommodate dissenting views, not on a random basis but as a steady and persistent ration in the daily diet. I now think I was excessively romantic. The umbrella is not broad enough, and there is no room for one who would like, as Willie Morris beseeched Chewing Gum Smith, "to go into a little more detail."

*   *   *

I wish I believed that the networks had the inherent capacity to change. But on the record the trend is toward still further retreat into the shell of safety and conformity. In the long run, of course, the more they retreat the more vulnerable they will become because the course they have chosen is a dead end.

Like the government, the networks have been neither educating the public nor effectively pacifying it. The caution that stultifies broadcasting is the product of fear — fear of government, fear of the new medium itself. The one sure way for journalists to deal with government is to challenge it, not wantonly, not recklessly, not irresponsibly, but in a steady, sustained pattern. We should proceed on the assumption that the media are a countervailing power charged with justly resisting attempts by any element of the society to exercise undue control over any other element. This, I take it, is what the First Amendment is about. But this requires that we stop identifying ourselves as part and parcel of established authority and face up to the difficulties and the rewards that could flow from the dissolution of what is basically an unnatural coalition.

Am I beating a dead horse? Am I asking for the impossible? I suspect that I am. There is no present way that I can see to change the situation as rapidly as I would wish to see it changed, as rapidly as I think it must be changed. Behind the brave façade of resistance, trepidation was reinforced in the corridors of network power by the recent clash between CBS and the House of Representatives over the "Selling of the Pentagon." Nor am I confident that the Public Broadcasting Laboratory is going to prove any more invulnerable if its influence mounts to the point where it invites similar pressures. The question, it seems to me, is not how to avoid the pressures but how to counter them.

Any change for the better may invite a fairly high mortality rate among commentators and producers of independent spirit. There are just so many experienced and talented people around, but all those are not likely to be driven out by their unwillingness to go along with things as they are. The even more disturbing question is: What difference would it make in the end? I doubt very much if the news programs we see each night would change materially. Many who feel as I do and stay on must do so recognizing that the routine they are following today is approximately what it was ten years ago — that innovation and creativity have been drained out of the presentation of news and documentaries as the price of sitting steady in the boat.

My personal dilemma arises from my belief that the inadequate manner in which we present television news is to a great extent responsible for the inability of our society to dispense with the myths that prevent it from coming to grips with realities. We cannot continue to shoehorn all those items into a half-hour evening news show without making it into a wire-service budget with pictures. Nor do we get anywhere by adding another half hour, for we simply fill it up with the same staccato fare. Just because we have been doing it that way for the first fifteen years is no reason why we have to continue doing it for the next fifteen. Events have become too complex to be explained away in a minute and thirty seconds; we must be aware by now that the pictures we put up every night do not necessarily portray reality.

I came to the end of the road at NBC trying, without success, to get the news executives to let me kick the habit of saying very little about everything and try instead to develop a pattern in which we could say a great deal about the more significant events and trends. I don't pretend that I had any master plan for effecting such a change. That could come only with trial and error, the exercise of imagination — qualities no longer accommodated by the present structure of the television industry.

I began by recalling the last time I was at the Center when Nick Williams, the editor who performed that remarkable rejuvenation job on the *Los Angeles Times,* advised, "Educate the elite and pacify the masses." Well, there is no doubt now that television is the preëminent mass medium — heir not only to all that patent-medicine advertising the mass newspapers used to carry, but the bland oversimplification that came with it. Still, I can't shake off the hunch that our viewers will accept a good deal better than what we are now giving them. There is only one way to find out and that is to try.

It was a sinking feeling that the effort is still a long way off, if it ever can be made at all, that led me to end a materially rewarding career in network television news. My problem had come down to this: I did not fear the unknown. What scared hell out of me was the known.

Mr. Crichton prepared the following remarks in response to an invitation to contribute to this volume. Surely the President of the American Association of Advertising Agencies should be heard from in a book about ethical and moral issues in mass communication.

Alongside the more verbal critics of advertising, Mr. Crichton's comments may seem of a minor key. Yet it is easy to overlook what the advertising industry has done and does do to regulate itself. There is no federal law banning the advertising of liquor in the broadcast media, for example; it is done as a matter of voluntary agreement by advertisers.

Yet, if The National Association of Broadcasters' Code Authority "inspects and clears all advertising for toys, premiums, and feminine hygiene products," why are we under the impression that there is much mischief and wrongdoing in these and other areas?

Some will feel that Mr. Crichton adequately answers his critics; others will not.

But *is* the problem merely one of self-regulation? Is the citizen who wants to sell his house, and describes it in the most favorable way he can, any more or less ethical than the advertiser of a national product? Are the "facts" for the seller the same as the "facts" for the buyer? Is the problem solved by regulating the seller's "facts"?

Then there are our modern myths about advertising. Are they based — is our negative image of advertising in America based — in "fact"?

And what are the problem areas as seen from Mr. Crichton's point of view? Does competition bring out "the best in products and the worst in men"?

Morals and Ethics in Advertising

JOHN CRICHTON

*President, American Association
of Advertising Agencies*

The problems of ethics and morality in advertising are partially those of any form of communications, and some are unique to advertising.

Advertising Restrictions

For example, advertising usually works in confined units of space and time. A poster relies on illustration and a minimum of words; the 30-second television commercial will probably have no more than 65 words of copy or dialogue; even the newspaper or magazine page is compressed and pruned to keep the written copy as terse and relevant as possible. In classified advertising, the language may be reduced to short-hand, or agreed-upon symbols, like "wbf" for *wood-burning fireplace*. So advertising tends to be brief, and perhaps alone of communications media is intended for the casual glance, the preoccupied ear, and the inattentive mind.

Further, advertising — with the exception of outdoor advertising and direct mail — usually occupies a subsidiary position to the news and entertainment and information of the medium which carries it. Its position adjacent to, or following, editorial matter presumes that the reader, viewer or listener will transfer some part of his attention to the advertising. Advertising *competes* with the editorial material which surrounds it for the attention of the audience.

It is clear that some advertising is as useful to people served by the medium as the bulk of its editorial material; on the other hand, by circumstance much advertising has to be *injected* into the reading or viewing or listening pattern of the audience. It is either an added benefit, or a burden, depending on one's viewpoint. As an example of the difference, it is an ominous development if a newspaper starts to lose department store advertising, which is an important part of its circulation allure. On the other hand, research suggests that the interruptive quality of television commercials is a major factor in the irritation some viewers report about television advertising.

Again, advertising as communication is preliminary to another transaction, or communication translation. Most advertising — mail order, or direct response advertising, is a notable exception — is premised on a subsequent visit to a supermarket, drug store, hardware store, book store, or gasoline station. As communication, then, it attracts interest and asks for action, but in most cases that action will be beyond the scope of the advertising.

Automobile manufacturers expect the advertising to build traffic in the showrooms, where the automobiles themselves, the sales literature, and the dealer's salesmen will be the convincing factors which lead to the sale. Grocery manufacturers expect that the coupons in their advertisements will be redeemed at the food store. Department stores sometimes offer mail and telephone service on items featured in advertising, while listing which of their branch stores have the items being advertised.

Finally, advertising alone among communication media has both statutory and self-regulatory mechanisms aimed at preserving its truthfulness. Some classifications of advertising are specifically required by law to state various pieces of language relevant to the real estate or financial community. The advertising of some products — cigarettes, for example — is circumscribed by law or self-regulation. Cigarettes were removed by law from broadcast advertising; they carry warning notices in advertising (Warning: "The Surgeon General Has Determined . . .") and tar and nicotine percentages in advertisements. Liquor advertising, by voluntary agreement, does not appear in broadcast media, and it is customary to clear advertising campaigns with a branch of the Treasury Department. State laws as well deal with liquor advertising, a reflection of the legislation which accompanied the repeal of the Eighteenth Amendment. Automobiles are required to use Environmental Protection Agency figures for gasoline consumption in advertising.

Most broadcast advertising is screened by individual networks, which require substantiation for individual advertisement claims. The National Association of Broadcasters' Code Authority inspects and clears all advertising for toys, premiums, and feminine hygiene products.

All national advertising may be challenged on a truth and accuracy basis through the National Advertising Review Board, an industry apparatus set up by advertising associations to handle complaints about specific advertisements or campaigns.

The federal government is represented by the Federal Trade Commission, which since 1914 has had a mandate to encourage competition by preventing unfair trade practices, of which deceptive advertising is held to be one. Since 1938, it has had specific powers over deceptive, misleading, and unfair advertising. Other government departments and bureaus have powers over specific segments of advertising (e.g., the Civil Aeronautics Board over airline advertising; the Food and Drug Administration over prescription drug advertising; the Department of Housing and Urban Development over some kinds of real estate construction and development).

The point is that advertising as communication operates in a much more circumscribed sense than most of the rest of communications. The circumscription comes in space and time, in its relationship to accompanying editorial or program material, in its prefatory role to a final selling transaction, and in an array of private and governmental bodies which exercise some control over its content and techniques.

Advertising in an Economy

It may be appropriate to look at the kind of economy in which advertising is likely to be established and to flourish. Usually the economy is industrial, or post-industrial. An essentially agrarian economy is likely to have relatively little use for advertising. Usually the economy is either growing or has the promise of growth; an economy of scarcity is unlikely to have much use for advertising. What little goods there are are quickly bought up by the populace, and no need for selling exists. An economy where advertising flourishes is likely to be an economy with considerable choice, and latitude for differentiation in life styles and products. A subsistence economy, or one in which (for any reason) all the people want precisely the same thing, is unlikely to be an economy where advertising is important.

An important exception is Soviet Russia, a country in which superior technology lives side-by-side with crude and primitive agriculture and village life. It has concentrated on military, scientific, and industrial growth at the expense of a consumer economy.

Accordingly, particularly because Soviet and Marxist dogma have long insisted that capitalism is doomed, and that advertising is merely one of the signs of capitalism's decay, recent history may be instructive.

In 1941, the Great Soviet Encyclopedia defined advertising like this: "Hullabaloo, speculation and a mad race for profits have made advertising a means of swindling the people and of foisting upon them goods frequently useless or of dubious quality."

Thirty years later, in 1971, the definition read: "[Advertising is] the popularization of goods with the aim of selling them, the creation of demand for those goods, the acquaintance of consumers with their quality, particular features, and the location of their sales, and explanation of the methods of their use."

Behind that shift in attitude is a long history. Fundamentally the Soviet government came to recognize that advertising could help in building the quality of goods through competition, and could help consumers to find products, and (in economic jargon) optimize shopping time and reduce search costs.[1]

The point is elaborated because advertising is essentially an economic process. It is not primarily a political or social process, although it has been used for both political and social ends. It is essentially an instrument for sellers trying to reach buyers.

The Buyer-Seller Relationship

This means that the first question about morality and ethics in advertising is whether selling is itself moral or ethical.

In primitive societies, where individual, family, or tribal units sustain themselves and provide all their own services, there is no selling, and no question arises about its ethics or morality. As work becomes specialized, and as transactions become the norm of life, with a medium of exchange — money — then buyers and sellers emerge.

With their emergence comes a discussion of morals and ethics. Plato saw the need of the market in *The Republic:*

"Clearly they will buy and sell.

"Then they will need a market place, and a money token for purposes of exchange.

"Certainly.

"Suppose now that a husbandman, or an artisan, brings some production to market, and he comes at a time when there is no one to exchange with him; is he to leave his calling and sit idle in the market place?

"Not at all; he will find people there who, seeing the want, undertake the office of salesman. In well-ordered states they are commonly those who are the weakest in bodily strength, and therefore of little use for any other purpose; their duty is to be in the market, and to give money in exchange for goods to those who desire to sell and to take money from those who desire to buy.

"This want, then, creates a class of retail traders in our state. . . ."

Nothing in recent times has changed the basic pattern. There are still sellers and buyers, even if the sophistication of each has enormously increased, and even if the selling now comes from a printed page, out of the air to an automobile radio, or on a television tube. The distance from seller to buyer has increased, but the transaction and the tensions are still the same. In fact, they may be increased, simply because of the lack of personal contact. The impersonality of the relationship may heighten the dissonance.

The morality of buyer and seller is best illustrated by real estate. The seller sees the house he owns as it ought to be.

"Brick colonial, 7 rooms, 2 baths, quiet neighborhood, old shade, gardens, brick patio."

The seller is an advocate. The virtues of the house are detailed. Its defects, whatever they may be, are unmentioned.

It has never occurred to him that the advertisement might read, "Brick colonial, 7 small rooms, 2 baths of which one needs new tile, old trees but the elm is dying, gardens which require much maintenance, brick patio which doesn't drain well, and a roof which will need replacement in two years."

Those additional facts — if they are facts — are left to be developed by the buyer. He may conclude that all these things are true, and the house is not worth the money. He may never see the brick patio on a rainy day, and then be surprised. Or he may have brought along a builder, discovered the patio problem, and the incipient problem with the roof. He may then have exacted price concessions from the seller, or gotten him to fix the patio or the roof as a condition of sale. Or he may have simply bought the house, allowing in his own mind the cost of additional repairs but still feeling the house was worth the money. Or he may have simply decided not to buy the house.

The point is that there is no moral requirement of the seller to disclose these "facts." "Facts" is an odd word; it is a matter of opinion about whether new tile is necessary; the amount of gardening may be dependent on how fastidious one is.

But when the present buyer becomes a seller of the property, his position and advocacy will be almost identical with those of the man from whom he bought the house.

I am suggesting here that the morality of buying and selling can be relative, and completely changeable, depending on which role is being assumed.

And the impersonality of modern selling is an additional strain on the already existing tensions in the buyer-seller relationship.

Myths about Advertising

Advertising often symbolizes that impersonality. It is received in an atmosphere of curiosity and skepticism. In recent years various occult powers have been imputed to advertising. These are deeply-held concerns about "subliminal" advertising, or "motivational research." The first suggests that advertising can be successful by operating beneath the ordinary level of comprehension; the second suggests that systematic exploration of the psyche can produce advertising which successfully manipulates people because it is directed toward their most susceptible areas of mind and personality.

Alas for the fable! The human mind is remarkable, and eye and memory can be trained to receive and retain and identify messages or objects flicked on for a split-second. The aircraft identification techniques of World War II are a good example. There is no recorded research which testifies in any respect to the successful use of subliminal advertising in selling. It remains in fact one of those hideous nonsense notions which haunt our fear-filled society.

The motivation research story is more complex. Research will reveal that products, services, and institutions have a personality. Their users and non-users have opinions about the products, sometimes from experience, sometimes from conversations with other users (particularly family and friends); [2] there are publications specializing in analysis of products and their performance, like *Consumer Reports;* some magazines and newspapers have analytical columns which test and review new products.

In short, experience with and opinions about products may be formed from many influences other than advertising.

It is, however, a marketing axiom that people buy satisfactions, not products. As Professor Levitt of the Harvard Business School has said, people don't buy quarter-inch drills, they buy quarter-inch holes. By extension, they don't buy soap, they buy cleanliness; they buy not clothing, but appearance. It is both efficient and ethical to study the public's perception of a product, and to try to alter or to reinforce it, and it may frequently lead to product reformulation or improvement in order to effect the desired change in attitude, buying, and satisfaction leading to repurchase.

Three Problem Areas

There remain three areas which are usually items of vehement discussion with regard to advertising, and its morals and ethics.

The first is *advocacy.* Advertising always advocates. It pleads its case in the strongest and most persuasive terms. It is neither objective nor neutral. It makes its case, as dramatically as possible, with the benefit of words, pictures, and music. It asks for attention, absorption, conviction, and action.

This disturbs critics, who feel that advertising ought to be objective, informative, and dispassionate. They wish advertising not to be persuasive, but informative. Their model for advertising is the specification sheet, and they have to some degree confused *advertising*, which must interest large numbers of people, with *labeling*, which is for the instruction of the individual purchaser, and performs a much different function.

If morals and ethics stem from public attitudes, it may be interesting that the public both perceives and appreciates the advocacy of advertising. It understands clearly that "they are trying to sell me something," and their attitude is appropriately intent and skeptical. Typically they are well-informed about the product and its competitors. It is a useful attitude in a democracy.

Research tells us that the public is both interested in and derisive about advertising. It is interested in the products which are being sold. It finds elements of the selling process entertaining. The public is, however, quickly bored and inattentive when the products or the way they are sold are unattractive to them.

The second problem area is *accuracy,* used here instead of "truth" because its elements are somewhat easier to define. Most advertising people believe advertising should be accurate; that is, they believe the product should not be sold as something it is not, nor should promises be made for its performance which it cannot fulfill.

In general, advertising's accuracy is good. The dress one sees advertised in the newspaper is available in the sizes and colors listed, and at the price advertised. The headache remedy will alleviate headache pain. It could hardly have been on the market for five decades if it did not. The orange juice looks and tastes like fresh orange juice. The instant coffee cannot be distinguished in blindfold tests from ground coffee which has been percolated. The anti-perspirant reduces perspiration.

Beyond accuracy, the question is often one of perception. It is true that the dress in the advertisement is available in the sizes, colors and price advertised — but will the dress make the purchaser look like the slim young woman in the ad? Answer, only if the purchaser looks like her already. There is no magic in advertising, and no magic in most products. The satisfaction with that dress cannot be literal, and most research suggests that in the public mind no such literal translation exists. It is not expected that the purchase of the dress will make the purchaser look like the person in the ad.

And while frozen orange juice may look and taste like fresh orange juice, it will not have the pulpy texture of freshly-squeezed juice, and therefore to many people will never be its equivalent. Therefore the purchaser must decide whether the texture means enough to him to squeeze the oranges. But the accuracy is not the question, it is the extended perception of what the words mean, so that accuracy becomes equivalency.

The third area is *acquisitiveness.* It is felt by many critics that advertising is a symbol of the preoccupation of our society with material things, and that preoccupation preempts the most important spiritual values. It is felt by critics that the steady drum-fire of advertising and advertising claims, the constant parade of products and services, serve to bewitch and beguile the viewer and reader, who gradually is corrupted into being either a hedonist or a consumptionist.[3]

Of this criticism, two things should be said. The first is that the more material a society has, the greater its support for matters and institutions of the mind and spirit. It is the affluent societies of history to which one must look for the art, architecture, music, universities, hospitals, and cathedrals.

The second is that man is acquisitive. Plato again, as the Athenian speaks: "Why, Clinias my friend, 'tis but a small section of mankind, a few of exceptional natural parts disciplined by consummate training, who have the resolution to prove true to moderation when they find themselves in the full current of demands and desires; there are not many of us who remain sober when they have the opportunity to grow wealthy, or prefer measure to abundance. The great multitude of men are of a clean contrary temper: what they desire they desire out of all measure; when they have the option of making a reasonable profit, they prefer to make an exorbitant one. . . ."

It is difficult to imagine that without advertising one would have an elevated society, one in which acquisitiveness had gradually disappeared. What one knows about such diverse tribes as the Cheyennes and the Kwakiutl of the Northwest is that both took individual wealth seriously, whether in stolen horses or in gifts to be given ostentatiously in a Potlatch. Acquisitiveness is innate, as Plato suggested; what advertising does is to channel it.

Daniel Bell, in "The Cultural Contradictions of Capitalism," argues that advertising is a sociological innovation, pervasive, the mark of material goods, the exemplar of new styles of life, the herald of new values. It emphasizes glamour, and appearance. While Bell concedes that a society in the process of quick change requires a mediating influence, and that advertising performs that role, he also sees that "selling became the most striking activity of contemporary America. Against frugality, selling emphasized prodigality; against asceticism, the lavish display." It is his judgment that "the seduction of the consumer had become total," and he believes that with the abandonment of Puritanism and the Protestant Ethic, capitalism has no moral or transcendental ethic, and he points to the conflict between the workaday habits which require hard work, career orientation, and delayed gratification, and the private life in which (in products and in advertisements) the corporation promotes pleasure, instant joy, relaxing, and letting go. "Straight by day," and a "swinger by night," in Bell's capsule summary.

But Bell also sees "in Aristotle's terms, *wants* replace *needs* — and wants, by their nature, are unlimited and insatiable."

Probably no more haunting problem exists for society than motivating people. The system of motivation and rewards within a society is critical to the kind of society it will ultimately be, and to the welfare and happiness of the people in it. The drive for material goods which characterizes most Western societies may be less admirable than a different kind of reward and motivation set of goals. The fact is that the system works, and that it does both motivate and reward people. If it appears to critics that the motivations are inferior, and that the rewards are vulgar, it must be remembered that at least the people have their own choice of what those rewards will be, and observation tells us that they spend their money quite differently. It is essentially a democratic system, and the freedom of individual choice makes it valuable to the people who do the choosing. One man's color television set is another man's hi-fidelity system; one man's summer cottage is another man's boat; and one man's succession of glittering automobiles is another man's expensive education of his children. In each case, the choice of the distribution of rewards is individual.

Three Important Reservations

Morals and ethics in advertising have engaged the interest of working advertising people as long as there has been an advertising business in this country. Much of the discussion has pivoted around three ideas:

1. While most advertising is accurate because the advertisers, the advertising agencies, and the media insist that it be so, there is a fourth compelling force. Almost all products depend upon repeat purchases for success. It is the experience of the consumer — his or her ultimate satisfaction with the product in relation to its promises in advertising, its packaging, its price, etc. — which is crucial. A satisfied consumer has future value, a dissatisfied consumer has none.

2. There are some problems associated with particular kinds of products and purchasers. There are people who feel strongly that advertising directed to children takes advantage of a child's trusting nature, and his inability to distinguish advertising from entertainment, and his undiscriminating wish for products simply because they are attractively presented to him. Further, the fact that the child is induced by advertising to bedevil parents to buy him or her products is annoying to parents. There are two solutions: one is to ban advertising to children, presumably still realizing that products will continue to be sold to children, that children will want these products, and that they will continue to cajole their parents for them. The second is to take the view that the child is socialized in the process — that learning about what to buy, learning to evaluate claims, learning to make discriminating decisions, is an important part of growing up, particularly in a free society which offers so many choices, political and social. The second choice seems more sensible.[4]

3. Advertising is a means of influencing the media of communication;

it distorts or subverts the publications and broadcast media which carry it. Experience suggests that this is an overblown issue. There have been publications which have foresworn advertising, in the belief that it would make possible a kind of journalism impossible so long as the "interests of the advertisers" had to be taken into account. None of the publications survived; the truth was that their editorial content was not sufficiently different from those which carried advertising to assure their success. There clearly is a problem with the demand of media for large audiences, because large audiences are able to command larger advertising support. But quality and responsiveness of the audience is also important. It is worth remembering that the *New York Times* survived in New York when it was the fourth largest in circulation in a seven-newspaper city.

Summary

Advertising has particular problems of ethics and morality among communications media because it is essentially a method of selling. It has the ethical obligation to be accurate, and it has the unusual circumstance of extensive voluntary and statutory restrictions, some arranged to protect competitors from unfair practice, others to be sure consumers are fairly treated.

Advertising is a weapon of competition, and it suffers from some of the defects of competition. The late General Sarnoff once said that competition brings out the best in products and the worst in men, and advertising's constant competitive effort is often wearing to people who wish for a quieter world.

Nevertheless, that competition is, in some respects, a public safeguard. The need for repeat purchases requires that advertising present the product so that the purchaser finds the product's performance satisfactory. The pressure of different products and services push and pull the public mind in different ways: fly and get there quickly, take the bus and save money; spend your money and go to the Caribbean, buy a savings certificate and earn 8¾%; try the newest coffee, switch to tea. What the consumer has is the misery of choice.

NOTES AND REFERENCES

[1] For a better description of the Soviet decision, see M. Timothy O'Keefe and Kenneth G. Sheinkopf, "Advertising in the Soviet Union: Growth of a New Media Industry," in *Journalism Quarterly*, Spring, 1976. See also the work of Marshall I. Goldman, *Soviet Marketing: Distribution in a Controlled Economy*

(N.Y.: Free Press, 1963), and *The Soviet Economy: Myth and Reality* (Englewood Cliffs, N.J.: Prentice-Hall, 1968). Dr. Goldman was a pioneer in seeing the change in Soviet attitudes toward advertising.

[2] George Katona, *The Mass Consumption Society* (New York: McGraw-Hill, 1964), Chapter 10, "Group Belonging and Group Influences."

[3] I have drawn from F. P. Bishop's *The Ethics of Advertising* (London: Robert Hale, Ltd. 1949), which is a comprehensive work on the subject.

[4] For more on the subject, see Seymour Banks, "Statement by Dr. Seymour Banks in behalf of the Joint ANA-AAAA Committee before the Federal Trade Commission, October 28, 1971"; and Scott Ward, Daniel Wackman, and Ellen Wartella, "Children Learning to Buy: The Development of Consumer Information Processing Skills," Marketing Science Institute, 1975.

One of the issues that Mr. Lacy points to stems from the fact that public awareness of what is going on, as "agendized" by the media, has wholly altered the kind of society we live in, and hence the *nature* of the responsibility of the media for the present and the future of that society. But there are inherent difficulties in meeting that responsibility.

That the media necessarily oversimplify, and necessarily "distort" their reports of what is going on, for example, is hardly to be doubted. Yet do we really want the media owners and operators to be socially "responsible" to those of us amongst the consumers who disapprove of what they do or do not do? Do we want the media operators to provide only what they think would be good for us?

Certainly whatever improvement we're likely to get is not going to come from lecturing the owners and operators of the media on their "social" or ethical responsibilities. Nor is the end sought to be gained by suppression or censorship.

How, then? Mr. Lacy's ideas are challenging, informed.

The Media and Social Problems *

DAN LACY

Senior Vice President,
McGraw-Hill Book Company

There can be no question that the responsibilities of communication have become awesome over the last generation. It's almost banal to say so.

Yet it's difficult to realize how small a role the media played in earlier crises in our history. At the time of the American Revolution, for example, there were probably not more than fifteen newspapers in the country, most of which were published but once a week, often with month-old news and printed on two sides of one sheet of paper. Probably none had a circulation of more than 1,000 copies. The total pages of newsprint used in newspapers produced in the United States at the time of the Revolution probably would not equal the number of pages in one daily issue of one ordinary middle-sized American city newspaper today. Nevertheless, that was the only organized mass medium that existed at the time. The great majority of American people never saw a word of print related to the Revolution, or heard anything about it except through personal contacts during the whole eight years of its duration. It is highly likely that there were thousands of people who lived in the United States during the Revolution who did not know it was going on.

The contrast today is enormous, and the responsibilities the media bear are correspondingly enormous. The media today must shoulder a

---

* Prepared from a taped transcript of a talk by Mr. Lacy at the University of Iowa.

completely new responsibility. That new and increasingly gigantic responsibility derives from the fact that what concerns us most today is beyond
the day-to-day experiences we have. A few hundred thousand Americans
gained some first-hand experience of Southeast Asia during the Vietnam
war. But for the many millions of American citizens, Southeast Asia remains a terribly remote region, about which they have absolutely no first-
hand experience, and practically no personal second-hand knowledge.
Their reactions are based entirely on what they have read in magazines, or
newspapers, or books, or hear on radio or television. Problems like atomic
energy or the control of nuclear weapons are matters that only a handful
of specialists have any independent personal knowledge of. Although all
of us can see smog, auto salvage yards, and can see or smell the pollution of
our rivers, the more subtle forms of atomic and thermal and chemical
pollution demand, for their apprehension, increasingly technical knowledge.
So in larger and larger numbers, we are all reacting not to the world as it
really is, as we know it to be in day-to-day experience; we're reacting to a
picture of the world that has been shaped for us largely by what the
media provide. How accurate and relevant and meaningful our responses
to this world are depend increasingly upon how accurate and how relevant
is the image of the situation the media provide.

    To take the most obvious example: Our response to the Vietnam situ-
ation was monstrously irrelevant and monstrously ineffective. Certainly
our nation's decisionmakers had access to information other than that presented by the media in this case. But the mass media can create a situation
in which it is very difficult for even the wisest decision-maker to be wiser
than the masses of people themselves.

    When the Constitutional Convention met in secret in Philadelphia, I
'would guess that not one in twenty people knew it was meeting, much less
what was going on in its deliberations. The conclusions that the members
reached were substantially free — for good or for ill — from the pressures
of public opinion. But no decision in government today is made free of this
pressure. However inadequate the mass media may be, they are our main
source of shared information about what is going on in the world, and
do mobilize public opinion to a degree that cannot help but have an
enormous impact on government decision-making.

    This situation has been true not only since the days of television. It
emerged after the development of mass journalism late in the last century.
Public opinion forced President McKinley's hand at the time of entry into
war with Spain in 1898, for example. Public opinion on the race issue, for
another example, was already highly sensitized by the early years of the
century, and President Theodore Roosevelt got himself into quite serious
"public relations" problems by inviting Booker T. Washington to dinner at
the White House. Spiro Agnew brought some criticism down on himself by

using terms to refer to racial minorities that are no longer publicly acceptable terms. The winds have shifted.

I think that this is essentially a benign phenomenon — that of imprisoning governments within the limits of an informed and vigorous public opinion. But it can do harm as well as good. Such polarizations as those between the East and the West, on which our whole foreign policy has been based for twenty years, is an example of the near disastrous consequences of an ill-informed public opinion which imprisons and captures even the highest officials of the government.

There are other reasons why the present circumstances of the mass media are exceedingly difficult. One of these is the problem of accuracy, or validity. How is anyone to provide a complete and correct enough picture of the world through a television screen or a newspaper, so that ever-increasing numbers of people can respond to it meaningfully and relevantly? To do so would depend upon providing a very sophisticated, very complex, mixed-up pattern of grays, instead of one of blacks and whites. What has typically been wrong with our views of what the world is like, beyond the ambit of our daily lives, is not only coming to think it is black when in fact it is white, or thinking it to be white when in fact it is black. We have gotten ourselves into all kinds of difficulties by tending to think of that world out there as either white or black, when in fact it is always a congeries of grays in widely shifting patterns.

Most of us can handle the actualities when we are talking about the complications of politics in something as simple as a mayoralty election in our own home town. We recognize that such things are not really western dramas with the good guys against the bad guys. We recognize in it all sorts of varied interplays of interests. But when the reporter and the cameraman extend our awareness out to the international scene, these complications become very much more subtle and difficult to follow; yet the mass media face limitations of time and space that make it almost impossible to avoid oversimplification. So no matter how sincerely the mass media job is done, the result is very likely to be a misrepresentation merely through the process of oversimplification. And all of us in the audience compound that, because we seize upon the more dramatic, the more oversimplified, the more vivid depiction as the one easiest to remember. It's a good deal easier to view Laotian politics as a simple case of the good guys against the bad guys than it is to memorize the baffling genealogy of the series of half brothers who head the various factions of Laotian politics, not to mention what goes on in the opium-trading monopolies (over which, in fact, most of the fighting in Laos seems to be done). So there is always the push to oversimplification.

Too, all sorts of decisions are made along the way in the whole process of acquiring, processing, packaging, and distributing information, and whether you call these decisions "control" or "distortion" would seem to me to be a matter of preference more than anything else.

There is no need to labor the point. It is obvious that the responsibilities of the people who manage our mass media of communication are enormous. Add to this the fact that the decisions as to what goes into the media are in the hands of private owners, for the most part. Without arguing for our own system, as contrasted with those in other parts of the world, it can hardly be overlooked that we have put a tremendous power in the hands of people whose motivations at least theoretically are not particularly social, but profit-seeking. We have left to the workings of the marketplace almost all of the decisions about what goes into our mass media. Let's just say that ours is a unique and most interesting experiment. So it seems to me natural enough for us to wonder about and talk about the problem of the ethical responsibilities of those few people who have editorial power over the mass media.

Yet I must say that I get a little frightened about some of the lectures I hear on social responsibility; they all sound good when you hear them for the first time. When you hear some highly placed individual saying that television should have a much more responsible attitude toward the exposure of children to scenes of violence, we would probably all tend to agree. Generally speaking, when we talk of responsibility in that way, what we are in effect saying is that the people who run the media should not permit things which you and I as critics disapprove of. Is it irresponsible to challenge religious orthodoxies on a national medium? Is the problem really solved by making the owner or manager of a mass medium responsible to his critics?

By and large, I suspect that one of the main protections of the freedom of the press is the cupidity of the people who run the press. They are trying to make as much money as they can, and this means producing what people want and have demonstrated an interest in by paying for it. Most of the people who say that the media should be more responsible are in effect saying that those who run the media should refrain from doing things which would be profitable to them and should begin to do things that would be less profitable for them — because it would be better if they gave people what the critic thinks people should have, rather than what the people have demonstrated in the marketplace they want. This implies that there are those who know better than people themselves what people should be getting in the mass media. Perhaps this has some truth in it, and perhaps it would be better for people to hear more Mozart than rock on the radio, to get science rather than astrology in the newspapers. Perhaps it would be more useful to devote the time that most newspapers give to recipes or chats about movie celebrities to the explication of the true complications of the African situation. At the same time, once you concede this elitist position, once you take the decision out of the marketplace and begin assuming a superior ability to decide, you slide into the "papa knows best" position of control of the media.

So I view this orientation to the "social responsibility" problem with considerable reserve. I really wouldn't feel comfortable in a situation in which what is available to me on television or radio would depend upon what Mr. Sarnoff or Mr. Paley think would be good for me. I don't even think what I get on television or radio should be dependent upon what the Ford Foundation thinks would uplift me, and certainly not on what an elected official thinks I'm old enough to know or hear about politics. If we move away from the chaos and irresponsibility and banality that fill our mass media, we may move at the risk of moving in the opposite direction, where the mass media become the instruments serving not the cupidity of their owners, but predetermined social purposes that in the long run may be far more harmful to the body politic than the anarchic mess we're in.

I think it is simplistic to believe we're going to get any substantial improvement of the mass media merely by lecturing to the people in control regarding their ethical responsibility. One can be as responsible as one chooses by one's own light in any one sector of the media without having any real effect on the total flow of information. The book publishing house I work for would never dream of publishing some of the pornographic junk you see in many places, but that does not keep it from being published. The problem is not one so readily solved by any change of attitude on the part of a few managers of the media.

What most people speak of when they speak of responsibility is suppressing something that is being said which they believe is irresponsible. I do not think that is our need. Our need is rather the reverse: To have a great deal said that now goes unsaid, mainly because of the lack of an audience or the inability to gain access to necessarily restricted channels of the mass media. This is likely to be solved only through changes in the framework of the media themselves. That is, the responsibility ultimately is in the kind of framework within which the media in this country operate. And this will be determined primarily by the sorts of public policies which are enacted in the next few years. I suspect that the present arguments over public policy with respect to cable television will have much more to do with the ability of television and radio to give us varied and informative and penetrating comment on world affairs than any amount of lecturing to newspaper publishers or TV producers about their moral responsibilities.

Thus it is through structural changes that we will find an opportunity to achieve a more responsive and responsible mass media. The FCC is in a position to bring about such changes. Another basic source of such changes is antitrust legislation. But we need to bring our attitude in line with current realities. For example, it is not necessarily true that the more radio stations or newspapers there are in a given locality, the better they are. The worst newspapers in any large city in the United States are probably in Boston. Why? Because they've got the most newspapers of any city in the United States. No one of them can make enough to afford decent news coverage on a day-to-day basis. And there is a desperate scramble for circulation. And how do you build circulation? With prizes, astrology, advice to the lovelorn columns, not with responsible coverage of world affairs. Most of the best newspapers in this country are in cities where there is a newspaper monopoly or near monopoly, and where a newspaper can afford to indulge itself in responsible reporting, instead of fighting desperately for circulation and advertising revenues.

If you think network broadcasting by the great networks is bad, I agree with you. But drive across the country and listen to the local competitive radio stations where there is continuous flow of used car ads, interrupted by replays of the top 50 tunes, and an occasional news bulletin on how the local basketball team did. Basically that sort of competition does not in practice produce responsible media performance.

I think some means of audience payment for broadcasting, along with a multiplication in the number of channels, is going to be the most promising method. Not the final answer, but the direction in which we will have to move. We have to move in this direction because the government is itself not without a vested interest in control of the media. In recent years, for example, it is precisely when the media have begun to behave responsibly, to have bite, to have an effect on public attitude, that the government begins to feel its position as the dominant force in the formation of public opinion challenged, and then there begin attacks.

Ultimately, we can look neither to the media nor to the government for our salvation. If we want responsible and effective media, our salvation depends in large part on the variety of media available, so that the most bigoted regional newspaper cannot protect its local citizens from the contamination of relatively more liberal national news. We need to reshape our thinking about broadcast policies in ways that would give each of us a chance for a wider choice and a chance to make that choice effective by laying down our money for what we want, just as we do so when we go to a movie or buy a book. If we want genuine audience-dominated, audience-controlled — for good or ill — mass media, we need to question those expressions of elitist control over the media by those people who have an *a priori* point of view, and who frequently mask these points of view behind demands for "responsibility."

Discussion

Q: *It seems to me that, as the U.S. population has grown, control of the media has become more centralized. What are the rights of "the public" even now?*

A: It is true that control of the media has become more centralized, and this does pose problems. Particularly is this true when one owner controls both the press and broadcasting stations in a community. Counter-balancing that are two factors. One is a belated but encouraging concern on the part of Congress and the FCC with common control of broadcasting, the press, and CATV in any community.

The other is the growing pervasiveness of national, as contrasted with local, media. Though at first look, this would appear to be an ominous trend toward national conformity, its actual effect is to increase diversity in individual communities. The treatment of racial problems in national newsmagazines and national TV programs, for example, had a major effect in Southern communities that formerly would have seen their problems only through the eyes of the local press.

Q: *You spoke in terms of changes in public policy. Are you saying there isn't anything individual citizens can do? You hinted that some decisions as to whether to publish a book or not are not purely marketing questions. What sorts of criteria other than market might your company use to refuse to publish a particular book?*

A: Individual citizens have a wide freedom to pursue their own intellectual freedom in their choice of programs, in the magazines they subscribe to, in the use they make of the library.

And many issues of public policy are decided at a local level where a few active citizens can unite to make their efforts realistically felt. One, for example, relates to local CATV franchises, which should require the dedication of one or more channels to "common-carrier" use and a specified amount of local public service programming. Adequate financial support of the public library and backing of the librarian in stocking a wide variety of controversial books is another local issue. So is pressure on local broadcasting stations for minority group and public service programming.

Though the impact of individual effort is less visible on the national scene, the aggregate of individual efforts — especially when exercised through groups, associations, churches, etc. — can have an important effect on Congress and on regulatory agencies.

As to the second question, we would not publish works that promised to be profitable if they seriously offended our taste. We aren't squeamish about sex or crude words when relevant, but we would not publish pornography. We happily publish both Senator Goldwater and Senator Fred Harris, Eldridge Cleaver and General MacArthur; but we would not have published *None Dare Call It Treason* or a comparable work on the left. Because of our position as a scientific publisher, we would avoid works of pseudo-science. We would not publish a book for laymen on diet or medical treatment unless assured by competent medical advice that its content was sound and not dangerous. But I can't imagine our refusing to publish a book we thought worthwhile because we feared it would be regarded as controversial.

On the other hand, we do publish a number of books that have little prospect of financial success because we think they are useful as improving or sustaining the company's "image" (horrible word!) or simply because we think they're good books.

Q: *I suppose it's possible that you might decide to publish a book or series of books which you anticipated would actually lose money. What sorts of criteria do you use to make that kind of decision? And isn't there something of what you referred to as "elitism" in such decisions?*

A: Generally a decision to publish such a book or series would be because it made an important contribution to a field in which we were active — e.g., the reports of the Carnegie Commission on Higher Education. Or it might be an early work of a writer who we thought showed great promise for the future. Or perhaps a book of little popular appeal by an otherwise successful author we wanted to retain on the list. Or, rarely, just from a belief that the book is one that ought to be published. But I would not want to exaggerate the number of such decisions, whatever the basis. We often publish books that lose money, but we don't often intend to.

As to elitism, I think we have nothing to fear from an elitism that enlarges the range of choices available to the public by issuing books that would otherwise go unpublished. I am concerned rather by the attitude that would restrict the public choice to works of which an elite approves.

Q: *Wouldn't it seem to you that the ethical problems faced by university presses would be different from those which commercial publishers face?*

A: Yes. University presses are supported, like their parent institutions, from public or endowed funds dedicated (to use words from the Smithsonian's charter) to the increase and diffusion of knowledge. And hence I think they have an overriding obligation to publish only works that serve that end and meet high scholarly standards. A commercial publisher is free to serve meaner ends. I think a secondary obligation of university presses is to use their privileged position to publish for the most part works that could not otherwise find publication.

Q: *I read somewhere that the majority of books published in this country come from ideas which originate with the publisher. Isn't there some ethical issue involved here or, if not ethical, some question of manipulation? Also, since you are more likely to undertake the publication of established writers, isn't there also a question of some kind of "elitism" at work here?*

A: I think there would be some problem if publishers generally refused to publish books they did not originate. But I see no problem in the fact that publishers perceive the need for books and recruit authors to write them. If this were not done, many excellent and useful books would not appear. Here, indeed, can be one of the publisher's most useful and creative functions.

Q: *Does it seem to you that there may be some shift in American reading habits in the direction of more serious non-fiction? And might this possibly*

be because people are turning more and more to television for what they might otherwise get out of novels?
A: Yes. I think this is clearly the case.
Q: *It is not at all clear to me why you think "serving pre-determined social purposes" is such a bad idea. Would you elaborate on this?*
A: It all hinges on pre-determined *by whom.* German radio in the period 1933–1945 served the social purposes pre-determined by Hitler. Spanish radio, television, and press served purposes pre-determined by Franco; the Russians, those determined by Mr. Brezhnev and his colleagues; the Chinese, those determined by Mr. Mao and his. These are extreme examples. But French television, in a non-totalitarian country, was harnessed to de Gaulle's ends too.

It's not a black-and-white question. As I tried to point out, what I called the "anarchic mess we're in" has its own evils. I'm sure that if they were my pre-determined social ends, it would be a good thing if the media served them! But I am nervous about other people's; and I think we ought to realize that calls for "social responsibility" in the media often mask a wish, perhaps a very sincere wish, to use them for the speaker's particular purposes and to foreclose criticism of those particular purposes.

Mr. Scanlon brings to bear a wealth of experience as a journalist, and as a professor of journalism. If it is not clear to an individual journalist just what may be the "proper" — i.e., the ethical, moral — decision in a particular situation, how meaningful is it to talk about what is ethical or moral at the collective level, at the level of the whole society?

Through a series of anecdotes, Mr. Scanlon opens up some of the ethical and moral issues involved from "below." Do journalists always align themselves with those newspapers or broadcast corporations whose "politics" are compatible with the journalist's own? What are the factors involved in all such decisions that journalists — and their employers — make?

And what of competition between journalists and among their employers? How does this affect what is done, and how it is done?

Should a journalist ever accept gifts? Even the gift of a prepared "news release"?

Is the journalist's discretion sufficient? Are individual journalists equally capable of *self*-regulation, or does a code of ethics involve the interests of consumers, even their participation in its formation, as well?

These are but some of the interesting questions Mr. Scanlon touches upon.

Some Reflections on the Matter of Ethics in Journalism

by T. JOSEPH SCANLON

Associate Professor, School of Journalism,
Carleton University

I am about to break a 10-year-old promise and reveal a well-kept secret.

During the dramatic Canadian federal election campaign of 1962 — when John George Diefenbaker was re-elected prime minister, though with a minority government — I took part in a game of bridge.

It's true the game was not all that spectacular. One of the participants neither gambled nor drank, so there were no stakes and no alcohol. But there were some genuinely newsworthy aspects: three of the participants were Toronto newsman J.J. Richards of CHUM, Toronto reporter George Brimmell of the *Telegram,* myself from the *Star,* and the fourth was Canada's 13th prime minister, Mr. Diefenbaker. It was the only time I've ever seen (or heard of) Mr. Diefenbaker playing cards.

I can no longer remember all the details of the game but I do remember two things. First, J.J. and I defeated George and the P.M. (George had terrible cards.) Second, my partner J.J. appeared terribly nervous — throughout the game sweat rolled down his brow. It turned out that he was actually airsick and spent the entire time trying to avoid vomiting on Canada's head of government.

The reason that I am breaking my pledge of secrecy at this time is not to boast of my prowess at bridge, not to make fun of J.J. or, for that matter, Mr. Diefenbaker, and not to demonstrate that I can't keep a secret. What I want to do is illustrate that journalists, in the normal course of their daily work, are constantly facing decisions about what they should or should not report and that most of these decisions can legitimately be described as decisions about appropriate behavior — in short, as ethical decisions.

In my opinion — and I have some evidence to support this opinion — such discretionary decisions are made by journalists no matter where or when or at what level they work (or worked). They are also made without any real reference points except some vague ill-defined ones and they are generally made without any opportunity for public review or public debate. (It is very difficult to have a public debate on a never-revealed decision not to report that something happened.)

I hope to support my arguments that this is the case by providing evidence from my own career (as a reporter based in Toronto, Ottawa, and Washington and on assignment elsewhere), and by supporting this evidence with some widely scattered references to indicate that I am not at all atypical. I think these examples will illustrate that the journalist — more than any other person in society — uses his daily judgment in a way that can and does enormously affect the health of the body politic.

The bridge game is, admittedly, in some ways, a bit of trivia. The reason we didn't report it was simple enough: it took place on the Progressive Conservative party's campaign plane and Mr. Diefenbaker agreed to play only after we all had pledged not to report either his participation or the results. (In fact, *we* were responsible for his taking part: we had persuaded one of his aides, John Fisher, later Canada's 1967 centennial commissioner, to persuade his Chief to join us for a few hands.)

Yet the very trivial nature of the bridge game — and the apparently unimportant decision not to report it — illustrates that discretion was involved and that that discretion was used by the reporters and that no one was there to judge whether or not it was used wisely and in the public interest.

Some years later — in London in 1969 — some of my colleagues got into a major row with another prime minister, Pierre Elliott Trudeau, when they, following the lead of the Fleet Street press, decided to report Mr. Trudeau's out-of-conference activities, dates, etc., during a Commonwealth prime ministers' conference in London. Objecting very strongly to these reports, Mr. Trudeau told the newsmen at a formal recorded news conference that some of them had exhibited "some pretty crummy behaviour in London" and he suggested that it might be better if the government had files on newsmen and useful "if the police could go and question some of the women you have been seen with." [1]

Later, Mr. Trudeau explained that he was trying to illustrate how strongly he objected to newsmen reporting what he considered to be his personal life by illustrating how they would be reacting if he pried into their personal affairs. The point here is not to question the rights or wrongs on either side but to underline the point that discretion is involved in reporting and that discretion without defined norms is a very tenuous thing.

Anyone like myself, who has worked for years as a political reporter at the municipal, provincial (state), federal, and international level can recall many incidents he did not write about for one reason or another. One night in the House of Commons, for example, I recall a former cabinet minister falling drunkenly over his desk as he attempted to bow formally to the Speaker and record his opposition to a government measure. To me — and apparently to all of my colleagues — the incident was irrelevant to the issues of the day and neither I nor they reported it.

Douglass Cater makes clear in his excellent book, *The Fourth Branch of Government*, that similar incidents occur in the United States:

> Senators have been seen to stagger drunkenly onto the Senate floor and deliver unintelligible harangues without creating a ripple in the press. Considering the great glare of publicity that beats down on Congress, the unillumined corners are the more curious.[2]

Sometimes, however, we did write about untoward behavior — usually with unexpected results. When I was assigned to City Hall in Toronto, first by the *Toronto Daily Star* and later the *Toronto Telegram*, it was at a time when the mayor of Toronto was an effervescent man named Nathan Phillips, a man who liked to be known as the "mayor of all the people." When the new Russian ambassador, Amasasp A. Aroutunian, arrived in Toronto, Mayor Phillips jovially addressed him as "Mr. Rootin' Tootin'" and the reports of that meeting got world wide coverage, much to the mayor's delight. (He personally showed me a clipping of the story which had been run page one by the *South China Morning Post*.)

From then on — since they and the mayor were both delighted at the play the stories got — city hall reporters including myself went to some trouble to record with great detail and meticulous accuracy all of the mayor's foibilistic use of language. The denouément came when I, spurred on by youthful enthusiasm and delight with regular front page coverage, stole (there is no other word for it) a cue card the mayor's staff had provided for him to help him avoid mispronouncing still another name. The *Star* ran a photo of the cue card; the mayor, now embarrassed and annoyed, protested at my theft; the *Star* ordered me to apologize* and the accurate but glossy reports came to an end.

The incredible part of the incident was not that we finally reported the mayor accurately but that our readers, accustomed to seeing a neat cleaned-up version of his language in the newspapers, assumed that the detailed reports were inaccurate attempts to embarrass the mayor rather than the first precise reports ever made of his diction.

The arrival of radio and television (though live broadcast coverage is

---

* My apology went rather well: the mayor patted me on the back, said "It's all right, Scanlon," and presented me with a silk tie to show there were no hard feelings.

still prohibited in the Commons) probably makes such edited coverage less uncommon, for the television media — even when edited — tend to pick up the hums and haws and hems; * but the point is the same one made earlier. Reporters, using their discretion, decide what shall and shall not be reported. Cleaning up a man's language as you translate it from spoken to written form is apparently an unwritten requirement of print journalism.

Having thought about this question for some time, I have come to the conclusion that the question of journalistic ethics arises in three areas — those of the relationships between the newsman and his competitors, the newsman and his editors, and the newsman and his sources of information — and that the problems increase as one moves along this list.

Given my own experience in highly competitive Toronto I can say, with complete assurance, that competition does lead to excesses. The rivalry between the Star (Canada's largest daily) and its afternoon rival, the Telegram, often pushed us to crude and boorish behavior. One habit of both papers was to acquire, as soon as a fatality occurred, all available photos of the person killed. The object of this exercise was to prevent the opposition from getting even a single picture. I can recall spending an entire weekend trying to clean out all available photos of four boys who had drowned to stop the Telegram from running a picture.

I can also recall an occasion (the day before I left Toronto to become the Star's Washington correspondent) when I talked a helpful policeman into obtaining the only existing photo of a girl who had been murdered by her mother. When he came out of the house with it, I took it from him and sprinted away as one of my colleagues, Lloyd Lockhart, threw a block to prevent the Telegram reporters from catching me. The incident led to an official protest from one of the editors of the Telegram to Harry Hindmarsh, my boss at the Star. Needless to say, Hindmarsh was not in the least irritated that I had beaten the "Tely" to the punch, and had no complaint to make about my competitive behavior.

Another epic clash occurred when a series of swims began across Lake Ontario. After the first dramatic swim by a young Toronto girl, Marilyn Bell, the papers tried to outdo each other with coverage. On one occasion one of my editors was commended for calling in the entire Toronto Diamond taxi fleet at Star expense to create a self-generated traffic jam in the harbor area and thus prevent the "Tely's" ambulance from leaving with a swimmer. Looking back, one must admit that much of the competition was nonsense, even if fun.

On occasion, this competitive instinct led to purchase of exclusive news. Once, in South America, I was one of a team of reporters who managed to convince the only English speaking person on a pirated ship (the Santa Maria) that for $500 he should talk exclusively to the Toronto

* This is not as true of radio. A good editor using a razor can edit a good deal of material from a tape (as the Watergate experience showed).

Daily Star and *Star Weekly*. (He lived up to his commitment — refusing to talk to British, U.S., or other Canadian papers.)

But competition — the desire to have your own story — has its benefits and these benefits are very real. One day at city hall the opposition *Telegram* flared a story about an incident involving a land deal. The "Tely" story was intriguing if vague. When I checked it out for the *Star* I discovered that the "Tely" had uncovered only about 20 per cent of it. The result of competition was better reporting all round. Another time after the *Star* had traced a stock scandal involving some members of the provincial cabinet, the *Telegram* broke the story as seen from the ministers' point of view. The result was more information and, in my opinion, more balance. Some years ago, when I went back to the *Star*'s city desk to keep in journalistic shape, I found myself one day waking up the premier of Ontario, John Robarts, in an effort to get him to tell me (for the *Star*'s benefit) what he had already told a Canadian press reporter, Rosemary Speirs. During my interview, Mr. Robarts disclosed that he had had a private meeting with John Young, the federal official responsible for prices and incomes policy (this was 1970 when Canada, like the United States, was debating price controls and income controls) and that he had told Young precisely what he had told me. This led to a disclosure that Young had been making coast-to-coast visits to provincial capitals, something that had not been public knowledge. Competition led to more detailed and better reporting.

The same thing can *not* be said for the kind of pressure that exists between editors and newsmen, the sort of informal yet terribly effective control that is so well documented in Warren Breed's classic article "Social Control in the Newsroom." Breed puts it quite succinctly and, in my opinion, quite accurately when he states:

> The newsman's source of rewards is located not among the readers, who are manifestly his clients, but among his colleagues and superiors. Instead of adhering to societal and professional ideals, he re-defines his values to the more pragmatic level of the newsroom group. He thereby gains not only status rewards, but also acceptance in a solidary group engaged in interesting, varied, and sometimes important work.[3]

When I moved from the *Star* to the *Telegram* (still covering City Hall) no one told me how to write differently but it was certainly true that for a time my stories got less play than previously. Then, very quickly, I adjusted to the "Tely style" and my stories once again regularly made page one. Every newsman is anxious to please his editors and quickly realizes what they want. I was well aware in 1962 therefore that when a series I had been asked to do on the New Democratic (Socialist) party in Canada did *not* suggest (as the *Star* believed) that the party was U.S. financed, and did *not* conclude (as the *Star* wanted to believe) that the New Democrats were really just a bunch of fast-moving Liberals and would soon become part of the *Star*'s favorite Liberal party, that I would be in disfavor with the editors of the *Star*. I was so much aware of what would happen in fact that I wasn't very anxious to do the series.

In his book, *The Washington Correspondents,* Leo Rosten reports that

> Extensive conversations with Washington correspondents for papers of diametrically opposed points of view have convinced this writer that many newspapermen (certainly not all) find their true journalistic level, and work for organizations in whose values and ethics they believe.[4]

My experience tells me that a similar statement could be made about most correspondents in the Parliamentary Press Gallery in Ottawa. I am a small 'l' if not always a large 'L' liberal and the *Star* is the same. I am a nationalist and so is the *Star*. Who can tell which came first — the paper's views or my own? Although my own experience (an interview with the *Star*'s editor Beland Honderich) was not exactly the same as Wilfrid Eggleston's in 1929, the unspoken instructions to a *Star* Ottawa correspondent were much the same in 1962 as they had been over 30 years earlier. Here, according to an article in *Queen's Quarterly,* is what Eggleston was told when he was sent by the *Star* to Ottawa on July 17, 1929:

> *The Toronto Star . . .* was broadly a Liberal paper, but it was not a ministerial organ. Its function was to develop and support liberal opinion, to some extent in advance and quite independently of the course of the Liberal party. Where there was divergence of opinion or policy, this could be noted and discussed without using it in such a way as to harm the party. Better . . . to have the Liberal party in office even if we didn't agree with its policies one hundred per cent, than to break with it on a minor issue . . . The current of opinion at Ottawa was to be interpreted as well as reporting events and transactions. Read the editorial page of the *Star . . .* so as to develop team-play with the editorial writers.[5]

Given this kind of "feel" between editors and reporters, it is perhaps not surprising that I can recall only half a dozen times in my career when I felt strongly that a story had in some way been interfered with.

One occurred when, after visiting the Royal Ballet in Detroit, I interviewed the premier dancer, Christopher Soames, about homosexuals in ballet. As I recall, Soames said he remembered many homosexuals when he began in ballet but by then (1958) they were uncommon. I believe the editors considered the story a bit distasteful for a family newspaper like the *Star*. It would probably run now.

Another occurred when, as a young *Journal* reporter, I wrote a story about a man who rebuilt artificial ears and noses for persons who had been disfigured by cancer. These substitutes at least allowed these persons the appearance of normality. A *Journal* editor said specifically he thought the story was distasteful.

A third occasion involved an interview with Glenn Gould, the distinguished Canadian pianist, the night he returned from a Russian tour. My story (which I still think was fascinating) covered mainly Gould's comments about the excellence of Russian pianos. I never heard why that story was disliked; but it never appeared.

A fourth story involved the dismissal of employees from a Toronto radio station which was cutting staff and moving to a pop, rock-and-roll style of broadcasting. I had checked and double-checked the story a bit too far — my last source was a golf partner of one of the publishers. The editor in charge told me the story was ordered killed, the only time I ever heard of specific outside interference.

The final incident was funny in retrospect: I was sent to interview the woman who writes under the name of Ann Landers. In the interview I asked questions about her background — education, religion, family, etc. My view was that our readers (we carried her column in the *Star*) were entitled to know from what viewpoint she advised others. She became very irritated and demanded I leave.

The next day the *Star* sent another reporter to interview her and ran a very complimentary, folksy and, in my opinion, dull story. No one ever spoke to me about the incident.

Given that I worked as a newsman for about eight years and with several different employers — the *Toronto Daily Star,* the *Toronto Telegram,* CBC, and the *Ottawa Journal,* this record — less than half a dozen killed stories — is not bad. It certainly backs up Breed's thesis that reporters learn to adjust to the needs of their editors and do not have to be told what to do.

Problems arising between newsman and competitor may be few and unimportant. Problems of conflict between editor and newsman may be rare because of that learning factor. But problems involving ethical decisions affecting a newsman's relation with his sources are everyday concerns and quite often insoluble.

Some years ago, I compiled a book of case studies for use in journalism,[6] studies that raised real problems based on real experience so the students could analyze and debate these. The project was patterned on the successful experiment with the use of case studies in Carleton's School of Public Administration and in the business program at Harvard. To my surprise, every single case involved a question of ethics and, in virtually every case, the writer informed me that he was not happy about his solution.

For example, journalists are constantly worried about their own social relationships in the community. Can a journalist belong to clubs, take an active part in community affairs, belong to a political party? Can he even have friends? The last one may sound silly but the problem is real. Joseph and Stewart Alsop wrote in their book, *The Reporter's Trade,* that they were reduced to isolating some persons from their working environment in order to maintain them as friends:

Our two best friends in Washington happen to be men in rather sensitive positions, who could no doubt tell us many things of extreme interest. But we long ago decided that the price of retaining these particular friends was never trying to discuss with them any matters within the area of their official responsibility, in office hours or out of office hours; and we have never done so.[7]

I never went as far as the Alsops but I did struggle many times with my conscience. A Toronto controller (the city executive was called the Board of Control) was always dropping in to the press room with some hockey tickets to Toronto Maple Leaf games: was it right to accept these tickets free? An alderman, Phillip Givens (later the mayor and later both a Member of Parliament and a Member of the Legislative Assembly of Ontario) was always good for a brighter and more 'newsy' quote than others, so I usually called him first if I wanted a reaction: was this fair or should I have devised some rotation system giving each council member in turn a chance for the publicity involved in commenting on the first news of some civic development? The City Hall Press corps was regularly invited to a free ride on the Toronto harbor ferry with free food and liquor for all (the ferry run by the transit authority normally operated from the harbor docks to the Toronto island which sheltered the main harbor basin): was this legitimate or did it put us in debt to the transit personnel? In Ottawa, a cabinet minister invited me for dinner and to his cottage: was this legitimate or should I have said, "Sorry, no"? The prime minister invited the press corps to his summer cottage for a relaxing afternoon — presumably at government expense. Was this legitimate? When my third child, Leslie, was born during the 1962 election campaign, Mr. Diefenbaker and his wife presented me with a small momento since I was travelling with them in British Columbia at the time: should I have refused such a generous and thoughtful gesture?

Underlying these difficulties is the fact that the reporter who is genuinely interested in the subject he covers probably shares that interest *most* with those who are most actively concerned in it as well. Thus it is not surprising that sports writers and athletes, and sports executives, get along well together: they are all knowledgeable and interested in sports. Writers about drama and drama critics obviously share common interests with playwrights, producers, and performers. Political reporters share their interests with politicians and public officials. There is usually mutual regard and respect. One would lead a very lonely life indeed if one were prohibited as a political reporter from associating except in a very formal way with politicians and public servants.

Aside from the dilemmas involved in personal relationships, there are real dilemmas about material obtained in confidence, off-the-record, for background, and under all the other assorted ill-defined categories.

I can recall obtaining information from a Conservative cabinet minister on the understanding that I could use it as long as I attributed it to no source at all and on the additional understanding he would publicly deny it when asked. The story — about a U.S. loan sought by the Canadian government — later became a matter of public record; but I spent some uneasy moments wondering whether my editors would accept my assurance that my source was impeccable. (They did.) But what about the public — who were they to believe?

I recall talking one day to one of Canada's senior public officials about a financial crisis, and receiving his assurance that the needed remedies could be obtained. I informed my editors and our story of the crisis was played down as a result. His assurances were right as it turned out, so we were right too: but again what about the public interest? How were they to know?

I can recall being given the name of the man who was to be appointed chairman of the newly created Economic Council of Canada before the legislation to create the Council had been approved by the House of Commons, let alone the Senate. This deliberate leak was designed to facilitate the passage of the legislation, for the opposition Conservatives, like the government Liberals, felt the man in question, John Deutsch, to be an appropriate appointment. Again, however, no source was given for my story: how were the public to judge?

The reporter, of course, decides on the basis of experience and past relationships whether or not to accept unsourced material. Once I was faced with an outright lie from an assistant to a prime minister. Needless to say I never trusted this person again; but what about the public? They never learned why my story was wrong or why I refused to obtain information from the same source in the future.

And certainly newsmen do become privy to confidential information. Wilfrid Eggleston, whom I quoted earlier, said:

> While a reporter loves to be taken into the confidences of the great and
> near great, it frequently disturbed me to be invited to share secrets of the
> most indiscreet and embarrassing nature.[8]

And this problem isn't confined to the higher levels of reporting. This past year, at Carleton University's School of Journalism, we have had a series of problems with confidential material. One particularly adept faculty member has managed to effectively block reporting of a whole series of events by feeding to the student reporters as "off-the-record," therefore leaving the reporters unable to write about the subject in question. At one point this became so serious I issued a complete ban on anyone on the staff of our radio news operation accepting material on an off-the-record basis.

In my days as an entertainment writer, I got into a long and heated debate with an editor as to whether it was proper to show copy to a source before submitting it for publication. The editor, Bill Drylie (now dead), maintained that it was totally improper. I did not agree: it seemed to me to help improve accuracy as long as the source was allowed to check only for fact and not to argue about opinion or interpretation. And, as I learned later, the practice of having copy checked was not at all a new one on the *Star*. In 1922, one of my colleagues, Roy Greenaway (he was still there when I arrived in 1956) had checked every word of a story he wrote with the two persons involved — Frederick Banting and Charles Best. According to Greenaway:

> They made corrections and carefully weighed the wording of the most important statements that were being made.[9]

I hardly think Greenaway was hurt by the practice for, as he says himself in the start of chapter six of his delightful book, *The News Game:*

> The first announcement of the discovery of insulin was made in the *Toronto Daily Star*. The date was March 22, 1922. That day means something to me because I wrote the story.[10]

Finally, I recall the one occasion when ¡ took what must be described, I suppose, as a bribe. One of my editors informed me that I was to leave the next morning for Detroit to write a story about the Royal Ballet which was then in Detroit and was about to come to Maple Leaf Gardens in Toronto. All the expenses of my trip — plane ticket, taxis, meals, etc. — were paid by Maple Leaf Gardens. Arrangements were made for us to interview members of the company and then to go out for drinks with the prima ballerina, Dame Margot Fonteyn. And, to top it all, at one point the Gardens P.R. man handed each of us $10 in cash explaining that one of my colleagues, a former sports writer, would explain what was going on. (For years, sports writers everywhere lived by charging their employers for expenses which had already been paid by the organization they were covering. And junkets are still common among entertainment, travel, and food writers.) The fact is that I enjoyed the ballet, learned a great deal from the interviews and was charmed by Dame Margot, so my report was an extremely favorable one. But I have often wondered what I would have done if the ballet stank. (Fortunately no one ever again sent me on any kind of junket so I never got the chance to further test my moral fiber.)

Looking back on what I have written, I suspect that the overall impression is that there are no rules at all relating to ethics and journalism. That would be unfair. There is one rule — and it is this: that if there are understandings between a journalist and a source (information is not-for-attribution, for background, off-the-record, whatever) then those understandings are not to be broken. A promise once made must be kept.

Recently, I interviewed a university president for a magazine piece. He said he would talk only on a not-for-attribution basis (meaning he wouldn't let me quote him). I said, "No, thanks." (I had enough material already.) He finally agreed to talk entirely on the record.

It is probably also true that times are changing. Cheque-book journalism is less common. Junkets are far more often frowned on. Public criticism — informal and formal — is more customary. The growth of press councils — first in the United Kingdom, now in North America — is making journalists more subject to public scrutiny. And codes of ethics are now no longer unheard of.

Yet it is still true that a journalist uses discretion in deciding what to write and what not to write. And that since the public sees only the end product — what is written — they never know what is omitted. And that the forces that lead to the use of discretion are difficult to ascertain.

Who would ever guess, for example, why I led this particular piece with an account of a bridge game? The reason — quite simply — was based on the fact that I have always wanted to match the delightful stories recounted by one of my early journalistic heroes, Quentin Reynolds, who used to write about card games in books such as *Only the Stars Are Neutral*.[11]

NOTES AND REFERENCES

[1] Quoted from a paper delivered by the author to the Canadian Industrial Editors' Association, January 23, 1969. The quotes were originally obtained from a transcript kept by the Prime Minister's office.

[2] Cater, Douglass, *The Fourth Branch of Government* (Boston: Houghton Mifflin, 1959), p. 56.

[3] Breed, Warren, "Social Control In The Newsroom: A Functional Analysis," *Social Forces*, Vol. 33 (May, 1955), p. 335.

[4] Rosten, Leo C., *The Washington Correspondents* (New York: Harcourt, 1937), p. 223.

[5] Eggleston, Wilfrid, "Leaves From a Pressman's Log," *Queen's Quarterly*, Vol. LXIII, No. 4, 1957, p. 550.

[6] Scanlon, T. Joseph (ed.), *Case Studies for Discussion*, Ottawa: Carleton University, 1968.

[7] Alsop, Joseph and Stewart, *The Reporter's Trade* (New York: Reynal, 1958), p. 16.

[8] Eggleston, *op. cit.*, p. 556.

[9] Greenaway, Roy, *The News Game* (Toronto: Clarke, Irwin, 1966), p. 59.

[10] *Ibid.*, p. 59.

[11] Reynolds, Quentin, *Only the Stars Are Neutral* (New York: Random House, 1942). "Because Ambassador Saed spoke no English we played in French. French is well fitted for poker. A flush in French is quite logically *couleur* while a straight is even more logically *sequence*" (p. 224).

Mr. Safford sees the reach — the technology — of our present-day mass media as creating a wholly new set of problems, without precedent. How are we to understand the influence of this wholly new phenomenon on the culture and the future of American society?

Briefly, Mr. Safford reviews the history of the notion of the freedom of speech and press in America, seeking clues to the answer. Clearly, local opinion-shaping influences have shrunk as our national and international reach has expanded. And our *sources* of information resources have increasingly clustered. Is this centralization "good" or "bad"? And, "if this country moves more and more into a leisure-oriented society, away from deep involvement with personal production, then a different set of mass communication responsibilities emerge.

Given these and other trends, are we heading for an "emotional, judgmental trap"? And what *is* the responsibility of the media in all this?

Mr. Stafford's answers are not the usual ones and perhaps therein lies their appeal.

The Need for a Public Ethic in Mass Communication

E. S. SAFFORD

President and Publisher,
Mountain Empire Publishing, Inc.

There is mounting evidence that the rapid advances in communication technology are leading our country into an emotional, judgmental trap. The possible effects of this trend can be so far reaching, and the consequences seem so imminent, that the situation warrants, right now, the attention of the best minds available.

I am speaking about the influences of the mass media of this country — primarily televison, the wire services, and the large consumer magazines — upon the attitudes and opinions of the citizens of this country. I am speaking about the increasing efficiency of communication technology and the compelling influence this has on how people view their country, how they view their country's position in the affairs of the world, and how the individual views himself in relation to the world in which he lives.

The emotional judgmental problem stems from the fact that we are complacently conditioned in the concept of the Constitutional Rights given by the First Amendment to the Constitution, literally unaware of the totally new influence which a different communication technology can have upon the country, its culture, and its future.

I

In order to consider the aspects of the new communication problems — these totally new problems without precedent — it is important to review the past. The framers of our Constitution recognized the importance of communication by writing the First Amendment on the freedom of speech and press, and they did so primarily out of the pressures of political problems that existed at that time. These wise men recognized that the very foundations of a democracy depended upon the right of the individual to make his views regarding the political system heard without fear of reprisal. They carefully protected the rights of each citizen to speak out in dissent against his government, against his government's policies, and against his government's leaders. The First Amendment was neither a license to destroy the government, nor an intention to give absolute freedom of speech, no matter what its consequences, to other individuals or to the state.

Justice Holmes said it this way, "The character of every act depends upon the circumstances in which it is done. The most stringent protection of free speech would not protect a man in falsely shouting fire in a theater and causing a panic." The concept was to permit free expression of individual opinion, for in this expression lay the vitality of the democratic system. Since that First Amendment was established, the courts of the land have translated this Constitutional protection to meet the changing needs of the society as conditions changed.

To understand the First Amendment, and to preserve this important individual freedom in the emerging communication technology, it is interesting to look at the interpretation of this concept through the eyes of some prominent jurists. Blackstone, in his *Commentaries,* said this about the freedom of speech and press: "The liberty of the press is indeed essential to the nature of a free state. To subject the press to the restrictive power of a licenser, as was formerly done both before and since the Revolution, is to subject all freedom of sentiment to the prejudices of one man, and to make him the arbitrary and infallible judge of all converted points in learning, religion, and government." Justice Reed stated, "The preferred position of freedom of speech in a society that cherishes liberty for all does not require legislators to be insensible to claims by citizens to comfort and convenience. To enforce freedom of speech in disregard to the rights of others would be harsh and arbitrary in itself."

The concepts of free expression were Jeffersonian in nature — the right of the individual as opposed to the majority.

As we moved from cracker barrel arguments and town hall meetings into the community newspapers, and then into nationwide newspaper chains, the right of free expression followed logically and appropriately. The individual was protected. Personal expression was influential.

Not too long ago, every city of substantial size had at least two prominent newspapers and, more frequently than not, these two newspapers (reflecting the views of their owners, publishers, or editors) subjectively presented their views and positions on important events. The regular, and frequently vociferous, feedback from their readers either reinforced and encouraged the papers' philosophies and reporting or, by massive reaction, forced alternative philosophies. In any event, more than one viewpoint was available to the individual seeking information, and from divergent sources a semblance of objectivity could be rationalized by the reader. By sensing and reacting to its readers' reactions, the papers identified — and crystalized — consensus. The individual's opinions and attitudes still counted and were influential.

II

As the ability to communicate quickly, and to increasingly larger audiences, changed through the introduction of telegraph, the wire services, radio, and TV, the existence of many strong local opinion-shaping influences began to shrink. Today many large cities have only one important newspaper, and radio and TV outlets have not characteristically identified themselves as crusading spokesmen for a specific political philosophy. The insidious effect of this policy is far more dangerous than a proclaimed political allegiance that identifies for the reader, listener, or viewer the bias that may exist. While the defense of this policy undoubtedly would be that the communication media are responsible for unbiased objective reporting, such a technique is patently impossible. Lee Thayer, former Director of the Center for the Advanced Study of Communication at the University of Iowa, puts it this way:

> First, there is no such thing (empirically speaking) as unbiased or 'objective reporting.' Every person must see the world in and through himself. There is no alternative, either empirically or logically. Objectivity can be nothing more than some mode of subjectivity. What a great many people in our country do not realize is that every item, on every page — not just the 'editorial' page — of every newspaper is neither more nor less than somebody's opinion about something. History is never just history; it is somebody's interpretation of what happened.

As the size of the media, in terms of audience served, increased, the influence of the individual's opinion tended to decrease. His right of expression under the Constitution remained without challenge; however, his effectiveness was diluted. Freedom of expression became more and more that of a large organization rather than an individual, and the corporation, as a legal entity, was accorded the same protection of expression as the individual. Through economic evolution, then, the organization became the spokesman. Corporate policy — the "publishing philosophy — established the tone, direction, and emphasis of the content. The cloak of the First Amendment was extended to cover the corporate entity as well as the individual, and this has been pulled and stretched to permit maximum profitability under the guise of free speech (reference the earlier Supreme Court ruling on pornography).

When opinion sources were formerly highly individualized, they contributed a valuable service to the organization and administration of our society. Local editors, to a very substantial degree, accurately represented the opinions and reactions of the readers whom they served. It must be remembered that newspapers are, first of all, a business and, as such, are in business to make money. The fact that newspapers make money is certainly not immoral. Quite the reverse has been true: when that very economic pressure necessitated that the newspaper respond to the audience, it served in an acceptable fashion, and in so doing reflected the opinions, prejudices, and the desires of that audience. This view may be challenged by our good friends in the newspaper business; however, Mr. Cecil King, formerly Chairman of the Board of the International Publishing Corporation of London, the largest English-language publishing organization in the world, was quoted as follows:

> You have got to give the public what it wants; otherwise you go out of business, as we have seen recently in the case of two or three newspapers. You try and raise its standards as well. The trouble is the critics imagine the Great British Public is as educated as themselves and their friends, and that we ought to start where they are and raise the standard from there up. In point of fact, it is only the people who conduct newspapers and similar organizations who have any idea of quite how indifferent, quite how stupid, quite how uninterested in education of any kind, the great bulk of the British Public is.

Mr. King is renowned for his directness, and also for his success. As long as newspapers exist as a product that must be sold, the logical conclusion is: people must continue to buy the product, or the enterprise will go out of business.

III

If we pursue this logic, the hazards become more apparent. As the number of principal information sources decreases, the strong diversity of opinion slowly shrinks. The cycle becomes self-serving and reinforcing.

The purchaser of newspapers, the viewer of TV, the radio listener, lets his interests and desires be known through many channels of feedback. This occurs through letters, through purchasing of goods and services sold by ads carried in the media, and through subscription payments. The decision maker at the information source understands and is sensitive to these audience likes and dislikes and, therefore, influences reporters, programmers, and creative people to produce the kind of information output which will be most generally acceptable to the audience at that point in time. The audience gets what it wants, the medium continues its success, and the result is a progressive redundancy in the system.

One might ask — is this process — this clustering of information resource — this evolution of information dispersal — really dangerous or undesirable? Isn't a centralized system as effective in portraying the average character, desires, and opinions of the mass as a multiplicity of small information systems might be?

To answer this question, it is necessary to step outside of tradition, or experience, to get the full perspective. Two new elements exist which have not characterized mass dispersal of information before. One of these elements is the rapidly increasing numbers of people influenced by a medium. The second element is the fact that TV has replaced the newspaper as a reporting and opinion-shaping device to a degree almost beyond the scope of understanding. This compelling new medium, with its capability of sound, action, and color simultaneously has broadened the base of the numbers of people exposed to the information presented and has, at the same time, inserted a character of credibility that cannot be equalled by any other communication medium. It is this medium, more than any other present development in communications technology, which offers the greatest hazards and greatest opportunities in the further orderly progress of our society and our culture.

TV has, for the first time in the history of man, permitted personal involvement by multitudes of individuals in a selected event as it happens. TV is a participant; every other medium is an historian or translator. The participation capability of TV created the almost unassailable credibility of the medium. It is this factor which is new and hazardous.

I discussed this subject with George Gerbner, Dean of the Annenberg School of Communications at the University of Pennsylvania. He related to me an example of the problem confronting TV in its reporting of current events. He described a TV clip made at the time of the "Hippie" march on the Pentagon in Washington. The complete and brief sequence went something like this: During the Pentagon "sit-in" a young man with long hair and unconventional wearing apparel was sitting on a curb. A policeman approached him, and with his night stick prodded the boy in the back, with the instructions to move along. The "Hippie" leaped up, grabbed the night stick, and tussled with the policeman in an effort to wrest the club from him. He was not successful, however, and the policeman, in the tussle, shoved the boy away, and gave him a swat across the back with his night stick to move him along.

Dr. Gerbner stated that this sequence was shown in three different versions by eastern TV stations. One version merely presented the young man leaping from the curb, grabbing the night stick, and tussling aggressively with the policeman. To the viewer who saw this brief sequence, it was apparent that the younger generation had no respect for law and order, and it implied that the marcher assaulted the policeman.

The second version, presented by some TV stations, showed only the policeman roughly shoving the boy and hitting him across the back with his night stick. To the viewer of this second clipped version, it was implied that there was substantial police brutality during this "sit-in."

The third version showed the entire sequence as it occurred.

The TV business itself recognizes the great difficulty it has in properly reporting live events. Richard S. Salant, then President of CBS News, in a talk before The American Society of Newspaper Editors in Washington in April, 1968, is quoted as saying: "I am opposed to live coverage because it is impossible to be accurate. You can get small sporadic action, and it can look like Armageddon, but it isn't." Mr. Salant brought out another very interesting aspect of TV coverage of live events when he stated that the mere arrival of TV equipment on a scene of a demonstration can set off crowd action that had not occurred before. In other words, once a TV camera crew is set up, some of the mob inevitably feels obligated to "go on stage," just because the TV is there. As pointed out before, however, TV producers are in business and, consequently, have to produce things the public wants to see. Again, Mr. Salant recognized this when he said, "When a demonstration begins because a camera has been set up, my orders to cameramen are in such cases, 'Cap your cameras and get out of there.' Those are our orders, but they cannot be enforced from a head office. The decisions are up to the men working on the story, and no newsman wants to quit on a story when it is happening."

A third example: A vice president of Cahners Publishing Company, J. V. Carey, was in New York at the Waldorf-Astoria at the time when Dean Rusk, then Secretary of State, was there for a meeting. Mr. Carey happened to be at the entrance of the hotel at the time Mr. Rusk arrived and saw a demonstration of perhaps 250 peace marchers with placards who were picketing the Waldorf in anticipation of Mr. Rusk's arrival. Mr. Carey said there seemed to be two policemen present for every marcher, and that the entire activity was confined to the immediate area in front of the Waldorf-Astoria. He returned to his hotel room shortly after Mr. Rusk arrived and received a frantic telephone call from his wife in Cleveland, who said that she had just seen on TV the terrible riots going on in New York City. She urged her husband not to leave the hotel, as it was most dangerous to be out in New York at that time due to the thousands of people who were roaming the streets. She understood that a great wave of anti-administration protests were erupting all over the city. Obviously, this was not the case; however, the excited announcements, the focused films, the dramatic news flash, made it appear that a major uprising was occurring. In reality, of course, only a handful of people were involved.

TV, by its very nature, must be highly selective in its coverage. The lens is a highly discriminating device, an instrument of severe limitations capable only of microscopic coverage of any one event at any one point in time. Its activities must, therefore, be the result of highly censored input, from the program director who identifies the general subject matter to the cameraman who selects, in his opinion, the most desirable immediate action.

This very limitation, however, presents the TV medium with a paradoxical problem. If the event is not covered at all, the public makes its dissatisfaction known vehemently by complaining that TV has covered up the story. Mr. Salant stated, "If we don't give live coverage, we give rise to this question: 'If you are not covering this, what else are you not telling us?'" Mr. Salant concludes, "We know the problem; we don't yet have an answer."

IV

Up to this point, I have touched briefly upon the mass media with respect to so-called news events, and their gradual disassociation from political bias. With the rapid economic development of our country, however, another dimension of communication influence has been occurring, which may become more important than the news and political implications. I refer now to the cultural changes occurring in our society. In their book, *The Year 2000*, Kahn and Wiener predict that our post-industrial society will experience some substantial changes, including the erosion in the middle class of work-oriented, achievement-oriented, advancement-oriented values, and an erosion of "national interest" values. They see more sensate, secular, humanistic, perhaps self-indulgent, criteria becoming central in our scheme of things. They suggest that "for the first time since his creation, man will be faced with his real, his permanent problem: How to use his freedom from pressing economic cares, how to occupy his leisure which science and compound interest will have won for him, how to live wisely and agreeably and well."

America is in a great transitional phase. It is a conceptual transition, as well as an economic transition, and it is imposing a set of problems for which our traditions and experience hold no ready answers. If the things that Kahn and Wiener predict come true, a new kind of planning and a new kind of implementation must occur. If this country moves more and more into a leisure-oriented society, away from deep involvement with personal production, then a different set of mass communication responsibilities emerge.

In the business world, it is frequently said there are two kinds of management: those that act, and those that react. Some businesses seem to be forever "putting out fires," as they react to the daily pressures and problems of their business. Other businesses seem to grow smoothly, rapidly, and profitably because they have planned a course of action, prepared for various alternatives, and utilized their resources on an anticipated basis. As a country, are we prepared to plan our cultural future? If the world our children will live in is to become more predominately a cultural environment than an economic environment, are we ready to try to chart a course of cultural improvement which should lead to a constantly better world?

If we are, then our mass communication facilities are the core implementers. How do we stand today in regard to mass media and their contribution to a better culture? From the standpoint of entertainment and cultural offerings, is there a plan, is there an ambition, is there a goal? Certainly there is a Code of Ethics by the National Association of Broadcasters; but how goal-oriented is this code? Ernest Lee Jahncke, Vice President of Standard Practices at the National Broadcasting Company is quoted on this subject. He stated in an interview with the *Chicago American,* "I do believe that America is growing up, so TV has to keep pace. We have a new awareness, a new permissiveness. The things that used to be unmentionable are now on top of the table, such as venereal disease, pregnancy, sexual behavior. We judge from trial and error, from our mailings, and other forms of communication to us." Mr. Jahncke said further, "TV is as big as life, literally. It's a mirror that reflects the tastes of the society it serves. It is important that the reflection not be disturbed. TV must stay in focus." In other words, TV, like the newspaper earlier, must produce what sells, and its internal test of censorship is oriented to the expressed tastes of the public as the censor understands it. Dan Lewis, a columnist for the *Chicago American,* in his interview with Mr. Jahncke stated, "TV, with its new era of permissiveness, also must acknowledge it now has the ability effectively to influence the mood of the public, and can infiltrate the minds of people with excessive exposure." He asks, "What then is TV's obligation to the public in general as it begins to accept this power and distributes the influence?"

We must remember that the original concept of free speech was considered as a means for developing larger policy. In recent years, however, with the fantastic growth of TV capability, the new wire services, and the large mass consumer publications, communication is no longer the primary instrument of policy, but rather an enterprise for profit. Raymond Williams, in his book entitled *Communications,* states:

It is clear that the extension of communication has been part of the extension of Democracy, yet in this century, while the public has extended, the ownership and control of the means of communication have narrowed. In the modern trend towards limited ownership of communication, the cultural conditions of Democracy are, in fact, being denied: sometimes ironically in the name of freedom. We have to recognize the contradictions we have been following: between Democracy and limited ownership; between genuine extension and the drive to sell.

V

At the beginning of these comments, I suggested there is increasing evidence that our developing communication technology is leading America into an emotional, judgmental trap. The trap is simply that our great new mass communications technology will inevitably change the future of our country; that the growth and success of monstrous new centralized information sources claim, and exist under, the same constitutional protections designed for the individual. And lacking societal, cultural goals, with a plan to reach such goals, only entrepreneurial success will construct the future culture. The ability of this communications technology substantially to influence the attitudes and opinions of the citizenry of this country will surely shape the kind of country, the kind of culture, the kind of aspirations, the kind of success this entire society ultimately achieves.

If this new technology offers tools for shaping attitudes and opinions in remarkably more controllable ways, are we really obligated to see that such tools are not misused? As these new technologies permit compelling persuasion, provide seemingly incontestable evidence, and rationalize so convincingly almost any philosophy or action, they will certainly be used, for good or for ill. Should we assume that this emerging new capability, the capability to influence and eventually to control human behavior, must find its level of application by trial and error in the whole scheme of things? In other words, shall this civilization, like certain inept managements, merely react, and through a period of violent oscillations of censorship and gross permissiveness eventually develop an acceptable norm for mass communications? Or should we try to anticipate, try to employ these enormous new information and knowledge powers toward agreed upon cultural goals which, hopefully, will contribute to a happier, more stable, progressively better world?

If we should try to construct such goals, lofty, yet practical, demanding, yet rewarding, challenging, yet do-able, it will be a big order for any "think tank." Certainly we can't ask a segment of the business community, namely, the mass communication media, to undertake such a responsibility. They are the implementers of cultural development, not the innovators. Their responsibility, by the very essence of their existence, must be profit-oriented, and this is not always consistent with cultural improvement.

Is now the time for our statesmen, our scholars, our philosophers, to start to work on cultural goals for our society for the next 50 years? A wealth of economic and scientific data exists with which to work. Is it possible to extrapolate with reasonable optimism certain trends that must inevitably occur in this country in the next 50 years? Building on these materialistic and sociological prognostications, is it possible to construct a road map for a great culture? If this can be accomplished, then it will surely require the complete cooperation of the mass media to make such a dream come true.

The first step, the very first step, is the voluntary creation of a New Ethic for America's mass media by the thought leaders of these media. We need now an ethic which recognizes the opportunities which this society has ahead of it, an ethic which understands the elements which can contribute to or detract from building a better world. We need now to bring together the leaders in the field of mass communication who will voluntarily subscribe to this concept, and who will set up the machinery by which such an ethic can be verbalized and then implemented. We need to see true leadership coming out of this most important segment of our society; a leadership capable of visualizing long-range greatness against short-range profits; a leadership which need not sacrifice the building of private enterprise; but a leadership which can recognize that building long-range values is far more profitable than satisfying short-range appetites. With great responsibilities come great opportunities. The mass media of this country have such opportunities in unbelievable abundance, if they will accept the corresponding responsibilities.

Finally, it seems to me that we must anticipate the methodology which must ultimately be involved. The construction of a New Ethic alone will never totally achieve the advantages that a great new technology offers. We must consider at some date, reasonably soon, a position in the President's Cabinet for a Secretary of Communications. The objective of this office would not be to censor, but to provide an arena in which can be brought together all of the new influences available in this new technology and to apply them for the progress and good of this country. This concept is not intended to encroach upon the First Amendment, as we have known it. Instead, this is an extension in which we protect the individual's right of opinion, his right of recourse to independent information, and his opportunity to develop his own opinion without the hazards that new technology can impose.

The First Amendment was written to protect the individual's right to initiate his own expression, and to publicize his own opinion. For the first time in the history of man, we need now to protect the individual from such compelling and overwhelming opinion-shaping forces that he cannot effectively generate and publicize his own unique opinions.

Our communication problems in this country are more critical, our need for action more demanding, and our time for solution is far shorter than most people understand. I earnestly hope that the inspired leadership necessary to do this critically important job will soon come forward.

Discussion

Q: *You seem to feel that those who peddle pornography, among others, have taken advantage of the First Amendment. Mightn't the best solution to this be a legal one, and not an ethical one?*
A: The legal route for controlling pornograpic material has already been tried and apparently without success insofar as stemming its flow. The old adage which has stood for so long, namely, "It is impossible to legislate morality" is probably as true today as it ever was. Good character or good taste are not functions of an imposed regulatory system. The value standards of a society must come from agreed-upon ethical commitments and not from imposed legislation. The communication gatekeepers, the organizations, the systems and the people who are responsible for distributing information, opinions, and ideas must come to grips with concepts, not legal interpretations. If national cultural goals can be agreed upon, then ethical commitments will eliminate the need for legal definitions and regulatory tests.
Q: *Your suggestion that it is not the responsibility only of the communication media — but one segment of the business community — to solve these problems is an interesting one. Also, I believe you said that the business of the media is to make money. Isn't it possible that any ways of shifting the major responsibility off the media would lead to further control or censorship of some type?*
A: Yes, I believe that shifting major responsibility could lead to increased censorship. Because the mass media form a totally new major system in our society, they probably warrant more than the entrepreneurial censorship which already exists. The question is not one of whether we should have censorship or not; the question is, what kind of censorship is practical for today's expanded communication systems? The codes of ethics constitute a first step, but certainly not the total answer. Some method must surely be developed that will monitor and enforce agreed-upon ethical standards which could very well create entrepreneurial difficulties.

What *I* would like to see now, given some events of recent years, is an assembly of a select group of the principal officers of the media in the U.S. in a summit seminar to review the subject of ethical issues and practices. Hopefully from such an event might come a steering committee that would undertake the job of designing a program that would lead to an acceptable — and used — New Ethic in Communication. It would require the input of futurists, psychologists, sociologists, and philosophers — as well as pragmatic communicators. Properly done it would be a monumental task, because it would essentially be describing what the future of this society *should* be. It could be a "Declaration of a Society," with future implications for the country as important as the "Declaration of Independence" was 200 years ago.

Because communication is the foundation of the future society, such an effort would not be just for communication. It would in reality be describing the concept of the future society. An action of this nature should bring recognition of statesmanlike character to media. It should generate a concept of leadership, responsibility, and credibility for all media, and ultimately truly contribute to a better world for all.

Q: *In your paper, you seem to be saying that the main ethical issues in mass communication today are those of television. But you are involved in the publication and sale of technical and trade magazines, which, I would imagine, are paid for largely from advertising revenues. Haven't you run across any ethical problems in your own business?*

A: I have stressed television because it is a large mass communication system that is having the principal influence on our total society. You asked if we have run into ethical problems in the area of technical and business publications. The answer is certainly yes. As with any business there are some unorthodox or perhaps unethical publishers who will produce favorable editorial copy on behalf of organizations that will buy advertising in their publications. For the most part, this kind of practice has not existed in the United States for some time; however, it cannot be ruled out totally. Almost three thousand business magazines exist in the United States today, and from time to time evidence will pop up indicating unethical publishing practices being followed. The American Business Press, which is the association for business publications, and its member companies have made earnest efforts to eliminate any of this kind of practice, and it probably does not exist in quality publications.

As was Mr. Crichton, Mr. Fox was invited to prepare his remarks especially for this volume. Although the field of public relations is not always considered an aspect of mass communication, it seemed to the editors as relevant as advertising and public opinion polling to our overall objective of surveying the ethical and moral issues involved in mass communication and the media in America.

As past President of the Public Relations Society of America, Mr. Fox is eminently qualified to describe the ethical considerations in public relations today — as seen from the point of view of the practicing professional. As one who has observed the critics (of public relations) for several years, Mr. Fox finds their criticism "frequently irrational." But is it the case that "the only evil publicity is that which advocates a point of view with which the observer disagrees"?

The author attributes some of that irrationality to "a deep-seated fear of being manipulated. . . ." His definition of public relations will be of interest to all of those who are concerned about ethical issues in the media, and may help to qualify the assessment he makes of present performance in the public relations field.

Again the matter of self-regulation is raised. Is a "code of ethics," or a set of "professional standards," enough to guarantee ethical or moral judgments by professional communicators? Mr. Fox's answer may not surprise many, but his argument may.

Yet "by what value system will we judge?"

Public Relations: Some Ethical Considerations

JAMES F. FOX

President, Fox Public Relations, Inc.*
New York

It is not uncommon for individuals to express their low regard for the business of public relations. Some people, indeed, consider it unethical, a view sufficiently prevalent that the Public Relations Society of America (PRSA) in 1976 hired a full-time public relations director to guard its image and carry out a planned program of rebuttal to the critics.

What makes these condemnations of public relations so puzzling — they frequently come from academics or journalists — is that most educational institutions and communications companies — newspapers, periodicals, broadcast media — employ public relations staffs. Many of the heads of these institutions spend a major share of their time in what could be considered "public relations" activities. Business and industry may be the prime consumer of public relations talents, but churches, foundations, the military, government, and other institutions in our society have placed the function on their organization charts.

This is not the only contradiction. Such departments of the federal government as the SEC and HEW insist on greater accountability from the institutions they supervise. They are strongly buttressed in this by the activists who want full disclosure and detailed consumer information on

---

* At the time he prepared this statement, Mr. Fox was President of the Public Relations Society of America, and had served as chairman of its Counsellors' Section.

products. Yet, the same activists denounce the flood of communication that has resulted as self-serving propaganda, manipulation, or an effort to subvert public opinion.

For their part, the communicators say they are only seeking familiarity and understanding. At the same time, at least as it relates to industry, they observe that newspapers with young, opinionated reporters can not be depended upon to tell a company's story. The result is that most institutions seek other means of reaching the audiences most critical to them. Even then, in the event the other means is paid advertising, the corporate communicator may be frustrated, as the oil companies discovered with their television spots during the fuel shortage.

One who observes the critics for very long finds the criticism frequently irrational. It is easy to conclude that the only evil publicity is that which advocates a point of view with which the observer disagrees.

Publicity is one of the most cleansing functions in our society. We speak not only of "sunshine" laws, but of "the white light of publicity." When a corporation or other institution seeks a high profile, it must be prepared to live with the resulting public scrutiny and analysis, which will ultimately and inevitably spotlight the blemishes as well as the good. A low profile, while not necessarily deceitful, is the posture of those who distrust public attention, and may even signal a "cover-up." Is publicity a cosmetic? It can be, but its absence may be more ominous.

A Roper organization survey concluded that public relations was regarded more favorably than advertising, and in about the same measure of esteem as journalism.[1] Why, then, the negative attitudes in public expressions by writers and speakers?

There must be a difference, first of all, between the generalization and specific situations. Otherwise, how does one explain the formal and widespread acceptance of the function and the continuous use of public relations techniques by non-professionals (who probably aren't aware that they are practicing public relations)? How does one explain the critic who denounces public relations, but in the process of doing so is himself engaging in propaganda activity?

There seems to be a deep-seated fear of being manipulated which, one can speculate, may derive from the centuries-old aversion to "propaganda."

The current attitude perhaps more directly derives from the pejorative use of the term "public relations." The term "public relations" was employed by the critics of the Nixon administration, for example, and was repeated in newspaper and television accounts of the proceedings. It was a popular put-down. Yet, the truth is that there were no public relations professionals in the Nixon inner circle, only advertising men and lawyers. Many public relations professionals believe it is quite possible that had Mr. Nixon heard and heeded sound public relations advice on the importance of performance, honesty, and candor, he would have been forgiven his errors at the beginning of the revelations. Is public relations good or bad? That may be a simple question, but it has a complex answer.

The problem in defining the ethics of public relations begins with the problem of defining public relations. Raymond Simon comments that "ethics is unclear, generally murky, and usually highly personal." [2] So is public relations.

There may be as many different "brands" of public relations as there are practitioners, but there is a developing body of knowledge. Much of it has been recorded by qualified scholars. Simon's book is a recent example. Professor Simon teaches at Syracuse University. The stacks of the Information Service of the PRSA contain hundreds of books on the subject and hundreds more file drawers of periodical clippings and pamphlets. There are three major journals published in the United States, one of which is published under the academic auspices of the University of Maryland. [3]

To 8,500 members of the Public Relations Society of America, public relations is an emerging profession with not only a body of knowledge, but a code of ethics, academic recognition in courses and accredited sequences, student chapters on four-score university campuses, and high standards of professional and moral conduct.

By the professional's definition, if a practice is dishonest, less than candid, or distorts the truth, it may be advertising, promotion, or persuasion, but it is not public relations.

At its best, public relations is the function of management which evaluates public opinion, assists institutions to adjust their policies to conform to social standards, and mounts programs of communication or action to create understanding and acceptance. Top-level public relations people today spend more of their time evaluating public attitudes and identifying and tracking trends and advising on public policy than on the communications function. Some organizations today issue few press releases that are not required by legal statutes. Institutions are necessarily trying harder to adjust to society's requirements rather than to mold society to their model.

Some institutions resort to euphemisms to try to make their use of "public relations" more palatable to themselves. It may be called corporate communications, information, public affairs, public policy counselling or what you will — but it is still public relations. The banning of the term by Congress has resulted in the burgeoning of "information offices" in government bureaus. Both industry and the government use the term "public affairs." Sometimes this describes legislative liaison; more often than not it is a synonym for public relations.

We could argue whether persuasion itself is immoral. Father Thomas J. Burke, director of the Fairfield (University) School of Corporate and Political Communications, says that "human beings cannot not communicate." Ever since Eden, much of human communication has been carried out for the purpose of influencing another person or group. Questions of the morality of persuasion are best left to the clerics and philosophers.

We cannot concern ourselves here with the use of persuasion and propaganda by non-professionals. These users cannot easily be identified, although it is probable that anyone who is engaged in mental activity uses persuasion in his or her interpersonal or group relations. There is no way short of the public's resistance by which society can limit or control the legal use of communication by anyone—regardless of what that person calls himself — so long as the Bill of Rights is the law of the land.

Here we can consider those individuals who profess to be in the public relations business and who earn their income either as public relations employees or advisers. The largest organized body of such people is the membership of PRSA.

Public Relations Society of America

The activities of the members of the PRSA are circumscribed by a Code of Ethics, which first came into existence in 1952. Although non-members of the Society are not controlled by this code, they are unquestionably influenced by its existence.

A major hope of the members of the Society is that employers will come to recognize membership in the Society as a qualification for employment, and accreditation by the Society as an essential for advancement.

Professional standards which employers, editors, legislators, and the public will recognize are particularly important because — like it or not — public relations is one of the fastest growing functions of management. It is expanding in business and industry, but its growth is even faster in government and the not-for-profit sector. The very people who are critics of public relations are increasingly engaging in the practice they condemn.

Advocacy

Public relations is sometimes criticized because it is equated with propaganda, because the term has taken on a pejorative meaning, and because people innately fear what may be manipulation (although they seem to enjoy it in advertising and in the theater).

Part of the difficulty is that public relations people oftentimes insist that they deal in facts. They will tell you that honesty is good economics, that the communicator who deceives quickly loses credibility. The public seems to doubt anyone who too avidly proclaims his purity.

There are two problems with the public relations man's traditional view of himself. One, of course, is that even with regard to simple topics there is room for conflicting opinions on what is factual. No one has a monopoly on the truth. Far more relevant to the subject of ethics is the matter of advocacy. Most public relations specialists will admit today that they are advocates, although still claiming that they work equally for the public interest.

While vehemently rejecting the suggestion that they are in the business of the "engineering of consent" or in any manner manipulating people, they sometimes admit to partisanship on a personal level toward the cause they espouse. If all goes well other views will be expressed, there will be discussion, and the public will arrive at the right conclusion.

Unfortunately, ideas are not so logically sorted out. The weight of interests, the pressure of emotions, the negotiating power of authorities and constituencies, economic, legal, cultural, social, and technical factors are a tangle from which the public decision must emerge. Not everyone has equal access to the media; some forms of communication — television, for example — are too senselessly powerful in their impact. All of the barriers to communication that Walter Lippmann pointed out to us half a century ago in *Public Opinion* are still in place.[4]

That is why professionl public relations people see their role as more that of analyst and planner, as enabling their institutions to foresee change and adjust to it rather than to influence it.

To the extent that he continues to be a communicator, the public relations professional no longer sees himself as an "information" channel dealing in absolutes. Some of that attitude developed because in the past most public relations specialists were former newspaper reporters and editors who belonged to the age that preceded advocacy journalism; their mission was to report "the truth." Today, public relations is peopled with former lawyers, university professors, marketing executives, and lawmakers to whom advocacy comes easy; they have never thought of themselves merely as objective observers.

The acceptance of the advocate's role is particularly prevalent in the voluntary and non-profit sectors. Most often the institution itself — a church or a foundation — exists to advocate ideas rather than to make a product or to provide a service. It should not be surprising that advocacy is increasingly the role, too, of the corporate public relations specialist.

Licensing

From time to time someone outside the public relations field will suggest licensing by the state as the solution to the ethical problems of public relations. It is even put forward by experienced and sometimes prominent persons in the field as a means to promote competency. One must assume either that they want licensing to protect their own vested position, or that they have not studied the implications of licensing.

There is no legislation now in the United States licensing public relations, although measures to do so have been introduced in a few state legislatures. A bill which failed when introduced in the New York State legislature sought to license psychological counsellors. It was intended to put unqualified marriage counsellors out of business, but included "public relations" in a laundry list of counselling positions based on the social sciences.

The subject of licensing has been explored formally on three separate occasions by the Public Relations Society of America, and informally for at least a score of years. During all this time, no one who has studied the data and thought carefully about the matter has concluded that licensing is wise. To the contrary, many who went into the study committees or task forces as avowed advocates did a total about face. Should it seem in any state that licensing is inevitable, the Society has a draft bill ready which it will ask to have introduced at that point.

The easiest type of legislation to devise would be to protect the use of the words "public relations." Such a law would simply force people to use other designations. In 1913, the Congress decreed that no government agency would carry out "public relations" activity unless the funds were specifically appropriated by Congress. Thus, government public relations today is called either "public information" or "public affairs."

Legislation which would define public relations and incorporate sound means of testing would stand a better chance of being effective. The only trouble is that no one has yet devised a precise definition of the term, and it is not likely to happen soon.

The most telling argument against licensing is that any such legislation most likely would be declared unconstitutional. An editor of the *New York Times* told a public relations group some years ago that *The Times* will accept no restrictions as to what news sources it uses and will oppose any legislation which tends to curb freedom of speech or expression.

If licensing is not the answer, what can be done?

A great deal already has been done in the form of SEC regulations, the disclosure rules of the FDA, lobbying legislation, libel laws and the like, all of which have an impact on how the public relations person conducts himself.

PRSA offers professional training and since 1965 has accredited members deemed qualified, based on independently administered testing. The Code of Ethics and judicial process help to enforce standards. An increasing number of universities offer courses of study, some of them approved by the American Association for Education in Journalism, which prepare students for careers in public relations. What is urgently needed is for those who pay for and those who use public relations services to recognize and insist on professionalism, as they do in other specialized fields.

The PRSA Code of Ethics

The Public Relations Society of America is the major professional association for public relations practitioners. It is the largest association of its kind in the world.

Membership in PRSA requires that individuals adhere to the principles of the Society's Code of Professional Standards for the Practice of Public Relations.[5]

Enforcement of the code is monitored by the Society's Grievance Board, which has nine members. The Society's judicial structure consists of six-member panels in each of nine districts throughout the United States. The panels investigate and hear complaints relating to violations of the PRSA Code. Recommendations of the panels are made to the Board which may warn, admonish, reprimand, censure, suspend, or expel any members found in violation of the Code.

One of the interesting aspects of the Code is that complaints may be filed either by members or by non-members.

While the Society has enforced the Code against violators, its importance is greater than that. It provides guidelines for those in doubt, sets standards for non-members and members alike, provides a benchmark for employers, and serves as a deterrent to any member tempted by shady practices.

The Code, and also the Society's education and accreditation programs, will be more effective once the consumers of public relations services, editors and employers, learn the difference between a professional public relations specialist and a self-styled practitioner, and give preferential treatment to those who subscribe to a Code of Ethics.

The Society's Declaration of Principles dedicates its members "fundamentally to the goals of better mutual understanding and cooperation among the diverse individuals, groups, institutions and elements of our modern society."

Individual members are pledged to conduct themselves both privately and professionally in accord with the public welfare and to be guided in all their activities by the generally accepted standards of truth, accuracy, fair dealing, and good taste.

(One critic has suggested that the principle as stated is faulty because of the low level of "generally accepted standards" in today's society.)

Contrast the public's perception of the term public relations with this statement which introduces the Code:

This code is adopted "in order that membership in the Society may be deemed a badge of ethical conduct; that public relations justly may be regarded as a profession; that the public may have increasing confidence in its integrity; and that the practice of public relations may best serve the public interest."

The Code refers to "fair dealing," the public welfare, high standards; it outlaws "front organizations" with an unidentified source, advocates accuracy and truth, discourages conflicts of interest, and sets forth standards for relations with employers and fellow practitioners.

Some clauses deal specifically with the media. For example, a member shall not engage in any practice which tends to corrupt the integrity of the channels of public communication, or disseminate false or misleading information.

The PRSA Board of Directors also has issued a more specific interpretation of the Code as it applies to financial public relations which has the full force of the Code itself. This interpretation was worked out with the counsel of the Securities and Exchange Commission. There is an official interpretation of the Code as it applies to political public relations, adopted in 1974.

While all these rules may deter a public relations person from wrongdoing, an equally powerful deterrent is the press itself.

While some editors and reporters still denigrate public relations, all of them are dependent on the work of public relations representatives to a degree that is difficult for them to acknowledge—for leads to news, for certain basic fact compilation, and for time-saving assistance even when the final story can honestly and freely be accredited to the newspaper reporter.

The press criticism of public relations is frequently justified, either because there are incompetent public relations people or because a competent public relations person may be unable to perform his job for reasons beyond his control.

In a sense, the negative attitude of some members of the press is odd because so many public relations people in the past were former colleagues on newspapers.

Some editors today acknowledge the role of public relations, albeit approaching "canned news" with suspicion and exercising caution in its use. Representative of the more rational attitude is Joseph Shoquist of the *Milwaukee Journal*, and an officer of the Associated Press Managing Editors Association. Recognizing the advocacy role of public relations, he has said, "Of course we are adversaries. But it does not follow that we must be hostile adversaries."

An experienced public relations person knows that the quickest road to oblivion is to try to "con" the press. He is seldom able to do it twice, and that may be the safeguard the public needs.

One of the provisions of the Code requires that "A member shall, as soon as possible, sever his relations with any organization when he knows or should know that his continued employment would require him to conduct himself contrary to the principles of this Code." This provision may be difficult to understand, but it is probably clear to most public relations people, whose personal ethics would probably interfere long before the Code violation became a constraint. Remember that a large number of public relations people trained in the media have brought their editorial skepticism (if not their cynicism) over into their new vocation.

In the decade and a half that my own counselling firm has existed, we have twice terminated financially rewarding relationships because we found ourselves dealing with people who were less than candid. Within the last year we rejected an opportunity to submit a proposal to a prospect whose source of financing has been questioned by the courts.

But this does not mean, in my judgment, that a public relations person should be required to reject an assignment simply because the cause he is asked to advocate is unpopular. Were that so, advocacy would have been denied in recent years to many products, industries, and causes that are controversial and unresolved, including most of the reform movements which are characteristic of public discussion today.

The Preamble to the PRSA statement on political public relations says that the consultant may serve his client or employer "without having attributed to him the character, reputation or beliefs of those he serves." Nevertheless, most members of the Society would no doubt find it dificult to advocate a cause alien to their own convictions.

There is no question that many people in the public relations field have been shaken by the revelations of corporate wrong-doing over the past several years. Whether, as a result, they have determined to stay and work from within or to move on to another organization, they are now less apt to accept management's infallibility and more apt to insist on a policy role.

By what value system will we judge? Will we judge by today's standards, or yesterday's? Are ethical values universal or do they change from one society to another? Are the values different for theatrical publicity and industrial publicity?

Ultimately, as Raymond Simon told us, ethics is a highly personal matter. You must judge.

I still believe in public opinion. In the end we will discover that the public writes the social code. In the end, it is the public which will decide whether public relations and the points of view it advocates are ethical.

NOTES AND REFERENCES

[1] In 1974, at the height of Watergate, the Roper Organization asked respondents to say whether they had a clear idea or knew little about some of the major fields of work within the communications industry. Those who indicated some familiarity with advertising people, public relations people, or people in the press were then questioned about their image of communicators.

Commenting that advertising people "are least likely to be thought ethical and most likely to be called dishonest," the report then said, "Public relations people, on the other hand, come out rather well. They are also considered intelligent, though not as outstandingly as the other two groups of communicators. They are considered more concerned with the public welfare and to perform a more useful social function than advertisers, though less so than the press. They are considered somewhat less ambitious and hard-working than the other two. But they are rarely called dishonest, though there is a certain low level suspicion that they are mercenary and slick."

The Roper staff concluded that ". . . charges that public relations people are there to paper things over and give the public false impressions are not supported. The manipulative aura of Watergate has not rubbed off on the public relations field. By and large the public thinks public relations people perform a useful and straightforward function of spreading information where it is needed, and of concerning themselves with the public's interests." (This information is from a restricted report, and is used here with the permission of The Roper Organization, Inc., One Park Avenue, New York, N.Y. 10016.)

[2] Simon, Raymond. *Public Relations: Concepts and Practices* (Grid, Inc., Columbus, 1976).

[3] The three publications are:

The Public Relations Journal, Leo J. Northart, Editor. 845 Third Avenue, New York, N.Y. 10022. Sponsored by PRSA.

The Public Relations Quarterly, Howard Penn Hudson, Editor. 44 W. Market Street, Rhinebeck, N.Y. 12572.

The Public Relations Review, Dr. Ray E. Hiebert, Editor. University of Maryland, College Park, Maryland 20742. Sponsored by the Foundation for Public Relations Research and Education Inc.

[4] Lippmann, Walter. *Public Opinion* (Free Press, 1965).

[5] After a year-long study, the Board of Directors of the Public Relations Society of America in February 1977 proposed language changes to strengthen and clarify the Code's 17 paragraphs that specifically define ethical behavior. After consultation with the Federal Trade Commission, they also called for elimination of a prohibition against a public relations counselor's soliciting clients of other members and of a ban on fees contingent on specific results.

Mr. Koop describes a number of legal and ethical problems that have plagued print and broadcast journalism in recent times, before he comes to the conclusion that the "American people can indeed place their their trust in the news media, which have not failed them in the history of the Republic."

Isn't this exactly the problem? In a society where all institutions have come under severe criticism from the public, why should the news media be exempt from the scrutiny of a disenchanted, even frustrated, public — particularly when the mass media also claim to be the "representatives" of the people?

Doesn't trust rest on the assumption of knowing about the other? And doesn't it develop over long periods of time and only after one has experienced understanding, responsiveness, and an attitude of caring about the other? Given the current structure of the news media, it can hardly be said that their audiences have participated in a dialogue with them that would encourage the development of such trust.

It has been suggested that media councils be established to help both the public and the media understand their roles and to make the operation of the media, as far as the news and public affairs coverage is concerned, available to review and criticism. To argue, as Mr. Koop does, that media councils are not desirable because their existence would involve seeking the advice of "amateurs," a step "that degrades professional judgment," reflects a point of view that may seem incompatible with the idea of the news media as a responsible institution. Is the "professional judgment" of journalists to take precedence over the interests of the consumers of the media, however "amateur" those interests may be? Is the one more *ethical* than the other?

While little needs to be said about the idea that the news media and the government are operating in an adversary position, and have been since the beginning of modern journalism, it seems that this condition has often been used as an effective argument to ward off those who would like to see some accountability on the part of the mass media. If, as many spokesmen for the mass media claim, they represent the people, public opinion, or the mood of the country, is there any reason to believe that they should not be interested in the ideas of those they serve?

Unfortunately, as Mr. Koop makes clear, there have been very few attempts on the part of the mass media to develop a theory which would allow them to define their freedom in terms of the participation of the publics which they profess to serve. What is to be done in the absence of such a definition?

Evolving Standards
of Broadcast Journalism

THEODORE F. KOOP

Retired Washington Vice President,
Columbia Broadcasting System

When I was editor of the student newspaper at the University of Iowa, I was invited to speak at Sigma Delta Chi's annual chapel service at nearby Grinnell College. My subject was awesome: "The Ethics of Journalism." Just before the program I met a Grinnell profesor who said, "I'm fascinated by your topic. It is the first time I have heard that journalism had any ethics." His remark was unsettling to a starry-eyed neophyte, but in retrospect I would have to acknowledge that the professor had a point.

At that time, in the late 1920's, journalistic ethics could readily be challenged. The characters of "The Front Page" were alive and thriving in city room after city room. It was nomal practice for a reporter to filch a photograph from the home of a dead man. If certain facts would spoil a good story, it was easy to overlook them. Crime was the big news, and it was handled in sensational fashion.

Professional standards have risen tremendously in the intervening decade. Whether as a cause or a result, the concept of what is news has changed. The depression of the early 1930's created a need for economic information that affected the pocketbook of every American. Then the rise of Mussolini and Hitler and the Japanese war lords caused the United States — and its news conduits — to discover the rest of the world. Ever since, events of international or national significance have held priority in newspapers and news broadcasts. They are matters of life and death — basic issues of society that require ethical coverage.

If ethics can be defined as "the basic principles of right action," I would equate journalistic ethics with professionalism. For professionalism, to my mind, is reporting available facts in an objective manner, making every effort to be as accurate, complete, and fair as possible. It would be nice to expand that definition to say that professionalism means reporting the truth, but as Supreme Court Justice Benjamin Cardozo wrote in *The Growth of Law:* "General truths are hard to grasp. Most of us have all we can do in accumulating, by dint of toil, the knowledge of a few particulars."

In general, I would label current journalistic practices as ethical as human frailties permit. One trend within the profession, however, strikes me as dangerous: the avant garde theory that newsmen can — and should — become advocates rather than impartial reporters. I talked with a young man who was getting an M.A. in political science and who said he wanted to go into broadcast journalism. I inquired if he had any reporting experience. "Oh, I don't want to handle news," he replied: "I want to tell people what I think and believe in."

At least that 23-year-old was more forthright than reporters who would distort spot news stories to peddle their own prejudices. In their zeal to advance pet causes they would spurn any notion of fairness and balance. To them a news event has only one side — their side, which is obviously the truth. They claim to be liberals, yet they are completely illiberal in ignoring expression of opposing views.

These embryo Tom Paines should be writing pamphlets (with scads of four-letter words) rather than news stories. In that case their difficulty, of course, would be economic. Who would pay the printing bill? If they are willing to report for a commercial news operation, they must acknowledge the professional discipline and standards that go with the job. Modern journalism cannot afford to be subverted by a comparative handful of rebellious newcomers. It is a simple fact that advocacy and news coverage have nothing whatever in common. If they are joined, the news stories lose their integrity and are no longer credible.

Broadcast journalism has encountered special ethical problems in addition to those inherited from the older print media. They are peculiar to the fantastic electronic technology and to the impact — an overworked word — of television and radio news on viewers and listeners. There are several reasons:

First, both radio and television news are comparatively infant media. Television news in particular has soared to a pre-eminent place of influence in a very short time — less than a quarter-century. The growing pains have been difficult. Although its standards were built on the foundation of newspaper ethics, much of the development into professionalism has been by trial and error. It is still maturing; its ethics are still evolving.

Second, television news so arrests its audience that relationships with newsmen become highly personal. A top network anchorman is regarded as a guest in the home, on a first name basis. If he errs, criticism becomes immediate and direct. He must surpass Caesar's wife in freedom from suspicion. A newspaper reporter, on the other hand, is only a vague name to his readers. His byline, indeed, is apt to be recognized only by his relatives and creditors.

Third, federal regulation of radio and television leads many an American to conclude erroneously that they are and should be less free than the printed press. Critics cry that the air waves belong to the people, and that licensees therefore have certain obligations and restrictions which take precedence over the First Amendment guarantee of fredom of speech. The great endeavor of broadcast news is to demonstrate that it cannot be half free.

Finally, special problems of ethics are created by the very presence of television cameras. The appearance of pencil-and-paper reporters often can affect the course of an event. It is only to be expected, therefore, that the high visibility of cameras will bring reaction from onlookers. As cameras pan across a sports arena, fans wave gaily at them. As they record a demonstration or a riot, participants may be tempted to step up their action.

Conscious of the danger that their equipment will be "used" to distort the actual occurrence, responsible broadcasters do everything possible to minimize their presence. Many have adopted guidelines: place cameras in unmarked cars, avoid special lighting, obey the police even if their orders seem unduly restrictive, and as a last resort, cap the lenses or remove the cameras from the scene.

At times, rather than escalating disturbances, the presence of cameras has served to restrain persons not eager to be shown in a posture of violence. Of Southern disorders in the early 1960's, Clarence Mitchell of the National Association for the Advancement of Colored People said, "I believe that even though there was a great deal of brutality against persons staging sit-ins, etc., it would have been worse if cameramen had not been on the scene making a record." Walter Cronkite once commented, "Is it not salutary that the government servant, the politician, the rioter, the miscreant knows that he is operating in the full glare of publicity, that the whole world is watching?"

If television cameras are obtrusive, it is an unfortunate fact that cameramen sometimes intrude to an unnecessary degree. They can be noisy, sloppily dressed, and discourteous, making themselves a general nuisance as they string cables, adjust lights, and set up their command posts. They come by this cock-of-the-walk attitude naturally, for they are ideological descendants of swashbuckling newspaper photographers who were never noted for restraint or the social graces. Their conduct can scarcely be classified as a matter of ethics, but it certainly is unprofessional. It demeans journalism. I have often wondered why editors of both print and broadcast media tend to overlook this crude behavior. I suppose the answer is that the bosses are always in the office and rarely witness their staff at work. They might profit by getting out on the street occasionally.

The most serious violation of ethics that can be charged against a broadcast newsman is the staging of a story — the deliberate, deceitful enactment of an incident that is presented as a spontaneous occurrence. This happens rarely, and it is strongly condemned by all responsible journalists. Here again we go back to the practices of the newspaper still-photographers, who posed their subjects and their scenes. They squeezed Rotary Club officers close together to avoid an expanse of white space, they re-enacted award ceremonies when a flash bulb failed, and they persuaded Hollywood starlets to hitch up their skirts — even miniskirts — just a little more.

Such conceits are harmless, for there is no attempt at actual falsification. The same can be said in regard to broadcast news when, for example, a microphone is set up for an interview. The interview is being "staged," in a sense, because the microphone did not happen to be already on the scene. But there is no reason to complain.

On the serious side, Chairman Harley Staggers of the House Commerce Committee repeatedly charged television networks with staging news events. He held sporadic public hearings, and in 1972 presented a parade of witnesses from West Coast network news bureaus. Among incidents involving accusations of staging were the following:

— For a story on Las Vegas, models posed as gamblers because casino rules forbade filming of actual customers.

— A film crew induced high school students to leave their building and climb a fence, thus causing a further clash with police.

— A college student posed as a purchaser of dynamite.

— For a story on "pop wine," young people were posed drinking in various surroundings.

Of eight examples presented on one day, a *Washington Post* reporter wrote that only two indicated any deliberate effort to slant a story. And the stories were "soft" features rather than "hard" spot news. Testimony also showed that in most cases news executives already had punished offenders, which is not surprising, for any attempt at staging is not going to get very far.

A minor offshoot of staging which I deplore is the practice of filming or videotaping "reverse questions." This often takes place after a television reporter has finished a long interview. The reporter may not have been photographed at the best angle, and he may have phrased some of his questions awkwardly. So he sits facing a camera, and wearing his best interrogating expression, asks the same questions again, this time with carefully prepared language. These "reverse questions" are then edited into the interview at the proper places. They are filmed in the presence of the interviewee or his representative, lest the reporter be acused of twisting a question. All the process does is add a little glamour to the reporter's presentation, but it is a shoddy stunt that should be abandoned.

Another, unrelated practice which I consider unethical is the voicing of commercial messages by newsmen. This implies an endorsement, and a professional journalist has no business endorsing or selling products. Many broadcast executives properly do not permit their news staffs to engage in this performance, but a minority allows newsmen to make a little more money by so doing. It is enough that a reporter receives additional pay when he appears at all on a sponsored program, where he may or may not be called on to give no more than a "lead-in" to a commercial.

First Amendment problems have plagued broadcast journalism with increasing frequency as the profession has grown in stature and hence in boldness in handling the news. Newsmen and their employers alike have faced repeated challenges to their ethical standards in this field. The most dramatic case to date involving broadcast news freedom was the contempt citation voted in 1971 by the House Commerce Committee against the Columbia Broadcasting System and its president, Frank Stanton. Again, the instigator was Chairman Staggers.

The confrontation grew out of a CBS News documentary, "The Selling of the Pentagon," a rather mild critique of the Defense Department's public relations operations. Congressional defenders of Defense cleverly diverted their censure away from the program's substance to allegations that it distorted — through improper film or videotape editing — statements by two Pentagon spokesmen. The principal complaint was that the answer to one question was spliced together with the answer to another question.

Although the Pentagon gave the Commerce Committee the full text of the edited material, Staggers issued a subpoena for CBS's outtakes — the unused portions of the filmed interviews. Stanton refused to comply, contending that CBS News had a right to protection under the First Amendment. Subjecting unused film to a Congressional review of editing, he said, would have a chilling effect on broadcast newsmen. Staggers insisted on taking the contempt citations voted by his Committee to the entire House, against the advice of both Democratic and Republican floor leaders. After heated debate, the House voted 226 to 181 to return the citations to the Committee, where they were quietly buried.

During the controversy, two important developments occurred outside the halls of Congress. The Federal Communications Commission held that the editing had been a journalistic judgment into which a government agency should not inquire. It also noted that CBS had been fair in presenting contrasting viewpoints on the air. And CBS issued a set of standards updating policies for all of its news operations. The document is, in effect, a statement of ethics. Among other things, it tightened instructions for

editing film which would specifically prevent procedures such as those
challenged in "The Selling of the Pentagon."

The lesson to be drawn from the unfortunate incident is that television documentaries, which sometimes are produced by movie men without
any news background, must be subject to the taut discipline of professional journalism. No two editors will cut film in exactly the same fashion,
but they should be expected to act with careful regard for accuracy and
honesty. And a documentary producer should undergo the same meticulous supervision that a reporter receives from a city editor. Too often he is
left to operate independently.

On the positive side, the episode illustrates the evolutionary process of
upgrading journalistic ethics. Stanton acknowledged that the documentary
was not flawless. He noted that the CBS standards could never be regarded
as final, and added, "Our central task is a continuing one — to re-examine
our past practices and improve our future performance in every way available to us."

Congress is not the only governmental body in which attempts have
been made to curb broadcast newsmen's protection under the First
Amendment. Prosecutors have taken to court the refusal of reporters to
testify before grand juries about the confidential sources of their information. Of three cases on this subject argued in 1972 before the Supreme
Court, two involved newspapermen and one a television cameraman, Paul
Pappas of WTEV(TV), New Bedford, Mass. During riots in New Bedford,
Black Panthers had invited Pappas to their headquarters to film a police
raid if one occurred. Otherwise his visit was to be in complete confidence.
The raid did not take place, and Pappas refused to tell a grand jury what
he had seen.

Attorneys for Pappas and the two newspapermen — Earl Caldwell of
the *New York Times* and Paul M. Branzburg of the *Louisville Courier
Journal* — told the Supreme Court the government must demonstrate that
the need for their testimony was so compelling as to outweigh any harm to
the newsmen's First Amendment rights. The Justice Department argued
that newsmen have the same obligation as other citizens to cooperate with
grand juries.

The Supreme Court's 5 to 4 decision upholding the government position was a blow to ethical newsmen. They received small comfort from a
concurring opinion by Justice Lewis Powell pointing out that a reporter
could try to get a grand jury subpoena quashed if he believed his testimony
was sought without a legitimate need of law enforcement.

In the minority opinion, Justice Potter Stewart declared the Court's
"crabbed view of the First Amendment" invited "state and federal authorities to undermine the historic independence of the press by attempting to
annex the journalistic profession as an investigative arm of government."
He added, "We cannot escape the conclusion that when neither reporter

nor his source can rely on the shield of confidentiality against unrestrained use of the grand jury's subpoena power, valuable information will not be published and the public dialogue will inevitably be impoverished."

The only recourse for journalists supporting the people's right to know was to seek protective legislation. Bills in Congress and in various state legislatures gave some hope of ultimate victory.

In still another First Amendment field, the Federal Communications Commission intervenes in broadcast public affairs coverage through its Fairness Doctrine. When a television or radio station decides that a public issue is controversial, the Fairness Doctrine provides that contrasting views must be presented. And when an individual is "attacked" on a station, he must be given time to reply.

On its face, this would seem to be a simple and orderly procedure to achieve fairness on the air. But in operation the Fairness Doctrine is complicated and meddlesome. At its best, it is a nuisance: whenever the FCC receives a complaint about fairness, it forwards the letter to the affected station or network, which must investigate and make a prompt reply. And if the FCC upholds the complaint, the file becomes a blot on the station's record at license renewal time. At its worst, the Fairness Doctrine is direct governmental interference with the broadcaster's journalistic decisions. Joseph DeFranco, Washington attorney for CBS, stated in 1972: "The Commission's course in recent years has been hostile to independent broadcast journalism — too often assuming the wholly inappropriate role of editor-in-chief of the nation's news . . . The replacement of journalistic judgment by mechanical rules of balance necessarily frustrates efforts to inform the public effectively, for it destroys the process of selection and emphasis that is the very heart of any journalistic enterprise."

No entity, private or governmental, should try to replace the responsibility of the broadcast licensee and his staff in determining questions of fairness. The next step would be to tell him exactly who should or should not have access to his station's facilities. Responsible broadcasters, like responsible newspaper editors, inherently seek to be fair. Why, then, should their First Amendment rights in this area be less than those of their print counterparts?

Thus we have attempts by various governmental agencies to take a hand in the professional operations of broadcast journalism. They add up to efforts to create a pattern for ethical standards, another function which should be reserved to the industry itself. Nixon administration officials, for example, from Vice President Agnew down began undertaking orchestrated criticism of journalistic ethics by charging a liberal bias on the part of network newsmen and the staffs of several Eastern newspapers. The media and the government have always been in an adversary position, as they should be, and the media have always been subject to criticism, as they should be. But, for broadcasters, criticism by high officials has serious implications, inasmuch as the threat of license revocation lies in the background. It would be unrealistic to claim that no broadcasters have bent to this type of criticism. In some instances, affiliates have pleaded with networks to curb their news coverage lest they incur even greater administration displeasure. Fortunately, the networks have not capitulated either to the government or to faint-hearted colleagues. Media critics close to the White House would do well to heed the words of U.S. District Judge Murray I. Gurfein of New York when he denied an injunction in the Pentagon Papers case: "A cantankerous press, an obstinate press, a ubiquitous press must be suffered by those in authority in order to preserve the greater values of freedom of expression and the right of the people to know."

The American people can indeed place their trust in the news media, which have not failed them in the history of the Republic. Both the National Association of Broadcasters and the Radio Television News Directors Association have adopted codes of journalistic ethics which pledge the highest standards of professional conduct. The RTNDA code sums up the case in its first article: "The primary purpose of broadcast newsmen — to inform the public of events of importance and appropriate interest in a manner that is accurate and comprehensive — shall override all other purposes."

If government should not become involved in setting news standards, should any other public body be formed to look over the shoulder of the media? There have been suggestions that councils of private citizens be established locally — and perhaps even nationally — to work with newspapers and broadcasting stations on ticklish problems of ethics, accuracy, and fairness. In a few communities such councils are already in existence. I am not an advocate of this system. It is always difficult if not impossible to reconstruct the circumstances under which a particular news story was handled. To seek the advice of amateurs, however well intentioned, strikes me as an unnecessary step that degrades professional judgments.

I would prefer to see an editor or broadcast news executive formally designate a member of his own staff to post-audit criticisms and complaints and come up with findings and recommendations. This internal procedure would leave both ethical and disciplinary control where it should naturally rest — with the responsible news department. After a half-century in the field, I am more than ever convinced that experienced, dedicated journalists are the best judges of their operations and their standards.

Mr. Bagdikian sees deceit and novelty as two major techniques used in commercial and political communication to penetrate our defenses against unwanted mass-communicated information. The ethical implications of these techniques, he feels, are compounded by the massiveness and speed of the media.

He describes information overload as a cause of many people rejecting "rationality and sequential systematic thought" and turning instead "to the instinctive and subjective life." Here he seems to equate rationality with linear, step-by-step processing of information. Yet McLuhan contends that the shift away from linear, sequential thought to Gestalt, mosaic, all-at-once, stream-of-consciousness thought stems precisely from the impact of the electronic mass media, especially television, in developing altered sensory reception habits in young humans. For an explanation McLuhan looks more to the nature of the electronic media than to the content or information conveyed to those media.

One ethical problem examined by Mr. Bagdikian is the "highly skilled and systematic perversion of words and ideas for purely commercial or ideological purposes" done "so efficiently through the mass media that in a very short time the symbol means nothing." As examples of ethically suspect shifts of meaning from an original context to a context rather different from the original, he reminds us of two Presidents who invoked slogans generated by black civil rights groups for use by those Presidents to support political programs in quite different contexts.

Mr. Bagdikian's ethical concerns here seem quite similar to those of Richard M. Weaver in his essay on "Relativism and the Use of Language."* Weaver argues that "language is a covenant among those who use it. . . ." While recognizing that some gradual evolution in word meanings in a culture are inevitable and desirable, he argues that any sudden shifts in meaning must be justified by right reason, not simply by quickly changing contexts and circumstances. Weaver particularly castigates two types of linguistic covenant-breaking as violations of "intellectual and cultural integrity" and as stemming from faulty reasoning and objectionable motives. One such "improper change keeps the old word but applies it to a new thing. . . ." The second improper semantic shift, which Weaver calls "rhetorical prevarication," attempts to "impose a change in the interest of an ideology."

Is this what Mr. Bagdikian is most concerned about?

* Reprinted in Richard L. Johannesen, Rennard Strickland, and Ralph T. Eubanks, eds., *Language is Sermonic: Richard M. Weaver on the Nature of Rhetoric* (Baton Rouge: Louisiana State University Press, 1970), pp. 115–36.

How Much More Communication Can We Stand?*

BEN H. BAGDIKIAN

Graduate School of Journalism,
University of California

In our brave new world of electronic gadgetry we are certain of one thing: the new communications machines are efficient and they work.

Today information comes into most newspaper offices on teletype machines with an effective rate of 45 words a minute. We already have a new generation of machines that can transmit at 2,400 words a minute, and in a short time we'll be able to transfer words, computer-to-computer, at 86,000 words a minute.

Today the average city has six channels of television. But already there is a 42-channel cable being installed in a city, and it is technically and economically feasible to provide each home with 80 or 100 or 200 video channels.

Computers will be able to store and retrieve this formidable quantity of information, at the rate of about 12 million words a minute, and turn it into usable microfilm at about 700,000 words a minute, and as a printed document at 180,000 words a minute.

Computers can even listen and talk. They can interpret a fair number of spoken syllables and figure out what they mean in words, and the com-

* Reprinted by permission of the author and the publisher, from *The Futurist*, October, 1971, published by the World Future Society, P. O. Box 30369, Bethesda Post Office, Washington, D.C. 20014. At the time this was written, Mr. Bagdikian was Assistant Managing Editor of *The Washington Post*.

puter can then compose its own spoken answer out of its store of sounds. So computers can talk better than they can listen, prompting male chauvinist . . . computermen to a hypothesis on the gender of computers.

But all of this mechanical ingenuity must ultimately lead to a human being. For all the millions of words and images that our cables and computers can deliver, the final recipient is a human being who can process about 250 words a minute, at most about 1,000.

The disparity between the capacity of machines and the capacity of the human nervous system is not a small matter in the future of communications. It has individual and social consequences that are already causing us problems, and will cause even more in the future.

The human being of the near future probably will need as much sleep as he does today. He will spend more time absorbing abstract information than he does today, continuing the trend of past generations. But there is a limit that is important in a number of ways.

Abstract Information Is Overwhelming Us

There may be a physical and psychological limit to living with an exclusively abstract intake. To be sure, we have been learning to take in more and more of this kind of information. In little more than a century in this country, formal schooling has gone from zero for the average person to more than 12 years. Reading and other image absorption takes up a majority of the waking hours of most middle-class people. This raises the question of what is left for . . . person-to-person communication, and the richness of non-abstract relations. It's not too much to suggest that we may already have reached an intolerable limit for many persons. Many people today reject rationality and sequential systematic thought, and turn instead to the instinctive and subjective life. It's not too much to suggest that they have been abstracted beyond human meaning, that there is a limit to how much you can withdraw the human personality from direct, emotional experience. So all the beautiful methods of inundating the society with abstract information could produce a starvation of emotion.

Furthermore, inundation of the individual with an overload of information de-sensitizes him. The American Association of Advertising Agencies tells us that there are 1,600 commerical messages a day directed at the average individual, that 80 are consciously noticed by the individual, and 12 provoke some reaction. Apparently we have become skilled in screening out the 1,588 unwanted messages a day and at selecting the desired or unavoidable 12. But at what cost? Don't we have to learn to ignore most sights, sounds, and smells that are persistently pressed upon us?

We put up defenses against the unwanted advertisement or radio chatter or television image or newspaper headline, or billboard, and do it by learning to detect subliminal clues that tell us to shut off our radar. But there is a multi-billion-dollar OR $30 billion industry, the advertising agencies of the country, who retain the highest paid talents of our society to penetrate this shield, with elaborate decoys and novelties to confuse our defenses. Their chief weapons are deceit — putting an acceptable package around an idea we have already learned to reject — or novelty. Novelty is a new weapons system for which we must construct a new defense. It comes toward us emanating none of the usual clues of previously rejected messages and before we have detected the true nature of this unidentified lying object, it has penetrated into our brain and caused us to place in our consciousness something we don't want.

The human personality has always had a basic instinct to communicate. So the impulse to use a variety of methods to attract attention and to overcome the individual defenses against messages is as old as, I suppose, the cave of Altamira.

Mounting Problem of Information Overload

But today we have some new factors and in the very near future the revolution in electronic communication could make even a greater difference.

First, we live in huge urban complexes. This means we are surrounded by a mass of complex sensations previously unknown to man. I suppose that walking down the densest neighborhoods of ancient Rome was a rich sensuous experience, almost as walking through Rome today is a rich sensuous experience. But the expanse of this density was relatively small. The primitive ability to illuminate the night in ancient Rome meant that it was only during daylight hours when the individual was confronted with a flood of impressions. And very few people in the population had occupations that put a high value on formal education and abstract knowledge, which meant that people seeing ancient urban scenes had a relatively simple way to integrate their daily experiences into previous knowledge.

Today we live in huge complexes of people, man-made sights and sounds. Our careers force us to thread our way through this public scene while avoiding it, so that we can concentrate on our more remote interests. We absolutely must learn to not see and not hear and not smell and not feel most of the sensations that impinge on our daily lives.

We also have a very elaborate system of artificial communications that adds to the real sensations. Newspapers, radios, television and all the other conduits of artificial messages are added to our daily diet of faces and personalities and sounds that our nervous systems must navigate daily.

And finally, we have a mass medium, driven by advertising, whose sole purpose is to break through our protection against the crushing overload of urban sensation. Never in history has there been a society that spent so much money and highly skilled talent to implant unwanted messages into its citizens. One small measure is the fact that a minute of prime television time can cost an advertiser something like $65,000. But this gives him access to perhaps 50,000,000 brains. The attention of the American media audience, whether it is achieved by the President of the United States or by Procter and Gamble, is one of the most stunning political and commercial prizes in history.

Since the chief weapon of this system of penetrating our defenses is novelty, the operatives grasp whatever new item they can to confuse our protective shields. This includes the stealing of images, so that not only new things get by our learned rejection, but old things concealed in friendly but false packages. It was no accident that Lyndon Johnson as he was escalating the war in Vietnam looked into the television cameras and said, "We Shall Overcome," or that Richard Nixon said he is for "power for the people." This was acceptable language of groups hostile to the presidential message, so it was necessary to put the real message inside a false cloak.

Symbols Soon Are Emptied of their Meaning

There is probably a serious social cost to this beyond semantic manipulation. The use of novelty to sell politics and to sell soap has meant that anything new is seized by people who pervert the original meaning of the new phrase or image. It is used cynically as a semantic trojan horse. It is then broadcast over the highly efficient mass media, and rebroadcast over and over, until both original meaning and the transmuted meaning are completely empty. The attrition in words and symbols in our time is frightening. It is not frightening because it proliferates new words, which is normal and good. It is necessary to keep a language pertinent to the changing society that uses it. What *is* frightening is the highly skilled and systematic perversion of words and ideas and images for purely commercial or ideological purposes, and doing it so efficiently through the mass media that in a very short time the symbol means nothing. It took only two years to spread the psychedelic style in language, graphics, and clothing from Ken Kesey's wired bus to the most respectable magazines, TV programs, and clothing manufacturers of the country. It was novel and it was exploited with mammoth electronic commercial efficiency by advertising agencies.

We hear a great deal about the decadence of our formal literature and entertainment media because of their emphasis on frank sex. But for years the advertising industry has been using emphasis on frank sex to sell commercial goods and this may have been more influential than the Yippie and sex education courses in Orange County to make sexual suggestions commonplace in public messages.

Commercial Exploitation Leads to Inability to Communicate

The problem, it seems to me, is not that somehow new ideas are spread rapidly. The problem is that the cynical political and commercial exploitation of these new ideas is so massive and so quick to divert them from their original meaning, that in a few years and even a few months, a phrase, an idea, a graphic pattern that may originally have had intense purpose and meaning has been burned out and becomes meaningless. And those who use it thereafter are not saying anything that can be reliably comprehended. After Mr. Nixon said his programs were for more power to the people, what does that phrase mean anymore? It used to mean more power to presently powerless people. It now means nothing.

I would suggest that this kind of advertising and political exploitation of symbols, to project them as having the opposite of their original meaning, has contributed to the breakdown in the ability of different generations and different political groups to talk to each other. In the old civil rights movement you could tell by language and dress whether someone was active. . . . In society in general you could tell the cultural conventionality of a person by his hairstyle and necktie. But advertising caught the novelty and since selling goods is politically acceptable, it is no longer a good index. One day we may even see ordinary FBI agents wearing sideburns and wide ties.

The problem, again, is not one of spreading ideas and styles, but their deliberate exploitation that brings meaninglessness.

Communications: Increasingly Efficient — and Meaningless?

Does this mean that when our future communications become even more efficient we will have an ever greater attrition in the meaning of the symbols by which we deal with each other.?

It could. If centralized systems driven by advertising continue to be the basic pattern of our mass electronic media, then we will see a deterioration of the ability of one American to be comprehensible to another.

If, on the other hand, we have most of our media non-commercial, not committed to playing the game of collecting mass audiences for sale, then the messages can say what they mean without fear that they may not be deceiving the uninterested citizen.

There is yet another perhaps more immediate problem. If we are lucky, we are going to have quick and inexpensive media, printed and electronic. Already, radical and eccentric groups know how to get things printed by offset and xerography that greatly increases their ability to spread their messages.

What happens if every home has 200 video channels and time on each, perhaps locally, costs only nominal amounts? What if anyone can buy half an hour of time on a community cable channel for $10? Then the PTAs, the vegetarians, and the single-taxers will be on the air regularly, taking their chances on an audience just the way they would if they hired a hall or spoke in a public park. But it won't be all sweetness and light. If our system is inexpensive and open, as it ought to be, then there will also be the Klan, the Birchers, the Panthers, and every other political and special interest group.

Could our society stand that? Today it could not. It could not because today we are in a period of contention and bitterness. There is in the government an ideological killer instinct in which the true believers feel that any method of quelling hateful voices is justified. There are revolutionary groups that speak the rhetoric of violence and killing, and in its own way, the government matches it with an assumption that it has some ordained right to ignore the American right to be rhetorically hateful.

Unless we can transform the present political atmosphere in the United States, our new mass media could become the most efficient instrument of official power in history. No leader of the past — Genghis Khan, Alexander the Great, Caesar, Napoleon, even Hitler and Stalin — had the power to mobilize the attention of so many millions of subjects as the President of the United States has today through television. . . .

The basic American ethic of tolerance of dissent no matter how hateful is in danger of dying at precisely the moment when the authorities are about to inherit more powerful systems of mass communications.

There is no point in having new communications systems unless they are open and unauthoritarian. As usual, we don't have much doubt that we can produce and operate the technology. And as usual, we are not so sure that we can put the technology to work for humane and creative purposes.

In an article published in 1958, Mr. Levitt advanced the position that ethical and moral issues related to advertising *should not be the concern* of management generally and the advertiser specifically. While he admits that someone in society should grapple with these ethical questions, "it should *not* be the businessman." [1] When the advertiser consciously considers moral aspects of advertising, claims Levitt, that advertiser inappropriately tries to influence our social, spiritual, and ethical values; also that advertiser dilutes his occupational function — success in selling the product. At one point in his 1958 article Levitt summarizes his pragmatic view:

> The cultural, spiritual, moral, etc., consequences of his actions are none of his occupational concern. He is in business for his own personal edification — neither to save nor to ruin souls. His job is perfectly neutral on these matters. Besides, the minute he become preoccupied with the deeper purposes and consequences of what he does, he becomes the conscious arbiter of our lives. He will be trying consciously to decide what is good or bad for us. . . .

But aren't ethical issues *inherent* in advertising? Don't the originators of messages, in this case the businessman and advertiser, bear at least partial responsibility for the ethical level of their communication?

Potential ethical issues are inherent in any instance of communication between humans to the degree that the communicator consciously chooses specific ends and communicative means. Because advertising clearly involves attempted impact on humans and because it clearly involves conscious selection of persuasive means and ends, potential ethical issues would seem to inhere in the symbolic efforts of the businessman and advertiser.

In the present essay, Mr. Levitt undertakes a philosophical defense of advertising techniques often viewed by others as ethically suspect. While admitting that the line between distortion and falsehood is difficult to establish, his central argument is that "embellishment and distortion are among advertising's legitimate and socially desirable purposes; and that illegitimacy in advertising consists only of falsification with larcenous intent."

Mr. Levitt grounds his defense in "a pervasive . . . *universal*, characteristic of human nature — the human audience *demands* symbolic interpretation of everything it sees and knows. If it doesn't get it, it will return a verdict of 'no interest.'" Because he sees humans essentially as symbolizers, he can justify "legitimate" embellishment and distortion. He contends:

Many of the so-called distortions of advertising, product design, and packaging may be viewed as a paradigm of the many responses that man makes to the conditions of survival in the environment. Without distortion, embellishment, and elaboration, life would be drab, dull, anguished, and at its existential worst.

Thomas Garrett argues that a person becomes more truly human in proportion as his behavior becomes more conscious and reflective.[2] Because of the human capacity for reason and because of the equally distinctive fact of human dependence on other people for development of potential, Garrett suggests there are several ethical obligations. As humans, we are obliged, among other things, to behave rationally ourselves, to help others behave rationally, and to provide truthful information. Suggestive advertising, in Garrett's view, is that which seeks to bypass human powers of reason or to some degree render them inoperative. Such advertising is unethical not just because it uses emotional appeal, feels Garrett, but because it demeans a fundamental human attribute and makes people less than human.

Is Mr. Levitt defending advertising which might have that effect? Or is he arguing that advertising has generally a more malevolent effect?

NOTES

[1] Theodore Levitt, "Are Advertising and Marketing Corrupting Society? It's Not Your Worry," *Advertising Age* (October 6, 1958), pp. 89–92. A direct rebuttal of Levitt's 1958 article is Clyde Bedell, "To the Extent that Advertising and Marketing are Corrupting Society — You'd Better Worry," *Advertising Age* (October 27, 1958), pp. 101–102.

[2] Thomas M. Garrett, S.J., *An Introduction to Some Ethical Problems of Modern American Advertising* (Rome, Italy: The Gregorian University Press, 1961), esp. pp. 39–47. Also see Clarence C. Walton, "Ethical Theory, Societal Expectations and Marketing Practices," in John S. Wright and Daniel S. Warner, eds., *Speaking of Advertising* (N.Y.: McGraw-Hill, 1963), pp. 453–458.

The Morality (?)
of Advertising*

THEODORE LEVITT

Professor of Business Administration,
Harvard University

In 1972 Americans consumed about $20 billion of advertising, and very
little of it because we wanted it. Wherever we turn, advertising will be
forcibly thrust on us in an intrusive orgy of abrasive sound and sight, all to
induce us to do something we might not ordinarily do, or to induce us to
do it differently. This massive and persistent effort crams increasingly
more commercial noise into the same, few, strained 24 hours of the day. It
has provoked a reaction as predictable as it was inevitable: a lot of people
want the noise stopped, or at least alleviated.

And they want it cleaned up and corrected. As more and more products have entered the battle for the consumer's fleeting dollar, advertising
has increased in boldness and volume. In 1971, industry offered the nation's supermarkets about 100 new products a week, equal, on an an-
nualized basis, to the total number already on their shelves. Where so
much must be sold so hard, it is not surprising that advertisers have
pressed the limits of our credulity and generated complaints about their
exaggerations and deceptions.

Only classified ads, the work of rank amateurs, do we presume to
contain solid, unembellished fact. We suspect all the rest of systematic and
egregious distortion, if not often of outright mendacity.

* *Harvard Business Review*, July–August 1972, pp. 84–92.

The attack on advertising comes from all sectors. Indeed, recent studies show that the people most agitated by advertising are precisely those in the higher income brackets whose affluence is generated by the industries that create the ads.[1] While these studies show that only a modest group of people are preoccupied with advertising's constant presence in our lives, they also show that distortion and deception are what bother people most.

This discontent has encouraged Senator Philip Hart and Senator William Proxmire to sponsor consumer-protection and truth-in-advertising legislation. People, they say, want less fluff and more fact about the things they buy. They want description, not distortion, and they want some relief from the constant, grating, vulgar noise.

Legislation seems appropriate because the national action of competition does not seem to work, or, at least not very well. Competition may ultimately flush out and destroy falsehood and shoddiness, but "ultimately" is too long for the deceived — not just the deceived who are poor, ignorant, and dispossessed, but also all the rest of us who work hard for our money and can seldom judge expertly the truth of conflicting claims about products and services.

The consumer is an amateur, after all; the producer is an expert. In the commercial arena, the consumer is an impotent midget. He is certainly not king. The producer is a powerful giant. It is an uneven match. In this setting, the purifying power of competition helps the consumer very little — especially in the short run, when his money is spent and gone, from the weak hands into the strong hands. Nor does competition among the sellers solve the "noise" problem. The more they compete, the worse the din of advertising.

A Broad Viewpoint Required

Most people spend their money carefully. Understandably, they look out for larcenous attempts to separate them from it. Few men in business will deny the right, perhaps even the wisdom, of people today asking for some restraint on advertising, or at least for more accurate information on the things they buy and for more consumer protection.

Yet, if we speak in the same breath about consumer protection and about advertising's distortions, exaggerations, and deceptions, it is easy to confuse two quite separate things — the legitimate purpose of advertising and the abuses to which it may be put. Rather than deny that distortion and exaggeration exist in advertising, in this article I shall argue that embellishment and distortion are among advertising's legitimate and socially

[1] See Raymond A. Bauer and Stephen A. Greyser, *Advertising in America: The Consumer View* [Boston, Division of Research, Harvard Business School, 1968]; see also Gary A. Steiner, *The People Look at Television* [New York, Alfred A. Knopf, Inc., 1963].

desirable purposes; and that illegitimacy in advertising consists only of falsification with larcenous intent. And while it is difficult, as a practical matter, to draw the line between legitimate distortion and essential falsehood, I want to take a long look at the distinction that exists between the two. This I shall say in advance — the distinction is not as simple, obvious, or great as one might think.

The issue of truth versus falsehood, in advertising or in anything else, is complex and fugitive. It must be pursued in a philosophic mood that might seem foreign to the businessman. Yet the issue at base *is* more philosophic than it is pragmatic. Anyone seriously concerned with the moral problems of a commercial society cannot avoid this fact. I hope the reader will bear with me — I believe he will find it helpful, and perhaps even refreshing.

What is reality?

What, indeed? Consider poetry. Like advertising, poetry's purpose is to influence an audience; to affect its perceptions and sensibilities; perhaps even to change its mind. Like rhetoric, poetry's intent is to convince and seduce. In the service of that intent, it employs without guilt or fear of criticism all the arcane tools of distortion that the literary mind can devise. Keats does not offer a truthful engineering description of his Grecian urn. He offers, instead, with exquisite attention to the effects of meter, rhyme, allusion, illusion, metaphor, and sound, a lyrical, exaggerated, distorted, and palpably false description. And he is thoroughly applauded for it, as are all other artists, in whatever medium, who do precisely this same thing successfully.

Commerce, it can be said without apology, takes essentially the same liberties with reality and literality as the artist, except that commerce calls its creations advertising, or industrial design, or packaging. As with art, the purpose is to influence the audience by creating illusions, symbols, and implications that promise more than pure functionality. Once, when asked what his company did, Charles Revson of Revlon, Inc. suggested a profound distinction: "In the factory we make cosmetics; in the store we sell hope." He obviously has no illusions. It is not cosmetic chemicals women want, but the seductive charm promised by the alluring symbols with which these chemicals have been surrounded — hence the rich and exotic packages in which they are sold, and the suggestive advertising with which they are promoted.

Commerce usually embellishes its products thrice: first, it designs the product to be pleasing to the eye, to suggest reliability, and so forth; second, it packages the product as attractively as it feasibly can; and then it advertises this attractive package with inviting pictures, slogans, descriptions, songs, and so on. The package and design are as important as the advertising.

The Grecian vessel, for example, was used to carry liquids, but that function does not explain why the potter decorated it with graceful lines and elegant drawings in black and red. A woman's compact carries refined talc, but this does not explain why manufacturers try to make these boxes into works of decorative art.

Neither the poet nor the ad man celebrates the literal functionality of what he produces. Instead, each celebrates a deep and complex emotion which he symbolizes by creative embellishment — a content which cannot be captured by literal description alone. Communication, through advertising or through poetry or any other medium, is a creative conceptualization that implies a vicarious experience through a language of symbolic substitutes. Communication can never be the real thing it talks about. Therefore, all communication is in some inevitable fashion a departure from reality.

Everything is changed . . .

Poets, novelists, playwrights, composers, and fashion designers have one thing more in common. They all deal in symbolic communication. None is satisfied with nature in the raw, as it was on the day of creation. None is satisfied to tell it exactly "like it is" to the naked eye, as do the classified ads. It is the purpose of all art to alter nature's surface reality to reshape, to embellish, and to augment what nature has so crudely fashioned, and then to present it to the same applauding humanity that so eagerly buys Revson's exotically advertised cosmetics.

Few, if any, of us accept the natural state in which God created us. We scrupulously select our clothes to suit a multiplicity of simultaneous purposes, not only for warmth, but manifestly for such other purposes as propriety, status, and seduction. Women modify, embellish, and amplify themselves with colored paste for the lips and powders and lotions for the face; men as well as women use devices to take hair off the face and others to put it on the head. Like the inhabitants of isolated African regions, where not a single whiff of advertising has ever intruded, we all encrust ourselves with rings, pendants, bracelets, neckties, clips, chains, and snaps.

Man lives neither in sackcloth nor in sod huts — although these are not notably inferior to tight clothes and overheated dwellings in congested and polluted cities. Everywhere man rejects nature's uneven blessings. He molds and repackages to his own civilizing specifications an otherwise crude, drab, and generally oppressive reality. He does it so that life may be made for the moment more tolerable than God evidently designed it to be. As T. S. Eliot once remarked, "Human kind cannot bear very much reality."

. . . into something rich and strange

No line of life is exempt. All the popes of history had countenanced the costly architecture of St. Peter's Basilica and its extravagant interior decoration. All around the globe, nothing typifies man's materialism so much as the temples in which he preaches asceticism. Men of the cloth have not been persuaded that the poetic self-denial of Christ or Buddha — both men of sackcloth and sandals — is enough to inspire, elevate, and hold their flocks together. To amplify the temple in men's eyes, they have, very realistically, systematically sanctioned the embellishment of the houses of the gods with the same kind of luxurious design and expensive decoration that Detroit puts into a Cadillac.

One does not need a doctorate in social anthropology to see that the purposeful transmutation of nature's primeval state occupies all people in all cultures and all societies at all stages of development. Everybody everywhere wants to modify, transform, embellish, enrich, and reconstruct the world around him — to introduce into an otherwise harsh or bland existence some sort of purposeful and distorting alleviation. Civilization is man's attempt to transcend his ancient animality; and this includes both art and advertising.

. . . and more than "real"

But civilized man will undoubtedly deny that either the innovative artist or the *grande dame* with *chic* "distorts reality." Instead, he will say that artist and women merely embellish, enhance, and illuminate. To be sure, he will mean something quite different by these three terms when he applies them to fine art, on the one hand, and to more secular efforts, on the other.

But this distinction is little more than an affectation. As man has civilized himself and developed his sensibilities, he has invented a great variety of subtle distinctions between things that are objectively indistinct. Let us take a closer look at the difference between man's "sacred" distortions and his "secular" ones.

The man of sensibility will probably canonize the artist's deeds as superior creations by ascribing to them an almost cosmic virtue and significance. As a cultivated individual, he will almost certainly refuse to recognize any constructive, cosmic virtues in the productions of the advertisers, and he is likely to admit the charge that advertising uniformly deceives us by analogous techniques. But how "sensible" is he?

And by similar means . . .

Let us assume for the moment that there is no objective, operational difference between the embellishments and distortions of the artist and those of the ad man — that both men are more concerned with creating images and feelings than with rendering objective, representational, and informational descriptions. The greater virtue of the artist's work must then derive from some objective element. What is it?

It will be said that art has a higher value for man because it has a higher purpose. True, the artist is interested in philosophic truth or widsom, and the ad man in selling his goods and services. Michelangelo, when he designed the Sistine chapel ceiling, had some concern with the inspirational elevation of man's spirit, whereas Edward Levy, who designs cosmetics packages, in interested primarily in creating images to help separate the unwary consumer from his loose change.

But this explanation of the difference between the value of art and the value of advertising is not helpful at all. For is the presence of a "higher" purpose all that redeeming?

Perhaps not; perhaps the reverse is closer to the truth. While the ad man and the designer seek only to convert the audience to their commercial custom, Michelangelo sought to convert its soul. Which is the greater blasphemy? Who commits the greater affront to life — he who dabbles with man's erotic appetites, or he who meddles with man's soul? Which act is the easier to judge and justify?

. . . for different ends

How much sense does it really make to distinguish between similar means on the grounds that the ends to which they are directed are different — "good" for art and "not so good" for advertising? The distinction produces zero progress in the argument at hand. How willing are we to employ the involuted ethics whereby the ends justify the means?

Apparently, on this subject, lots of people are very willing indeed. The business executive seems to share with the minister, the painter, and the poet the doctrine that the ends justify the means. The difference is that the businessman is justifying the very commercial ends that his critics oppose. While his critics justify the embellishments of art and literature for what these do for man's spirit, the businessman justifies the embellishment of industrial design and advertising for what they do for man's purse.

Taxing the imagination to the limit, the businessman spins casuistic webs of elaborate transparency to the self-righteous effect that promotion and advertising are socially benign because they expand the economy, create jobs, and raise living standards. Technically, he will always be free to argue, and he *will* argue, that his ends become the means to the ends of the musician, poet, painter, and minister. The argument which justifies means in terms of ends is obviously not without its subtleties and intricacies.

The executive and the artist are equally tempted to identify and articulate a higher rationale for their work than their work itself. But only in the improved human consequences of their efforts do they find vindication.

The aesthete's ringing declaration of "art for art's sake," with all its self-conscious affirmation of selflessness, sounds hollow in the end, even to himself; for, finally, every communication addresses itself to an audience. Thus art is very understandably in constant need of justification by the evidence of its beneficial and divinely approved effect on its audience.

The Audience's Demands

This compulsion to rationalize even art is a highly instructive fact. It tells one a great deal about art's purposes and the purposes of all other communication. As I have said, the poet and the artist each seek in some special way to produce an emotion or assert a truth not otherwise apparent. But it is only in communion with their audiences that the effectiveness of their efforts can be tested and truth revealed. It may be academic whether a tree falling in the forest makes a noise. It is *not* academic whether a sonnet or a painting has merit. Only an audience can decide that.

The creative person can justify his work only in terms of another person's response to it. Ezra Pound, to be sure, thought that ". . . in the [greatest] works the live part is the part which the artist has put there to please himself , and the dead part is the part he has put there . . . because he thinks he *ought* to — i. e., either to get or keep an audience." This is certainly consistent with our notions of Pound as perhaps the purest of twentieth-century advocates of art for art's sake.

But if we review the record of his life we find that Pound spent the greater part of his energies seeking suitable places for deserving poets to publish. Why? Because art has little merit standing alone in unseen and unheard isolation. Merit is not inherent in art. It is conferred by an audience.

The same is true of advertising: if it fails to persuade the audience that the product will fulfill the function the audience expects, the advertising has no merit.

Where have we arrived? Only at some common characteristics of art and advertising. Both are rhetorical, and both literally false; both expound an emotional reality deeper than the "real"; both pretend to "higher" purposes, although different ones; and the excellence of each is judged by its effect on its audience — its persuasiveness, in short. I do not mean to imply that the two are fundamentally the same, but rather that they both represent a pervasive, and I believe *universal,* characteristic of human nature — the human audience *demands* symbolic interpretation in everything it sees and knows. If it doesn't get it, it will return a verdict of "no interest."

To get a clearer idea of the relation between the symbols of advertising and the products they glorify, something more must be said about the fiat the consumer gives to industry to "distort" its messages.

Symbol & substance

As we have seen, man seeks to transcend nature in the raw everywhere. Everywhere, and at all times, he has been attracted by the poetic imagery of some sort of art, literature, music, and mysticism. He obviously wants and needs the promises, the imagery, and the symbols of the poet and the priest. He refuses to live a life of primitive barbarism or sterile functionalism.

Consider a sardine can filled with scented powder. Even if the U.S. Bureau of Standards were to certify that the contents of this package are identical with the product sold in a beautiful paisley-printed container, it would not sell. The Boston matron, for example, who has built herself a deserved reputation for pinching every penny until it hurts, would unhesitatingly turn it down. While she may deny it, in self-assured and neatly cadenced accents, she obviously desires and needs the promises, imagery, and symbols produced by hyperbolic advertisements, elaborate packages, and fetching fashions.

The need for embellishment is not confined to personal appearance. A few years ago, an electronics laboratory offered a $700 testing device for sale. The company ordered two different front panels to be designed, one by the engineers who developed the equipment and one by professional industrial designers. When the two models were shown to a sample of laboratory directors with Ph.D.'s the professional design attracted twice the purchase intentions that the engineer's design did. Obviously, the laboratory director who has been baptized into science at M.I.T. is quite as responsive to the blandishments of packaging as the Boston matron.

And, obviously, both these customers define the products they buy in much more sophisticated terms than the engineer in the factory. For a woman, dusting powder in a sardine can is not the same product as the identical dusting powder in an exotic paisley package. For the laboratory director, the test equipment behind an engineer-designed panel just isn't as "good" as the identical equipment in a box designed with finesse.

Form follows the ideal function

The consumer refuses to settle for pure operating functionality. "Form follows function" is a resoundingly vacuous cliché which, like all clichés, depends for its memorability more on its alliteration and brevity than on its wisdom. If it has any truth, it is only in the elastic sense that function extends beyond strict mechanical use into the domain of imagination. We do not choose to buy a particular product; we choose to buy the functional expectations that we attach to it, and we buy these expectations as "tools" to help us solve a problem of life.

Under normal circumstances, furthermore, we must judge a product's "nonmechanical" utilities before we actually buy it. It is rare that we choose an object after we have experienced it; nearly always we must make the choice before the fact. We choose on the basis of promises, not experiences.

Whatever symbols convey and *sustain* these promises in our minds are therefore truly functional. The promises and images which imaginative ads and sculptured packages induce in us are as much the product as the physical materials themselves. To put this another way, these ads and packagings describe the product's fullness for us: in our minds, the product becomes a complex abstraction which is, as Immanuel Kant might have said, the conception of a perfection which has not yet been experienced.

But all promises and images, almost by their very nature, exceed their capacity to live up to themselves. As every eager lover has ever known, the consummation seldom equals the promises which produced the chase. To forestall and suppress the visceral expectation of disappointment that life has taught us must inevitably come, we use art, architecture, literature, and the rest, and advertising as well, to shield ourselves, in advance of experience, from the stark and plain reality in which we are fated to live. I agree that we wish for unobtainable unrealities, "dream castles." But why promise ourselves reality, which we already possess? What we want is what we do *not* possess!

Everyone in the world is trying in his special personal fashion to solve a primal problem of life — the problem of rising above his own negligibility, of escaping from nature's confining, hostile, and unpredictable reality, of finding significance, security, and comfort in the things he must do to survive. Many of the so-called distortions of advertising, product design, and packaging may be viewed as a paradigm of the many responses that man makes to the conditions of survival in the environment. Without distortion, embellishment, and elaboration, life would be drab, dull, anguished, and at its existential worst.

Symbolism useful & necessary

With*out* symbolism, furthermore, life would be even more confusing and anxiety-ridden than it is *with* it. The foot soldier must be able to recognize the general, good or bad, because the general is clothed with power. A general without his stars and suite of aides-de-camp to set him apart from the privates would suffer in authority and credibility as much as perfume packaged by Dracula or a computer designed by Rube Goldberg.

Any ordinary soldier or civilian who has ever had the uncommon experience of being in the same shower with a general can testify from the visible unease of the latter how much clothes "make the man."

Similarly, verbal symbols help to make the product — they help us deal with the uncertainties of daily life. "You can be sure . . . if it's Westinghouse" is a decision rule as useful to the man buying a turbine generator as to the man buying an electric shaver. To label all the devices and embellishments companies employ to reassure the prospective customer about a product's quality with the pejorative term "gimmick," as critics tend to do, is simply silly. Worse, it denies, against massive evidence, man's honest needs and values. If religion must be architectured, packaged, lyricized, and musicized to attract and hold its audience, and if sex must be perfumed, powdered, sprayed and shaped in order to command attention, it is ridiculous to deny the legitimacy of more modest, and similar, embellishments to the world of commerce.

But still, the critics may say, commercial communications tend to be aggressively deceptive. Perhaps, and perhaps not. The issue at stake here is more complex than the outraged critic believes. Man wants and needs the elevation of the spirit produced by attractive surroundings, by handsome packages, and by imaginative promises. He needs the assurances projected by well-known brand names, and the reliability suggested by salesmen who have been taught to dress by Oleg Cassini and to speak by Dale Carnegie. Of course, there are blatant, tasteless, and willfully deceiving salesmen and advertisers just as there are blatant, tasteless, and willfully deceiving artists, preachers, and even professors. But, before talking blithely about deception, it is helpful to make a distinction between things and descriptions of things.

The question of deceit

Poetic descriptions of things make no pretense of being the things themselves. Nor do advertisements, even by the most elastic standards. Advertisements are the symbols of man's aspirations. They are not the real things, nor are they intended to be, nor are they accepted as such by the public. A study some years ago by the Center for Research in Marketing, Inc. concluded that deep down inside the consumer understands this perfectly well and has the attitude that an advertisement is an ad, not a factual news story.

Even Professor Galbraith grants the point when he says that ". . . because modern man is exposed to a large volume of information of varying degrees of unreliability . . . he establishes a system of discounts which he applies to various sources almost without thought. . . . The discount becomes nearly total for all forms of advertising. The merest child watching television dismisses the health and status-giving claims of a breakfast cereal as 'a commercial.' "[2]

This is not to say, of course, that Galbraith also discounts advertising's effectiveness. Quite the opposite: "Failure to win belief does not impair the effectiveness of the management of demand for consumer products. Management involves the creation of a compelling image of the product in the mind of the consumer. To this he responds more or less automatically under circumstances where the purchase does not merit a great deal of thought. For building this image, palpable fantasy may be more valuable than circumstantial evidence."[3]

Linguists and other communications specialists will agree with the conclusion of the Center for Research in Marketing that "advertising is a symbol system existing in a world of symbols. Its reality depends upon the fact that it is a symbol . . . the content of an ad can never be real, it can only say something about reality, or create a relationship between itself and an individual which has an effect on the reality life of an individual."

Consumer, know thyself!

Consumption is man's most constant activity. It is well that he understands himself as a consumer.

The object of consumption is to solve a problem. Even consumption that is viewed as the creation of an opportunity — like going to medical school or taking a singles-only Caribbean tour — has as its purpose the solving of a problem of how to lead a relevant and comfortable life, and the lady on the tour seeks to solve the problem of spinsterhood.

The "purpose" of the product is not what the engineer explicitly says it is, but what the consumer implicitly demands that it shall be. Thus the consumer consumes not things, but expected benefits — not cosmetics, but the satisfactions of the allurements they promise; not quarter-inch drills but quarter-inch holes; not stock in companies, but capital gains; not numerically controlled milling machines, but trouble-free and accurately smooth metal parts; not low-cal whipped cream, but self-rewarding indulgence combined with sophisticated convenience.

The significance of these distinctions is anything but trivial. Nobody knows this better, for example, than the creators of automobile ads. It is not the generic virtues that they tout, but more likely the car's capacity to enhance its user's status and his access to female prey.

Whether we are aware of it or not, we in effect expect and demand that advertising create these symbols for us to show us what life *might* be,

---

[2] John Kenneth Galbraith, *The New Industrial State* [Boston, Houghton Mifflin Company, 1967], 325–326.
[3] Ibid., p. 326.

to bring the possibilities that we cannot see before our eyes and screen out the stark reality in which we must live. We insist, as Gilbert put it, that there be added a "touch of artistic verisimilitude to an otherwise bald and unconvincing narrative."

Understanding the difference

In a world where so many things are either commonplace or standardized, it makes no sense to refer to the rest as false, fraudulent, frivolous, or immaterial. The world works according to the aspirations and needs of its actors, not according to the arcane or moralizing logic of detached critics who pine for another age — an age which, in any case, seems different from today's largely because its observers are no longer children shielded by protective parents from life's implacable harshness.

To understand this is not to condone much of the vulgarity, purposeful duplicity, and scheming half-truths we see in advertising, promotion, packaging, and product design. But before we condemn, it is well to understand the difference between embellishment and duplicity and how extraordinarily uncommon the latter is in our times. The noisy visibility of promotion in our intensely communicating times need not be thoughtlessly equated with malevolence.

Thus the issue is not the prevention of distortion. It is, in the end, to know what kinds of distortions we actually want so that each of our lives is, without apology, duplicity, or rancor, made bearable. This does not mean we must accept out of hand all the commercial propaganda to which we are each day so constantly exposed, or that we must accept out of hand the equation that effluence is the price of affluence, or the simple notion that business cannot and government should not try to alter and improve the position of the consumer vis-à-vis the producer. It takes a special kind of perversity to continue any longer our shameful failure to mount vigorous, meaningful programs to protect the consumer, to standardize product grades, labels, and packages, to improve the consumer's information-getting process, and to mitigate the vulgarity and oppressiveness that is in so much of our advertising.

But the consumer suffers from an old dilemma. He wants "truth," but he also wants and needs the alleviating imagery and tantalizing promises of the advertiser and designer.

Business is caught in the middle. There is hardly a company that would not go down in ruin if it refused to provide fluff, because nobody will buy pure functionality. Yet, if it uses too much fluff and little else, business invites possibly ruinous legislation. The problem therefore is to find a middle way. And in this search, business can do a great deal more than it has been either accustomed or willing to do:

It can exert pressure to make sure that no single industry "finds reasons" why it should be exempt from legislative restrictions that are reasonable and popular.

It can work constructively with government to develop reasonable standards and effective sanctions that will assure a more amenable commercial environment.

It can support legislation to provide the consumer with the information he needs to make easy comparison between products, packages, and prices.

It can support and help draft improved legislation on quality stabilization.

It can support legislation that gives consumers easy access to strong legal remedies where justified.

It can support programs to make local legal aid easily available, especially to the poor and undereducated who know so little about their rights and how to assert them.

Finally, it can support efforts to moderate and clean up the advertising noise that dulls our senses and assaults our sensibilities.

It will not be the end of the world or of capitalism for business to sacrifice a few commercial freedoms so that we may more easily enjoy our own humanity. Business can and should, for its own good, work energetically to achieve this end. But it is also well to remember the limits of what is possible. Paradise was not a free-goods society. The forbidden fruit was gotten at a price.

Among the various attacks on broadcast advertising described by Mr. Wasilewski is the petition of Action for Children's Television (ACT) which seeks abolition of all advertising on broadcasts directed to children. Does such advertising "constitute an immoral act which should not be permitted in our society?" This example can illustrate the more general matter of the possible *contextual* nature of ethical standards for mass communication ethics. Should ethical criteria be more stringent for communication aimed at children as opposed to adults? Should ethical standards for public communication differ between peacetime and time of war? Should ethical standards vary for communication in different fields, such as advertising, education, law, religion, and politics?

Jurgen Ruesch argues that at present "there is no single set of ethical rules that control communication." Instead, he contends, "we have to specify what purposes the communication serves." [1] Based on this assumption, Ruesch suggests that differing sets of ethical standards for communication would apply for the following different areas: (1) the interpretive, manipulative, and exhortative communication engaged in by advertisers, propagandists, and public relations experts; (2) the representational communication of scientists; (3) the political communication of government and candidates; and (4) the personal communication of individuals.

To what degree should criteria for assessing mass communication ethics be inflexible, universal, and absolute or to what degree should they be flexible, situation-bound, and relative? Surely the more absolute our standards are the easier it is to render simple, clear-cut judgments. But in matters of public communication and public decision-making, the ethics of communicative means and ends seldom are simple. Harley Shands asserts that in human affairs "there is no such thing as objectivity, and therefore no such thing as a universal system of morality or ethics." [2] But is this the case?

Mr. Wasilewski mentions that a South Dakota court differentiated between the "informational" advertising of a public utility and advertising aiming merely at "image building." By implication informational advertising would be acceptable while image-building advertising would be ethically suspect. Obviously one concern is the exact meaning of image-building; on that definition could hinge the precise ethical judgment to be rendered.

Should the ethical criteria appropriate for judging advertising differ depending upon the *function* which the specific advertisement serves? Some advertisements aim at justifying the claims of merit for a product or institution. They "make a case" for the superiority of the product. To such attempts at arguing the quality of a product, can the traditional standards for persuasion ethics be applied?

[1] Jurgen Ruesch, "Ethical Issues in Communication," in Lee Thayer, ed., *Communication: Ethical and Moral Issues* (N.Y.: Gordon and Breach, 1973), pp. 16–17.
[2] Harley C. Shands, "Morality and the Communicational Process," in *ibid.*, p. 147.

But what of advertisements which function primarily to capture and sustain consumer attention? Some advertisements function simply to create consumer awareness of the name of the product and to promote name-brand identification through association of the product with pleasant images and emotions. For assessing the ethics of advertisements whose prime goal is attention-getting, what criteria would be most appropriate?

These are but some of the questions that Mr. Wasilewski raises.

Advertising:
Does It Have a Future?*

VINCENT T. WASILEWSKI,

President,
National Association of Broadcasters

. . . The exchange of goods and services began before human history was recorded and certainly, shortly thereafter, some crude form of advertising appeared. And shortly after that, no doubt the first attack on advertising was made.

The conclusion might be drawn that as long as there are human beings there will be commerce and as long as there is commerce there will be advertising and as long as there is advertising there will be attacks on advertising.

That kind of a conclusion is comfortable because it seems to establish an equation of historical inevitability — that what has gone on for so long in the past will continue into the future.

Yet, just as nuclear weapons raise a question about the basic assumption that human beings will be around forever, so do certain events and trends raise a similar question about the assumption most of us hold — that advertising will be around forever.

Since advertising has been under attack for as long as it has been in existence, is there any reason to believe it is more seriously imperiled now than it has ever been?

---

* First presented as a talk before the Poor Richard Club, Philadelphia, Pennsylvania, in 1972. Printed here with permission of the author and the Club's President, Joseph P. McLaughlin.

In my opinion, there is.

The number and variety of the attacks have increased immensely. Different groups are attacking different elements of advertising for different reasons, so that advertising is, in the old phrase, in danger of being bit to death by ducks. More important for the future of advertising, however, are the signs that a massive shift in public attitudes may be taking place. The final conclusions are uncertain and the attitudes not fully formed but the direction is ominous — and if those who believe in advertising stand idly by much longer, providing neither explanation or defense, it will be too late.

Within recent times, there was one landmark event which may be regarded as the beginning of advertising's most recent and serious troubles. That was, of course, the ruling of the FCC that for the first time the Fairness Doctrine would be applied to a product — cigarettes. That represented the ultimate perversion of an already ill-advised, unworkable, and unrealistic doctrine. It was a prime example of an apparently common bureaucratic technique: if something works badly, rather than admit a mistake keep expanding it in the hope things will improve and the mistake will go unnoticed.

Then Congress stepped in and legislated an even more radical solution. It banned the advertising of cigarettes from the broadcast media. They didn't ban cigarette advertising from newspapers or magazines or billboards or in any way inhibit the ingenious promotions and methods which cigarette manufacturers were allowed to use to sell their product. They did not ban or restrict in any way the production, manufacturing, transportation, or sale of cigarettes. And, of course, they continued the Federal tax money subsidy to farmers to grow tobacco in the first place. And not only that, they even voted to continue the subsidy for the advertising of American cigarettes overseas. Here was an attack on advertising, an attack that was essentially a diversion, a cosmetic action which made no pretense of really getting to the heart of the matter but sought only to make a public scapegoat out of advertising and broadcasting.

One would have thought that members of the advertising community would have rallied round to oppose this flagrant discrimination and to help in the common cause because of the implications it had for everyone in advertising. As someone who was involved in the matter deeply, I must report to you that aid and assistance was minimal. The attitude seemed to be: "Watch out, your end of the boat is sinking." Indeed, magazines, fat with cigarette advertisements, ran less than objective columns by the dozen. The editorial pages of many American newspapers were filled with editorials about broadcasters promoting cigarette smoking and cancer. The only reason there wasn't a cigarette advertisement next to the editorial is the policy of most papers to separate advertising from editorial material.

They can separate the material but I do not think they can separate the morality.

So, this blow against advertising was struck. It fell on broadcasters alone but the implications for all advertising were obvous — and, by most involved with advertising — were ignored.

With that precedent, the enemies of advertising looked for new fields to conquer and they have discovered what they regard as a very fertile one. The drug crisis is a serious problem. All America is preoccupied with finding a solution. Advertising is again seen as a convenient pressure point. So there is a serious move to ban the advertising of proprietary drugs and medicines on radio and television. Considering that there is little, if any, scientific support for the contention that the advertising of drugs and medicines on the broadcast media promotes hard drug use in our society, the threat is serious. Here again, the thrust is directed at radio and television because broadcasting is regulated and thus the first and easiest target to reach.

But, here again, the implications are ominous for advertising. For, if the advertising of drugs and medicines on radio and television is branded as a contributor to a drug-oriented society, then all advertising stands convicted.

Here again, the initial pressure is on broadcasting. Here again, is the rest of the advertising world going to stand by and say, "Your end of the boat is sinking" . . . or are they going to recognize that it is one and the same boat?

We in broadcasting also face the ACT petition which is now before the FCC. ACT is an organization put together by a group of Boston women calling themselves Action for Children's Television. It has gained some nationwide support. The ACT petition is flatly anti-advertising in the most extreme sense. It seeks to abolish advertising entirely in one type of broadcast programming — those programs directed to children. And even though the petition applies to broadcasting, isn't the question that ACT is asking pretty basic to anyone involved in advertising, because the question is: should any advertising at all be directed toward children or does such advertising, in fact, constitute an immoral act which should not be permitted in our society? Make no mistake, the only reason they have concentrated on broadcasting is because they believe it to be the most effective, and because broadcasting is regulated and easier to get at. But if the principle is established that it is wrong to advertise to children, then goodbye *Boy's Life* and *Seventeen* and a large chunk of newspaper advertising and Christmas catalogues, and maybe even goodbye to Santa Claus in department stores at Christmas time.

We broadcasters are faced with the latest insanity — a word I choose deliberately because I think it accurately describes the proposal of the Federal Trade Commission made to the Federal Communications Commission — that radio and television stations be required to carry counter-advertising. If the FTC's proposals are followed, broadcasters would be required to provide both free and paid time for attacks on broadcast advertising. To us, this proposal seems so obviously destructive that we wonder if it is intentionally malevolent. Do those who make such decisions at the FTC so hate the American system of broadcasting and advertising that they are intentionally seeking to destroy it?

That is a strong reaction, I admit. Some may regard it as an overreaction, but let me describe to you what the FTC proposes. The FTC would require broadcasters to allocate free time to answer any statement in a commercial announcement that someone felt was controversial. For example, the Commission says: "In response to advertising for whole life insurance emphasizing the factor of its being a sound investment, the public could be informed of the views of some people that whole life insurance is an unwise expenditure."

A second quote from the Commission's proposals: ". . . In response to advertising for small automobiles emphasizing the factor of low cost and economy, the public could be informed of the views of some people that such cars are considerably less safe than larger ones. On the other hand, ads for big cars, advertising the factors of safety and comfort, could be answered by counter-ads concerning the greater pollution arguably generated by such cars."

The Commission, in an obvious attempt to put itself on the side of the angels, feels that products that raise ecological issues should also be the recipient of counter-ads. Ecology is the relationship between man and his environment and there is little that falls outside of that definition, particularly under the broad interpretation the FTC would give to the term. Under the FTC definition, all advertising for automobiles, gasoline, or any other product connected with automobiles would be subject to counter-advertising, as would advertising for soaps and detergents, foods, personal products, drugs and pharmaceuticals, appliances, toys and, as far as can be determined, most services. The Commission piously alleges that not all product commercials would be subject to counter-ads. It is very difficult to think of one that would not. Indeed, in the Commission's own words, "This list of examples could go on indefinitely."

This approach to the ecology problem seems to be perversely negative in yet another respect. It appears that the FTC seeks to punish American business corporations which are trying to assist in finding solutions to the ecological problems. Clearly, the news of progress that companies are making on environmental problems, and their attempts to engender goodwill by publicizing those actions, should be encouraged and not discouraged. But the FTC proposals would not only effectively prevent companies from informing the public of their concern and their accomplishments, they would discourage the companies from undertaking any such improvements at all. Does that make sense?

If the claims of the companies are true as to their ecological achievements or as to the benefits of their products, then those activities should be touted far and wide. If the claims are false and misleading, then the FTC should proceed against the offending companies, as Congress has charged it to do.

I said a moment ago that we may seem to be over-reacting. But let me ask you . . . : How many organizations would buy advertising time on radio or television when, adjacent to their message extolling the merits of their product, there would be a counter-ad telling people it was a bad product, don't buy it? Would companies with which you are acquainted continue to advertise under such circumstances? Many of them, obviously, would not. They would find other ways and other methods of convincing the public of the merit of their products., Even those who continued to advertise would, with justification, inevitably seek substantial reduction in the cost of advertising because the effectiveness of that advertising would obviously have dropped very substantially.

Here again, because the government has a handle on broadcasting, the proposal would apply only to broadcasting. They can reach us because we are regulated, but it is obvious that they can reach magazines that use the mails, and probably that they can ultimately reach newspapers as well. My hope and belief is that the Commission will recognize that the FTC's proposal is destructive to the American system of broadcasting and will reject it. . . .

As I am sure most of you are aware, the FTC's counter-advertising proposal is the offspring of the FCC decision which first applied the Fairness Doctrine to a product — cigarettes. This proposal would apply the Doctrine to all products, all advertising.

NAB protested violently that it was wrong in concept and dangerous in precedent when it was applied to cigarettes. We were assured that it would be so narrowly written that it could not be construed to apply to any other product. Well, they did try to draft it so that it did not, but the erosion began as soon as it hit print. The original wording of the Communications Act upon whch the Fairness Doctrine is based was not intended to cover advertising. The actual wording in the Act is that the licensee has an obligation "to afford reasonable opportunity for the discussion of conflicting views on *issues* of public importance."

It seems obvious that the wording and the intent of the Act contemplates discussions of issues and that the application to product announcements is an extension of the law beyond Congressional intent. There is no need or reason for the Fairness Doctrine to be applied to product advertising. If advertising is fraudulent or misleading, the Federal Trade Commission has powers to deal with it. If a company is making claims about its products that are not sustainable, those claims can be dealt with. If the Federal Trade Commission does not have powers to deal with those abuses, they should be given them. Neither advertisers nor media would object to providing better tools to deal with the shady practices that harm us all.

There is a pretty frightening catalog of anti-advertising actions which I think fully justifies the question I asked at the beginning: "Advertising — Does it Have a Future?"

But we are not finished yet.

Because there is one aspect of public attitudes toward advertising that overshadows even all these important issues which I have already discussed.

Advertising has throughout history been criticized, particularly in intellectual and academic circles. Some people have always regarded it as frivolous and always questioned its function. They have always attacked its economic utility. Does it really lower costs, as we claim — or does it, in fact, increase costs? Does it really promote mass production — or does it, in fact, promote monopolies? You have all heard those arguments. They have been debated inconclusively for at least a hundred years.

But recently a new argument has appeared. It is essentially this: even if we completely agree with you about the role advertising plays in our society, even if we accept completely all of the arguments about the efficacy and importance and need for advertising in promoting consumption and mass production, *that's bad.* It is bad because, from an ecological and environmental point of view, we have reached a time on this planet when constant increases in consumption are anti-social. If advertising is doing the job you claim it is doing, it is in fact a negative and evil force in society which encourages excessive and poorly directed use of limited resources. Therefore we should cut down or even cut out advertising.

Now, just so you won't think this is one of those academic arguments fashionable only for a moment, let me cite a small example of the practical application of it. The Sierra Club, an outdoor and environmental organization active in California, Oregon, and Hawaii, has been using this argument in a very sensitive area — state regulatory bodies for public utilities. They argue that utilities use up natural resources at an excessive rate by promoting consumption through advertising. They argue that advertising by utilities should be entirely disallowed or, at the very least, advertising expenses should not be allowed in determining the utilities' rate base. Now that's a pretty practical application of this new doctrine. It has even received some indirect judicial support. A South Dakota court made a distinction between the "informational" advertising of a utility and advertising it regarded as merely "image building."

Obviously this issue goes to the very heart of our advertising system. If this philosophy carries the day, then advertising has little future. But their questions are valid and we must ask ourselves: Do those people have a point? Are we really engaged in an act which is ultimately anti-social? after all, we all have to live in this world too. None of us wants to spend his life in work which is bad for the human race.

And they do have a point. There are excesses in advertising. There are extremes, and there are negative effects.

But I believe advertising's net effect is good. It helps promote the greatest good for the greatest number. I believe it helps to satisfy the needs and desires of human beings. I believe that it does make possible many more of the good things of life, not only for the affluent but also for those who can least afford them. If you believe that, as I do, then I don't think you can stand by and let advertising be destroyed. We need a cooperative effort among believers . . . a cooperative effort and a personal contribution toward educating people about the real truth of the value of advertising. . . .

All those who believe had better lend a hand soon — because it is not just broadcasting's end of the boat which is sinking, it is your end as well.

Mr. Gallup bases his views on more than "four decades of gauging and reporting public opinion on all of the important social, political, and economic issues of the day. . . ." But level of experience and reflection do not necessarily guarantee a complete or satisfactory answer to the ethical problems of behavior in this field any more than any other, as Mr. Edelstein, in his reaction, makes clear.

While "polling" and public opinion analysis are not always considered to be a part of what we refer to as "mass communication," their relevance is obvious. More and more the owners and operators of the media base their own policies and operating decisions on survey research of one form or another. How do people feel about "X" or "Y"? — whether those X's or Y's be politicians or products or programs. What survey researchers purport to know about how people feel about the X's and Y's of the world do affect the kinds of decisions that are made, and those decisions affect our social, economic, and political future.

It is also worth noting that more and more "news" about ourselves may be based on survey research. The media report to us how we feel about the X's and Y's of the world, based on some pool or survey research. Are people able to understand and interpret that research, or even the reports of that research in the media? "The layman, "Mr. Gallup writes, "should beware of all research that is undertaken to prove a point, whether this be in politics or any other field." But what of Mr. Gallup's point?

And how are people to "beware" of what is available to them in the media? Is it possible for large numbers of people to be sophisticated enough to read a newspaper competently?

This is part of the dilemma, as Mr. Edelstein assumes in his response. It is possible *methodologically* to avoid bias in polling? What we get is not what is going on, but what the "pollsters are capable of providing." Does this limitation constitute an *ethical* issue, or is it *merely* a matter of method?

"What *can* and should future polls reflect?" is Mr. Edelstein's central question.

The Ethical Problems of Polling

GEORGE GALLUP

Chairman, the Gallup Poll
American Institute of Public Opinion

In the development stage of any new field two problems must be faced: gaining acceptance for new concepts, and establishing credibility for its practitioners.

Every communicator has problems of objectivity that arise out of personal concerns. The reporter with liberal leanings knows that his advancement may depend on how well he pleases his conservative publisher. The author of a book knows that if he makes sensational charges and presents a lot of half-truths his book, hopefully, will command greater attention and sell more copies. The editorial assistant knows the prejudices of the name broadcaster and selects news accordingly. Even the college textbook author knows that his book will gain wider acceptance and sales if he caters to the views of certain leaders in his field.

Complete objectivity is a goal rarely reached by human beings. The problem, therefore, is to devise constraints, to establish standards, that will serve both as a guide to the communicator, and as a protection to his audience. Standards alone, unfortunately, do not provide complete protection. Much still must be left to the ethical and moral sense of the communicator.

Perhaps the best way to indicate some of the ethical problems of the poll-taker is to start with his first task — getting financial support for his efforts. In the field of survey research sponsors fall quickly into two categories: those who want to discover the truth, and those who want to prove a case.

Needless to say, the layman should beware of all research that is undertaken to prove a point, whether this be in politics or any other field. As the reader and viewer know, millions of dollars are spent to prove that Product X is the favorite with housewives; that Magazine A has twice as many readers in the middle-age groups as Magazine B; that the public opposes environmental controls that would cost industry millions of dollars. Not all of this kind of research is suspect, but certainly the burden of proof must rest with the research organization to establish objectivity.

Ideally a sponsor of research should have only one interest — to discover the facts regardless of how these facts conflict with his own views or interests.

The public opinion polls that are supported by the press have been fortunate in having sponsors who fall into this latter category. In the entire history of the Gallup Poll not one newspaper, to our knowledge, has ever distorted the findings or changed the results. Headline writers, because of the requirements of space, may find it difficult at times to write a headline that will fit and still give a correct reflection of the findings.

The fact that the newspaper sponsors of a poll typically represent all shades of political belief adds another constraint to the polling organization to present its findings in strictly neutral fashion. Any deviation from this policy would most likely result in cancellations from those newspapers who felt that their cause was being unfairly represented.

Bias can influence the selection of questions to be included in the survey, the wording of questions that are included in the interviewing form, and in the interpretation or analysis of the findings.

The selection of questions

Questions of a negative character may contain an unconscious bias even when they meet other tests of objectivity. It isn't necessary to ask the classic question: "Have you stopped beating your wife?" If the researcher asks only: "Do you beat your wife?" the poll-taker is implying that perhaps the respondent does, else the question wouldn't have been asked.

The question might be asked about a president: "Has President 'X' always lived a moral life?" The findings would almost certainly include some persons — maybe a lot — who would answer "No." A greater number would likely say they "Didn't know," and the overall impression left in the minds of readers could be one of doubt.

Questions asked in a poll at a time when delicate discussions are going forward with a foreign nation could prove embarrassing and could hamper progress in reaching solutions. Again, cases that are before a court and that have attracted great public interest pose a severe problem for the poll-taker who does not wish in any way to influence the course of justice. The early months of the Watergate affair presented just such a problem.

The wording of questions

Almost every critic of polls believes that a slight change in the wording of questions can make a great difference in poll results. On controversial issues, those which have been widely discussed by the public, this is seldom the case. Proof of this is seen in the public's response to official referendum issues in the United States and in other nations. Even when these issues are presented to the people in a form deliberately designed to influence or confuse voters, the effort invariably fails.

Questions that are put to respondents in a poll must be carefully pretested to see that persons with little education understand the wording and to ascertain the general level of knowledge about the issue. Unless questions are adequately pre-tested they are likely to contain words that aren't understood, and the question, or questions, asked may not get at the real core of the issue being polled. Biases may become apparent that were overlooked by the person who formulated the question.

The wording of questions is one of the most difficult tasks of the survey organization. Recognizing the problem of achieving a wording that is impartial, understandable, and that gets at the heart of the issue, responsible polling organizations follow the practice of including the exact wording of the question or questions asked when poll results are published. Each reader or viewer then is in a position to judge whether the question is fairly stated.

Interpretation of findings

Survey findings can obviously be looked at from many points of view. The interpreter can point to the finding that a majority holds a certain viewpoint; or he can look at the same finding to show that only a bare majority hold the same view — a proportion much lower than might be expected. Again it is a matter of whether the bottle is "half full" or "half empty."

The poll analyst can look at any of a dozen sub-group results and find something that he thinks is significant. But here again, as pointed out earlier, the reader or viewer is under no compulsion to accept the analyst's interpretation. The question — and the results — are there before him and he can reach his own conclusions.

*   *   *

After four decades of gauging and reporting public opinion on all of the important social, political, and economic issues of the day, I have come to a firm conclusion about the best way to insure impartiality. The best of all safeguards is to make certain that all shades of political belief — from extreme right to extreme left — are represented on the staff of the research organization; and that these persons be given the right and the responsibility to examine the questions selected for polling, the wording of questions, and the interpretation of the results. Any objection or criticism must not go unheeded; it must be carefully weighed.

This practice has been followed from the earliest days of the Gallup Poll. At least six senior members of the organization examine every wording, every question, and every article based upon the poll findings. In this manner, most of the biases, conscious or unconscious, can be detected.

I believe that the media might well follow this same practice. Most of the obvious bias in television news broadcasts, and in the press, could be eliminated if the selection of news and the reporting of news were subjected to critical examination by persons of widely different political viewpoints. When most members of a staff think alike, bias is inevitable.

Poll standards

A set of standards to be followed by polling organizations was adopted by the National Council on Published Polls in 1968. Membership in this organization is open to any survey research organization whose polls are designed for publication in the press or on the air. A somewhat similar code was established by the American Association for Public Opinion Research at an earlier time.

The codes require that in all poll reports these specific facts be provided: a description of the sample reached, the method employed for reaching the sample, the size of the sample, the exact wording of the questions asked, and the time of interviewing.

The standards adopted have, in general, been observed. Press releases dealing with poll findings include the information required by the standards although largely for space or time reasons, facts about the way the poll was conducted often are edited out of the release that the reader or viewer sees.

The greatest sinner in this respect is television. Often only poll findings are reported and the essential facts needed by viewers to judge the quality and the reliability of the poll are omitted. The excuse given is that viewers aren't interested in how the poll was taken — only the score. But growing sophistication about polls on the part of the public may force networks to give more data about the poll itself and how it was conducted.

Growth in polling organizations

In each new presidential election a new group of poll-takers appears, some of them properly trained to conduct polls, but many of them still in the novice stage.

Unfortunately, the layman does not have enough sophistication in this area to judge whether a poll is conducted properly or not, and what credence he should place on the poll findings.

The best protection and the best guarantee of a poll-taker's ability is his track record — the size of the errors he has registered in all of the elections in which he has reported his findings. Such a record should be available on request, and along with it, proof of publication prior to the election.

Often poll-takers claim accuracy when, in fact, their final reports do not tell how the undecided voters will vote. After the election they can claim that the undecided vote went largely to one candidate or the other, or that it divided evenly — whichever brings their figures closer to the mark. Others stop polling some two or three weeks before an election to avoid having their figures checked against the actual election results.

It is possible today to eliminate non-voters and to allocate the undecided vote by objective methods. There is, therefore, no excuse for not providing readers or viewers with a final estimate that can be checked down to the last decimal point against official election returns. Anything short of this is a cop-out, and a clear indication that the poll-taker hasn't learned how to take the final steps, or is unwilling to place his neck on the chopping block.

The standards agreed to by the polling profession should insist that any polling organization be ready to supply full details about its polling record, not only in the elections in which it may have been close, but in every election in which it has participated.

The private polls

Private polls, those conducted by candidates, parties, or others, to gain insight into the preferences of voters and their views on important issues, and not for publication in the press or on television, pose a special problem.

Individuals or organizations that pay for such polls run the risk of getting incompetent or inexperienced pollsters. But the principle of *caveat emptor* applies here. If the poll misleads the sponsor, he has only himself to blame for choosing the wrong poll-taker.

However, an important ethical problem rears its ugly head when the poll-taker, or the sponsor, leaks the poll to the press. When this happens, it is rare that any facts are given the public about the polling organization, or how the poll was conducted. And it can be taken as a certainty that no poll is ever leaked unless the candidate or party believes that such disclosure will give it an advantage.

If a poll is leaked to the press, then all details about it, including the name of the research organization that did the polling, the sponsor, and the procedures followed should be published at the same time. And if these aren't supplied, then the media should refuse to print the results.

Leaked poll results are of the greatest concern to the polling organizations that are trying to observe the highest standards and that have an interest in building public confidence in survey findings. Typically such polls are based upon shoddy research and often the results conflict with the findings of responsible polling organizations. On occasion, the results are faked and they are leaked only because a candidate or party is under the delusion that by reporting a candidate ahead of his opponent he will gain some advantage.

What has been said here should not be taken to mean that private pollsters are incompetent or dishonest. It is only the "leaked" poll that is harmful. Virtually all candidates for higher office today make use of polling to discover their voting strength and to find out the chief concerns of voters who make up their electorate. In fact, in the presidential election of 1976, for the first time, candidates openly boasted of their polling efforts. In earlier years, little was said about polling lest the people conclude that the "candidate doesn't know his own mind."

Legislation to control polls

For nearly fifty years, bills have been regularly introduced in Congress to control polling. And in more recent years many state legislatures have discussed laws that would control polls, or require that poll-takers be licensed. Such efforts have come to naught chiefly because they conflict with the right of a free press. After all, a poll is merely a formalized and systematic way of collecting information that political reporters themselves have gathered throughout the history of the nation. A reporter who goes out to talk to persons in different walks of life about their views, or their voting intentions, is taking a poll, whether he calls it a poll or not. And his right to report his findings in quantitative terms, whether these be percentages or not, is fully protected by the First Amendment.

Disclosure of operating procedures is another matter. Congressman Lucien Nedzi proposed legislation that would require published polls to disclose essential details about the procedures that were followed in taking a specific poll the results of which were published. This information would be supplied to the Library of Congress within a period of 72 hours after publication. I supported this bill and I believe it is both legal and desirable. The Gallup Poll, from its early beginnings, has taken the position that the public has the right to know how it operates, who pays for the polls, and essential facts necessary to interpret the findings. In fact, my book, *The Sophisticated Poll Watcher's Guide,* was written to supply detailed information to those who have questions about polling procedures, and the place of polls in a democratic society.

Since 1935 when modern polls first appeared, great improvements have been made in almost every department. But polls are still far from perfect. We can still learn much about public opinion and its measurement. We know, at the same time, that no other method has yet been devised to gauge public opinion with the same degree of accuracy.

Polls have gained wide acceptance throughout the world. No major country today is without at least one highly competent survey organization. And it is now possible to poll the entire free world — and in a surprisingly short period of time. The views of the developing world can be contrasted with those found in the advanced industrial societies. The quality of life can be assessed in both worlds.

Survey research has been widely accepted, not only by governments but in the social sciences and in business. One would like to think that an important reason for the wide acceptance of this new instrument of democracy has been the high ethical standards of its leading practitioners.

COUNTERPOINT:

Polling:
The State of the Art

IT WILL BE WHAT'S UP FRONT
THAT WILL COUNT

ALEX S. EDELSTEIN*

The question about the polls today is not what has been done but what needs to be accomplished. This was the thesis that Dr. George Gallup brought to polling almost half a century ago, and it is a thesis that needs to be restated. For while in some respects the polls haves succeeded, in many other ways they have failed. As the familiar phrase goes, it will be what is up front from now on that will really count.

How have the polls failed?

Two reasons: sins of commission and omission. The errors of commission are too many and too easy to recount. The polls have not been accurate in predicting outcomes of primary elections, they are experiencing increasing difficulties in eliciting responses, there are problems of timing, and there is a pernicious tendency to continue to ask questions that respondents can't and don't really answer. One example that comes to mind is the question that asks people to evaluate their institutions. The conclusion that comes from this study inevitably is that people value one institution more than they do another; yet that is not the question that is being asked. People evaluate different institutions on different bases. The church and the press are not really comparable for those who attend either or both.

* Director, School of Communications, University of Washington.

Or asking people if they "agree" or "disagree" with one statement or another, concluding from the answer that the person does or does not hold that "opinion." That was the methodological problem that hooked us on the war in Vietnam and caused even the academic pollsters to agree that there was "support" for the war when there was merely support for any seemingly viable alternative (as stated by the pollster) to bring the war to an end. Although Louis Harris said in *Time* magazine that the public was "confused," *Time* and the public demurred. There was suspicion that the public was getting a lot of "What do you think about what *I* think *you* think?" questions.

But some of the errors of omission are *more* critical. The polls are not reflecting a real sense of what the country is thinking *about, what* we are thinking, and *if and when* we are thinking. The pollsters have become addicted to horse races, so to speak. They wait sometimes until the horses are on the track, but if they are not on the track, the pollsters will put them there.

Because the polls do not represent, or even seek to provide, an overview of the thinking (so-called opinions) of individuals in society, we are lacking that vital data about ourselves that a society needs to communicate and, perchance, depending upon our skills, to communicate effectively. We are getting, instead, what the pollsters are capable of providing. One suspects, by looking at the subjects with which the polls concern themselves, that their repertoire is limited. Citizen participation (and repertories) in polls need to be increased: not in *answering* questions but in *asking* them.

Let us make the point. A report published by the *New York Times* (July, 1977) says that while Americans may not vote in great numbers, they increasingly are directly involved in government and are seeking still more (direct) participation. The report, entitled "Strengthening Citizen Access and Governmental Accountability," was done by the Exploratory Project for Economic Alternatives, a group of foundation-funded economists seeking new modes of coping with contemporary economic policies.

Place that finding in contradistinction to the flood of "opinions" that pollsters have been reporting which say that the public has "lost faith" in existing institutions, and the "conclusion" emerges that (associated with lower voting figures) Americans are "alienated" from their institutions.

The fact doubtless is that many of those who are reported by the polls to be "alienated" never at any time "identified" with the governmental process as *participants.* They understood their world as it *was,* as long as it was familiar and confined; they did not understand the new worlds that were bring created around them by the staggering forces of economic and social change — their world was no longer their oyster; it had become a Jonah's whale.

Participation is the key concept; one cannot be considered as holding an opinion unless one is participant in some sense. One doesn't participate in the opinion sense by being an onlooker unless, of course, it stimulates one later to participate.

There are many among those of us who purportedly are "alienated" for whom the church, the schools, and other institutions did, indeed, once serve basic needs. But many of us have developed *new* needs. Are we "alienated" in the sense of seeing all things as meaningless, and ourselves as powerless? Of course not. We want to gain more direct access to those institutions so that they can be more responsive to us. Where we conclude that the *institutions* are meaningless or powerless, we seek to create *new* ones.

Are the polls biased on the side of establishmentarianism; e.g., existing institutions? And are the polls capable of providing access to those of us who want to participate in the *asking* of questions?

The answers obviously are both "yes" and "no." Yes, the polls are establishment oriented, although not entirely so. They realize that they must move "opinions" *up* and *around* and not merely *down*. They can't permit themselves or other institutions to establish the full polling agenda, but they are, nevertheless, controlling too much of it.

The polls also appear to be somewhat incapable of permitting access to the questioning process. They ask questions out of habit, it seems. Does the question about faith in institutions need to be asked? Again and again? The pollsters argue that such questions permit "trends" to be observed and that these are "indicative." But *what* they indicate requires explanation. Why not go more directly to explanation? If one does not know what one is measuring, why measure it? Why also do we need repetitive polls on presidential "popularity"? Why do we need continuing polls on who the best known or admired people in the world are each year, particularly when we don't know what those findings really reflect?

It is easy to go over the mistakes that have been made in the history of any activity. Polling is particularly vulnerable, but it is also peculiarly intriguing. We could recite a litany of errors, just as Mr. Gallup has quite correctly pointed to a record of success. But what about the future?

What can and should future polls reflect? Who should inspire the questions, e.g., define the polling agenda? Or should public opinion continue to be primarily what the pollsters say it is? At present, the polls appear to be obsessed with politics. That's what makes the country run, it might be said. (Politics lends itself more than emerging social issues to the defining of alternatives — to so-called decisions or opinions.) But are we really so gifted as a nation, politically speaking, that each of us can and wishes to offer opinions on everything political? Many of us have more questions than answers; we wish to comment rather than to decide. Must we continue with the polling fiction that we all have opinions, or wouldn't it be better to admit that we need only know most times what the problems, or others' opinions about them, might be?

The basic question we return to is how public opinion can become more what the *public* says it is. The new information technology, as one example, may become a means by which publics will be able to ask questions as well as answer them. The pollsters know this, of course, and they may learn to ask questions that will help to answer the questions that *society* is asking. The the pollsters will become a part of the search for ways of organizing information that is amenable to technology, thus permitting technology to become more amenable to society. Should pollsters *not* adopt this societal perspective they may find themselves, twenty years hence, reporting that the public has lost faith in the polls and not know exactly what this means. There is, in fact, some evidence that the public already is losing faith in the polls. We need to discover what this means for now and for the future.

The criteria which Mr. Moran offers for distinguishing communication from pseudocommunication, genuine communication from double-speak, could also be applied as guidelines for assessing the ethics of mass communication.

In his comments and examples, Mr. Moran assumes that his framework for analysis applies to advertising as one kind of mass communication. In fact, most ethical standards which people suggest as applicable to mass communication are assumed to apply uniformly to advertising. But what of a distinctly contradictory view which argues that commercial and political advertising via the electronic media such as television are *not* subject to some of the traditional standards?

Tony Schwartz, a professional designer of commercial and political advertisements, argues that because our conceptions of truth, honesty, and clarity are a product of our print-oriented culture, these conceptions are appropriate in judging the content of *printed* messages. In contrast, he contends that the "question of truth is largely irrelevant when dealing with electronic media content." [1] In assessing the ethics of advertising via electronic media, Schwartz feels that the Federal Trade Commission should focus not on truth and clarity of content but on *effects* of the advertisement on receivers. But, he laments, at present "we have no generally agreed-upon social values and/or rules that can be readily applied in judging whether the effects of electronic communication are beneficial, acceptable, or harmful."

In one sense most of "reality" for us is a symbolic reality and one no less "real" because of its symbolic nature. In another sense, if rhetoric is seen as human attempts at influence through symbols, properly we can speak of rhetoric *as* reality rather than the stereotypical rhetoric *versus* reality, rhetoric versus action, or *mere* rhetoric. One explanation of such a view is that of Martin Marty who observes that

> . . . the communicator, more than anyone else in society today, symbolically constructs our social reality. None of us faces reality head-on. Reality, whatever that is, would be abstract. It would be a plotless sequence with an infinite number of random impressions. The communicator is the person who organizes that reality for us and in a sense gives us the world. [2]

Other scholars believe that reality, truth, and knowledge are *constructed by us* in and through communication as we attach meanings to the things we observe. [3] For example, Jurgen Habermas, a philosopher-sociologist, believes: "Reality is constituted in a framework that is the form of life of communicating groups and is organized through ordinary language. What is real is that which can be experienced according to the interpretations of a prevailing symbolic system.[4] And compare Mr. Moran's view with that of Kenneth Burke:

> But can we bring ourselves to realize just . . . how overwhelmingly much of what we mean by "reality" has been built up for us through nothing but our symbol systems? . . . And however important to us is the tiny sliver of reality each of us has experienced firsthand, the whole overall "picture" is but a construct of our symbol systems . . . Though man is typically the symbol-using animal, he clings to a kind of naive verbal realism that refuses to realize the full extent of the role played by symbolicity in his notions of reality.[5]

NOTES

[1] Tony Schwartz, *The Responsive Chord* (Garden City, N. Y.: Anchor Books, 1974), pp. 18–22.

[2] Martin E. Marty, "Ethics and the Mass Media," in Lee Thayer, ed., *Communication: Ethical and Moral Issues* (N. Y.: Gordon and Breach, 1973), p. 190. See also Peter L. Berger and Thomas Luckman, *The Social Construction of Reality: A Treatise on the Sociology of Knowledge* (Garden City, N. Y.: Doubleday, 1966), pp. 38, 89, 96, 119–120, 140–142.

[3] For one synthesis and analysis of such views see Barry Brummett, "Some Implications of 'Process' and 'Intersubjectivity': Postmodern Rhetoric," *Philosophy and Rhetoric*, 9 (Winter 1976), 21–51; also see Robert L. Scott, "On Viewing Rhetoric as Epistemic," *Central States Speech Journal*, 18 (February 1967), 9–17.

[4] Jurgen Habermas, *Knowledge and Human Interests*, trans. Jeremy J. Shapiro (Boston: Beacon Press, 1971), p. 192.

[5] Kenneth Burke, *Language as Symbolic Action* (Berkeley: University of California Press, 1966), p. 5.

Public Doublespeak: 1984 and Beyond

TERENCE P. MORAN*

As the countdown to 1984 continues it is well that we heed Ludwig Wittgenstein's warning about language and human behavior: "The limits of my language are the limits of my world." The point is that language, or any medium of communication, is an environment in which organisms and cultures live and die. And as Stanley Milgram notes in *Obedience To Authority*, ". . . the social psychology of this century reveals a major lesson: often, it is not so much the kind of person a man is as the kind of situation in which he finds himself that determines how he will act." In many aspects, much of the commentary, learned and otherwise, regarding the influence of language and the mass media on human thought and behavior is similar to the medieval theological arguments concerning free will and determinism; you will recall that the free will position held that individuals were responsible for their thoughts, their actions, and their souls; conversely, the deterministic position held that the individual's fate was predestined and controlled by outside forces.

In considering these polarities, it is well that we keep in mind the dif-

* Mr. Moran, at the time this essay was published, was Director of the Media Ecology Program at New York University and a member of the Committee on Public Doublespeak of the National Council of Teachers of English. Adapted from *College English,* 37 (October 1975), 223–227. Copyright © 1975 by the National Council of Teachers of English. Reprinted by permission of the publisher and the author.

ferences between *illusion* and *delusion,* between our symbol systems that are used to represent or recreate reality and actual reality; as the general semanticists like to put it, "Whatever I say something is, it isn't." This distinction between symbol and reality seems clear enough, even a bit simple minded. But in our increasingly technological society, much of what stimulates our sensory and nervous systems comes to us via such totally symbolic systems as television, the LP record, the transistor radio, electronic calculators, movies, and the various manifestations of print. The end result of this massive symbolization of our lives may be our confusing our illusions of reality with reality itself, in deluding ourselves into believing that our symbols are reality. . . .

If our illusions are to serve us in our quest for survival by providing symbolic representations of experience, then it becomes vital that we find ways to distinguish reality from illusion, illusion from delusion, communication from doublespeak. In a series of experiments with rats, animal psychologists placed some of the animals in environments that deprived them of food; after a time, half of the rats were fed a solution of sugar and water; the other half were given a solution containing saccharine and water. Both groups exhibited behavior that indicated that their hunger was satisfied. Eventually, however, the saccharine-fed rats died of malnutrition, all the while behaving as though their hunger was satisfied, as indeed it was—at the illusion level. The sugar-fed rats, of course, not only acted as though their hunger had been satisfied but survived as well.

It seems to me that, without committing oneself totally to a ratomorphic view of life, this experiment suggests certain analogies between the environments created for the rats by the scientists and the environments created for us humans by language and the various mass media of communication. Like the saccharine environment, an environment created by or infiltrated by doublespeak (or pseudocommunication, to use a more encompassing term) provides the appearance of nourishment and the promise of survival, but the appearance is illusionary and the promise false. Indeed, those who exist in such polluted environments rarely are able to distinguish between pseudocommunication and communication, between the illusion of survival and actual survival.

The following matrix (a word that comes to us from the Greek for womb, thereby implying a developing process rather than a fixed product) is one attempt to provide a methodology for distinguishing communication from pseudocommunication. I am indebted to my friend and colleague, Professor Christine Nystrom, for providing me with a systems perspective for analyzing communication, and to my graduate students in my classes in propaganda analysis for their contributions to this model. Obviously, reality cannot be represented totally by any model, certainly not an either-or one; therefore the following should be understood as representing tendencies toward which any message or message system might incline. Since these tendencies represent polarities on a continuum, most analyses will fall somewhere in between. Different types of analyses will fall somewhere in between. Different types of analyses could develop from this matrix. For example, those inclined toward critical analysis might use the categories as questions to be asked of any message system; those inclined toward content analysis might use a score sheet (Agree Strongly (+3), Agree Moderately (+2), Agree Slightly (+1), Unable to Decide (0)) for either side of the polar continuum to gather statistical data.

In Communication

1. Control tends to pass from sender to receiver in a sharing experience with power continually shifting via feedback, which influences both technique and goals, allowing the meanings of symbols to be all those involved in the transaction. If the passing of control is delayed it will be for a limited time.

In Pseudocommunication

1. Control tends to remain with the sender in a non-sharing experience with power held by the message sender who determines the meanings of symbols and with feedback limited to improving the technique only. Delays are always strategies for avoiding the passing of control.

This concept of control may be the single most important difference between communication and doublespeak. As Norbert Wiener writes in *The Human Use of Human Beings:*

. . . feedback is a method of controlling a system by reinserting into it the results of its past performances. If these results are merely used as numerical data for the criticism of the system and its regulation, we have the simple feedback of the control engineer. If, however, the information which proceeds backward from its performance is able to change the general method and pattern of performance, we have a process which may be called learning.

The New York *Times* of June 16, 1975 provided two interesting, and different, examples of control in politics. In Iran only one political party is legal and the premier, Amiie Abbas Hoveida, wisely told the people, "It does not make any difference which of the Rastakhiz candidates you vote for as long as you register your political coming of age through casting your vote." Obviously, our age of mass communication has made it convenient, perhaps even necessary in order to maintain an illusion of participatory government, to have the people "vote" even when the vote has no meaning, except as an approval of those in power. Interestingly enough, a failure to vote will have to be explained to the party since this would be regarded as "a breach of discipline." In our own country President Ford, on February 3, 1975, detected a consensus emerging from his policies, say-ing, "Most Americans are not only solidly agreed on the problems we must solve — but they are agreed that solutions must be forthcoming soon." Like his predecessor, he seemed to possess magical skills for dis-cerning the thoughts of some "silent majority." The *Times* of June 19, 1975 reports that Mr. Ford is currently planning a series of "Town Meet-ings" across the country to identify and solve domestic problems. As James M. Cannon, the President's senior advisor for domestic affairs, put it: "There is some kind of a current running against too much government interference not only in the lives of businessmen, but of ordinary citizens." Perhaps this is an accurate report but, as the *Times* points out, "Verifica-tion of such a trend through cross-country forums would coincide, by ac-cident or design, with the development of the theme on which Mr. Ford is expected to base his appeal for a full term in the White House." Some feedback. Some control.

In Communication

2. Language tends toward the technical in that meanings are clearly stated and relatively stable with precision used about the use of terms in that abstractions are based upon concrete examples, and conclusions are supported logically and critically.

In Pseudocommunication

2. Language tends toward the formal in that meanings are encoded in *do's* and *don't's* with little regard for precision of meaning and a ten-dency to rely on appeals to authority, high level abstractions and uncri-tical acceptance of ideas.

The abuse of language noted here is one with which the semanticists have long concerned themselves. Whether bureaucratese, gobbledygook, the examples cited by Orwell in "Politics and the English Language," or the "mind-chained manacles" of *1984's* Newspeak, the intent is the same, for as Orwell notes, "The purpose of Newspeak was not only to provide a medium of expression for the world-view and mental habits proper to the devotees of Ingsoc, but to make all other modes of thought impossible." A news item in the New York *Times* (April 29, 1975) contains relevant data. After testifying before the Rockefeller commission investigating the C.I.A., former director Richard M. Helms called to CBS newsman Daniel Schorr, "Killer Schorr! Killer Schorr!" Later, at a news conference, in a response to a question from Schorr, Helms said, "I don't like some of the lies you've been putting on the air. I just want to say one thing — I don't know of any foreign leader that was ever assassinated by the C.I.A. That's my honest belief."

Putting aside for the moment which lies Helms did like, consider the comparison of "I don't know . . ." and "That's my honest belief." Did Helms *know* anything or had he only *beliefs?*

In Communication

3. Stated and Observed Purposes tend toward similarity in that the stated purposes are clear and open to verification by empirical observation using methods of the choosing of all of those involved in the transaction.

In Pseudocommunication

3. Stated and Observed Purposes tend toward being different in that the stated purposes are unclear, hidden, or contradictory to the observed purposes, or in that the stated purposes are not verifiable by empirical observation, or in that the methods of analysis are determined by the sender only.

This is nothing more than a plea for openness and empiricism in our public utterances. As Charles Weingartner noted in an earlier issue of *College English,* in this technological society it becomes increasingly difficult to verify statements ourselves. It may be that given the widespread reliance on various mass media for our information that we are no longer able to verify much of what bombards our senses each day. Perhaps the answer here is to distrust most, if not all, "communication" that comes to us in unverifiable form. In short, we have to be wary of accepting statements and conclusions from people who claim secret or private knowledge, whether they be transcendental meditators, astrologists, fortune tellers, government officials, advertisers, teachers, or newsreporters. As a simple exercise, try verifying the following statements:

1. "Revlon, the people who help make the world a little more beautiful." (TV commercial)
2. "I don't think anybody could say we don't have some people who wouldn't want to overthrow the government." (Senator Barry Goldwater on investigating the C.I.A.)
3. "With your popularity at a peak now, you'll probably have more invitations than you can handle, so select thoughtfully. Instead of wasting time on several projects, figure out priorities beforehand and concentrate on the most important, worthwhile ones." (Horoscope for Cancer in June)
4. "Rockefeller Finds No Kennedy Link With Death Plots. But He Indicates White House Must Have Known About Major C.I.A. Actions." (Headline in *N.Y. Times,* June 16, 1975)
5a. "Does TV Violence Affect Our Society? YES." (article in *TV Guide,* June 14–20, Neil Hickey)
  b. "Does TV Violence Affect Our Society? NO." (article in *TV Guide,* same issue, by Edith Effron)

In Communication

    4. Thinking required tends to be individual and critical in that both sender and receiver are expected to reach their conclusions independently from observing the same information but by using their own methods of analysis.

In Pseudocommunication

    4. Thinking required tends to be collective and non-critical in that the sender tries to control both the information flow available to the receiver and the methods of analyzing that information available to the receiver.

Whether President Nixon or Chairman Mao, the Surgeon General or the Tobacco Institute of America, Ford or Volkswagen, Gleem or Crest, *Playboy* or *Ms.*, the message is the same: believe in me, do as I want. A half century ago another leader put it succinctly in *Mein Kampf:*

> The purpose of propaganda is not to produce interesting divertissements for blasé young gentlemen, but to convince the masses. The masses, however, are slowmoving, and they always require an interval of time before they are prepared to notice anything at all, and they will ultimately remember only the simplest idea repeated a thousand times over.[1]

    In a very real sense it may be that the best way to uncover "dishonest and inhumane uses of language" is to read the great propagandists themselves. Men like Hitler and Goebbels, as well as the lesser lights from American politics and Madison Avenue, frequently provide the rest of us with tremendous insights into how to corrupt language, thought, and behavior. Dr. Paul Josef Goebbels (Ph.D. in Romantic Drama from Heidelberg), a most attentive pupil of the master, wrote these words in his diary for January 29, 1942:

> . . . the rank and file are usually much more primitive than we imagine. Propaganda must therefore always be essentially simple and repetitious. In the long run only he will achieve basic results in influencing public opinion who is able to reduce problems to the simplest terms and who has the courage to keep forever repeating them in this simplified form despite the objections of the intellectuals.

Both Hitler and Goebbels, I suspect, could have had lucrative careers as communication consultants to either Madison Avenue or Washington, D.C.

---

[1] Adolf Hitler. *Mein Kampf. Trans. by* Ralph Mannheim (Boston: Houghton-Mifflin, 1942), p. 203.

In his review of Ellul's *Propaganda,* Mr. Lasch properly focuses attention on several definitional issues related to propaganda. How broadly or narrowly should it be defined? Should it be viewed as ethically neutral or as inherently unethical? In exploring such questions we might well bear in mind the warning of Stuart Chase: Propaganda "is a word in our heads, corresponding to no entity in the outside world, a word to which everyone probably gives a somewhat different meaning. It can, however, be a useful label to designate special kinds of behavior." [1]

Mr. Lasch questions Ellul's broadening of the meaning of propaganda from deliberate efforts to deceive to a pervasive sociological phenomenon of mass societies; he feels that Ellul has not presented a convincing rationale for such enlargement.

He also perceives Ellul as describing propaganda as "inescapable" and as an "ethically neutral" process. But Ellul believes that propaganda is pernicious and a "menace which threatens the total human personality." Ellul is explicit:

> As we proceed to analyze the development of propaganda . . . the reader will be tempted to see an approval of propaganda. Because propaganda is presented as a necessity, such a work would *therefore* force the author to make propaganda, to foster it, to intensify it. I want to emphasize that nothing is further from my mind . . . In my opinion, necessity never establishes legitimacy . . . To say that a phenomenon is *necessary* means, for me, that it denies man; its necessity is proof of its power, not proof of its excellence. [2]

Today one cluster of definitions of propaganda presents a *neutral* position toward the ethical nature of propaganda. A definition combining the key elements of such neutral views might be: Propaganda is a *campaign* of *mass* persuasion. According to this view, propaganda represents an organized, continuous effort to persuade a mass audience primarily using mass media. Such a view stresses communication channels and audiences and categorizes propaganda as one species of persuasion. Just as persuasion may be sound or unsound, ethical or unethical, so too may propaganda. [3]

Another cluster of definitions takes a *negative* stance toward the ethicality of propaganda. Definitions in this cluster probably typify the view held by many "average" Americans. A definition combining the key elements of such negative views might be: Propaganda is the intentional use of suggestion, irrelevant emotional appeals, and pseudo-proof to circumvent human rational decision-making processes. Such a view stresses communication techniques and sees propaganda as *inherently* unethical.

Mr. Lasch underscores the contention that governments use propaganda to give the masses an illusion of participation without the reality. Propaganda also thwarts critical judgment by citizens of public policies. In this process the press becomes not a countervailing force against arbitrary government power but one of its instruments.[4]

And we might compare Mr. Lasch's views with those of Murray Edelman:

> It is no accident of history or of culture that our newspapers and television present little news, that they overdramatize what they report, and that most citizens have only a foggy knowledge of public affairs though often an intensely felt one. If political acts are to promote social adjustment and are to mean what our inner problems require that they mean, then these acts have to be dramatic in outline and empty of realistic detail. In this sense publishers and broadcast licensees are telling the exact truth when they excuse their poor performance with the plea that they give the public what it wants. It wants symbols and not news.
>
> Even without much encouragement by the government, obsessive involvement with verbal accounts of political acts occurs in democracies, too, and it has the same numbing impact upon the critical faculties . . . A dramatic symbolic life among abstractions thereby becomes a substitute gratification for the pleasure of remolding the concrete environment.[5]

Should our ethical concerns therefore be directed at the *media?*

NOTES

[1] Stuart Chase, *Guides to Straight Thinking* (N.Y.: Harper, 1956), p. 169.

[2] Jacques Ellul, *Propaganda* (N.Y.: Vintage Books, 1973), p. 61. See also pages 38, 180, 188, 217.

[3] See, for example, Ralph K. White, "Propaganda: Morally Questionable and Morally Unquestionable Techniques," *Annals of the American Academy of Political and Social Science,* 398 (1971), pp. 26–35.

[4] Dennis Gouran offers seven standards for assessing the degree to which governmental communication is "inappropriate and irresponsible." Several of these standards focus on the government-news media relationship. See "Guidelines for the Analysis of Responsibility in Governmental Communication," in Daniel Dieterich, ed., *Teaching about Doublespeak* (Urbana, Ill.: National Council of Teachers of English, 1976), pp. 20–31.

[5] Murray Edelman, *The Symbolic Uses of Politics* (Urbana, Ill.: University of Illinois Press, 1967), pp. 2–3, 8–9.

A Profusion
of Information*

CHRISTOPHER LASCH**

Modern propaganda, according to Jacques Ellul, is not the work of un-
scrupulous men acting from evil motives but an inescapable means of governing. In mass societies, the state can neither govern without mass support nor govern in accordance with mass wishes, since the masses, unlike
conventional democratic electorates, are politically incoherent and incapable of rationally directing policy. Thus, "even in a democracy, a government that is honest, serious, benevolent, and respects the voter *cannot
follow* public opinion. But it *cannot escape* it either." Hence the need for
propaganda. By means of propaganda the state tries to give the masses the
illusions of participation without the reality. It not only informs them of
its decisions but subtly suggests that it is the masses themselves which have
demanded them.

The rest of Ellul's argument follows from this analysis of the function
of propaganda. Propaganda does not lie, according to Ellul; at least it does
not lie as to facts. But neither does the propagandist trust in the critical
judgment of the people he addresses. Everything he does has the effect of

* A book review essay of Jacques Ellul, *Propaganda: The Formation of Men's Attitudes*,
trans. by Konrad Kellen and Jean Lerner (New York: Alfred A. Knopf, 1965).
** At the time this essay was published, Christopher Lasch was a member of the History
Department at the University of Iowa. Reprinted with permission of the author and publisher from *The Nation*, April 4, 1966, pp. 397–398.

making it impossible for people to bring critical judgment to bear on the policies which he is trying to promote. He does not withhold or falsify information; he overwhelms the public with it, and the facts themselves demoralize the reader or listener by giving him the impression that he lives in a terrifying world in which the problems of government are too complicated for anyone but experts to understand. At the same time the reader craves to be informed and would object if he were deprived of access to the news. Information accordingly becomes a doubly effective means of propaganda: it sustains the morale of the reader by reassuring him that the state wishes to keep its citizens informed — thus fostering the illusion of participation — while at the same time terrifying the reader with the complexity and danger of events — thus setting him up for more propaganda (the state will protect him from a world of dangers). Outright falsehoods, however, play a very small part in all this.

It follows that the effectiveness of modern propaganda presupposes a certain standard of living — among its victims. Obviously it presupposes literacy; but more important, it presupposes precisely the "informed citizens" who are commonly regarded as the best resource of self-governing societies. Indifference, next to intelligence, is the propagandist's worst enemy; he needs people to be actively involved in following the course of affairs. Otherwise propaganda has nothing to work on. The poor, whose struggle for existence absorbs "all their capacities and efforts," cannot be very successfully integrated into the nation, but those who follow events — without, however, being able to understand them — become prey to the anxieties and guilts which it is the work of propaganda to palliate (even while reinforcing). "People . . . think that reading is a road to freedom . . . Actually, the most obvious result of primary education in the nineteenth and twentieth centuries was to make the individual susceptible to super-propaganda."

The purpose of propaganda, finally, is not so much to supplement policies abroad, by undermining the enemy's morale, as to integrate the nation from within, by reminding the masses of the need to resist the enemy's incessant efforts to overthrow it.

It may seem to the reader that none of this is particularly new. Ellul's ideas about the mass society, the loneliness of the mass man, and so forth, are familiar; nor does it come as a great surprise to be told that modern governments seek to give citizens the illusion without the reality of participation. The only novelty, one is tempted to say, lies in calling these efforts propaganda; and it may be argued that in thus enlarging the definition of propaganda to refer not merely to deliberate efforts to deceive but to "a sociological phenomenon" of mass societies, Ellul confuses things rather than clarifies them. It is certainly true, for instance, that the reader of newspapers is victimized by the way news — given the definition of news as disaster — is reported; but what is gained by calling this condition "propaganda," when all our associations with the word predispose us to think of propaganda as describing not an ethically neutral "sociological phenomenon" but the activities of people who deliberately seek to manipulate opinion for their own interest? If a writer intends to use a term in a sense radically different from its accepted meaning, he has to show that there is some decisive analytical advantage to be gained from doing so; and it is not yet clear, in this case, what the advantage is.

Whether or not the term "propaganda" helps to describe what Ellul wants to describe, and no matter how familiar some of his general ideas may appear, the reality they describe is still very imperfectly understood; and it is important, therefore, that Ellul's book should have been written and translated. Consider, as an example of the general confusion surrounding these subjects, the controversy about "managed news." Douglass Cater (*The Reporter,* March 19, 1959) describes a revealing conversation that took place between James Reston and Dean Acheson shortly before Acheson left office as Secretary of State. Reston regretted that Acheson had not maintained better relations with the press. He complained, as he has complained on so many other occasions, of the secrecy which shrouded the operations of the State Department. Acheson replied that diplomacy was incompatible with publicity. "Reston," according to Cater, "argues that Secretary Acheson failed to understand and make use of the creative power of the press to muster public support for sound policy and, alternatively, to gauge the full extent of public reaction to unsound or unrealistic policy."

In the context of the debate about official secrecy and "censorship," Reston emerges from this colloquy as the champion of the "people's right to know" and Acheson as a man who is actively thwarting it. But from the perspective offered by Ellul's analysis of propaganda, the antagonists appear in a very different light: the liberal, enlightened, "progressive" position appears the more sinister of the two. Reston, whatever his purpose, was urging Acheson, in effect, to exploit the propagandistic possibilities of "information" — "the creative power of the press" in mobilizing opinion. The press, once conceived as a check on arbitrary power, thus becomes one of its instruments, even though Reston's argument is still couched in the imagery of democracy: he imagines that the public has the option of accepting sound policies and rejecting unsound ones. But the choice is illusory, once the "creative power" of the press is used in this fashion; the very choices on which the public is invited to register an opinion will be defined with relation to an overall view of the world which is propagandistic in Ellul's sense — that is, a view of the world as filled with enemies and (as our experts keep reminding us) forbiddingly complex. The public will be invited to choose, say, between "containment" and "victory," while the image of the enemy and the definition of the national emergency confronting us — "Communist aggression" — remain unchanged.

Much of the clamor for a "free press" thus reveals itself as an unwitting demand for more propaganda. The controversy about government secrecy shows once again how the traditional safeguards of civil liberties have broken down in the face of centralized power which presents itself not as power at all but as benevolence — in this case, a government which (with many lapses, it must be admitted) conscientiously keeps its citizens "informed." We still think of the danger to freedom of thought as consisting of "censorship" and "propaganda." It is important to realize that a greater danger, whether or not we wish to discuss it under the heading of propaganda, lies in the very profusion of information which leaves the reader with a total impression of a world "that is astonishingly incoherent, absurd, and irrational," and which lends itself so easily to the promotion, both by government and by unofficial manipulators of mass media, of "sound policy." The withering away of the critical intelligence as a political force, under these conditions, is the subject of Ellul's book — a book that ought not to be ignored.

PART THREE

Conversations With . . .

In this section, we have tried to provide a sense of encounter with the minds of eight additional professionals. Included in these "conversations" are those with a television producer and filmmaker, a freelance journalist and author, a novelist and film writer, a newspaper editor, a "current affairs" commentator from the BBC, a popular magazine editor, a well-known advertising executive, and a popular film critic.

The interviews upon which these "conversations" are based were conducted over a period of time, and took several forms. What we have tried to capture here is the essence — the key points — of what were typically longer and more detailed interviews.

Aspects of the media not represented in Part II are represented here, and vice versa. For example, we were curious to know just what kinds of ethical or moral problems a novelist/screenwriter might come upon in the course of his/her professional work. Questions and answers seemed to be an ideal way of uncovering both some personal experiences and some thoughtful reflection upon the ethical and/or moral issues that may have been involved.

Again, more questions are raised than are answered. And, again, this is perhaps as it should be. The actual experiences of professionals in the mass media do not lend themselves to simple solution or even always to ready principle. Perhaps we have yet to forge an "ethic" for those who are professionally involved in the mass media.

And perhaps the first step is gaining some appreciation of the kinds of questions that these professionals raise as they reflect upon their own experiences in the media.

A Conversation with . . .

DAVID KEITH HARDY*

Film Producer

Q: *Would you talk a little bit in general first about your views on some of the ethical and moral issues involved in film-making?*
A: They would have to be very general, because they come from a very diverse background. As you know, I'm mainly a motion picture producer and run the film school at Brandeis. I came initially out of anthropology into radio, then into magazines, then took a job as a foreign correspondent, then back into magazines, television, documentary television, and so on. Well, where to begin? Last summer, six of my graduate students made a movie paid for by the Civil Rights Commission. We wanted to look at students — high school students — and we asked the question, don't students have rights? Unfortunately, you're not likely to see our film because the networks don't want it and the Civil Rights Commission which funded it and liked it has now realized that they don't want it seen because of their relationships with the National Education Association, etc., and that two million teachers around the country are going to get uptight if this film is put on, because it is a very savage attack on high school education as seen from the students' point of view. Is this censorship? If you're a journalist — and what we're concerned with is visual journal-

---

* Until his death, David Keith Hardy was Professor of Theatre Arts and Director of the Morse Center for the Study of Communications at Brandeis University. Prepared from a transcript of a seminar held with Professor Hardy at the University of Iowa.

ism — your function is to disclose. This is the whole concept of publishing, broadcasting, and of film documentaries. What you deal with is disclosure. That is the function of our business. Unfortunately, you will find that some of our best newspaper men give up their trade of raising hell and disclosing and digging and reporting, to go into the public relations business where their function is actually to manage the news.

Some years ago CBS did some specials on drugs in America. The third part of this program dealt with pricing, advertising, and related aspects of the drug industry. This wasn't shown, and the reason is that the drug companies didn't want it to be shown. That is censorship of the worst sort.

Some years ago before people started thinking about the environment and about ecology, I made two films. One was called "George Washington's Dirty River," which ran on NBC. In filming this, we came to the net conclusion that the Potomac was an open running sewer. To prove it, we started off the whole show with a beautiful shot of thousands of people walking through the cherry blossom festival around the tidal basin in Washington, and simply panned down slowly from this angelic scene into the water of the tidal basin. Given that there is an open sewer that discharges in front of the Jefferson Memorial into the tidal basin, there can be no question in your mind as to what the camera showed. But that shot did not in fact open the show on television; it got lost in the cutting room. The reason: We were putting our finger on four of NBC's sponsors located along the river.

Later we did another show on the interstate highway system. Essentially we wanted to inquire into how much money had rubbed off onto how many people's fingers in this massive project. You don't build a $44 billion highway system and not have some rub off on people's fingers. It turned out that our film was really a sweeping indictment of a lot of people, and some went to jail as a result. It turned out that the sponsor, one of the country's largest manufacturers of asphalt, withdrew from NBC sponsorship of the program. We lost some other sponsors for the same reason. I could go on and on with such personal experiences. I've gone through dozens of these, and from an ethical point of view have been compromised. One can go just so far.

Part of the problem is that the main function of television in the United States is to entertain — or I should say to make money for the stockholders. The secondary function is to entertain and to get high ratings. The third function is to try to disclose. But what I want to emphasize is that censorship is essentially political in nature. I suppose whatever form it takes, it does to some extent reflect what we think society's standards are. But it is the complicity that worries me. For example, the American movies of the 'twenties were fairly mature. Then the Hays office came in 1930, and the movies became more and more immature. You can't go back to the American movies of the 'thirties and find a mature expression of what people were thinking about in those times. There were three pressures: One, the religious pressure; another the industry's self-regulation — the Hays office; and the third, political pressure. You could shoot or bludgeon anyone; violence was fine; but when it came to anything people thought of as "dirty," or had anything to do with sex or such matters — then it was excluded. There was a conspiracy to make everything seem very wholesome, and it was therefore very unrealistic.

I want to emphasize, too, that I think all censorship is essentially demonology. I could give you all sorts of hair-raising examples from my experiences in Cambodia, and my personal friendship with Sihanouk. The story of the CIA's role in Cambodia is just simply not being told. Whether the media don't know of it or no one wants to discuss it or what, there is clearly a lot of censorship going on.

Q: *What is your reaction to what Denmark and other nations have done in removing censorship of pornography?*

A: Pornography is incredibly boring! You probably know that the Vatican has a huge library of pornography. The man who used to be curator and who is from near my home near Dublin said such things may have been fascinating to the Marquis de Sade, but incredibly boring when you look at them in great quantities. Pornography is such an incredibly boring subject that I don't see how it could be terribly dangerous. I suppose from a psychological point of view certain children should not be exposed to certain things, but this is not what I'm talking about. I'm talking about adults and their mature activities. I think "Oh! Calcutta!" is sententiously boring, but lots of people — instead of looking in the mirror — want to see other people take their clothes off in public. They don't have to join nudist colonies; now they can go to Broadway and do it. It's a fad. It will pass.

Q: *Then it might be functional in a positive sense to relax censorship — at least over pornography — so that everyone can get a bellyfull?*

A: Yes, that's true. It's the illicit that we desire.

Q: *Aren't there times, however, when such decisions might be more difficult? Isn't it possible that information made public could be destructive?*

A: We do live in a "free world" — in an "open society." Two examples. There was the Bay of Pigs invasion. The *New York Times* and the *Miami Herald* knew what was going on. They had films. A crew had been sent down there, and lots of people had seen the films. The *Miami Herald* decided not to publish the story, but the *New York Times* did decide to publish it. But a series of midnight conferences occurred which finally persuaded the *New York Times* not to publish this story. Another story was the Eisenhower heart attack in Denver, which was one of the most skillfully handled and manipulated stories of all times. The question was to disclose or not to disclose. As a matter of fact, and a lot of people knew this, Eisenhower was near death, but the public never got this impression.

They got the impression that he had a little indigestion. The press has a function to disclose, and I think that if we are going to have an "open society" this is what they have to do.

Q: *Do I understand you correctly that if one has access to information one should disclose it?*

A: If you are a journalist, that is your function.

Q: *No matter what happens?*

A: Are you trying to get me into a fictional argument? There was the U-2 incident. That was never really disclosed. Everyone knew we were over-flying Russia. Why shouldn't the American people have known? The Chinese knew. The Russians knew. If I know, it is my function to write a story or make a film about it. In this case, I didn't have to because someone else did so. I think the more digging, the better. But much so-called digging is going on now by the left-wing student press, and these people have absolutely no respect for facts whatsoever. I'm sure you all see these journals. They can't even spell people's names right. They have absolutely no interest in accuracy. Half-truth reporting is worse than no reporting at all.

Q: *To come back to the matter of television documentaries: If the networks are watering down documentary films, won't they eventually lose the intensity that documentary films should probably have with the public?*

A: Not only that. The problem of the documentary film in the United States today is that they just don't do them at all. If you want to do a really controversial documentary you do it on the breeding habits of the squid. Jacques Cousteau makes lovely movies, and I'm absolutely in favor of them. But when you say in your report to the FCC that we did several controversial public service programs this week — we did the CBS driving test, the NBC smoking test, the sex life of the squid, the private life of the white whale. . . .

America doesn't need to fritter away its television time on those sorts of subjects when, for example, some biologists are saying we have 10 years to live, at the outside maybe 35. About 80 per cent of the people in this country now get their news from television. What they're getting on a 30-minute news show with 7½ minutes of commercials is 22½ minutes. If one-third of that is film from other sources, the newscaster is left with about 1,500–1,600 words. Now, 1,500–1,600 words is exactly the number of words in the summary section of the *Wall Street Journal*, which is a good taste of what happened. But people watch this news and think that they know all about what's going on. And this, too, is a form of censorship. You just can't get the news into 1,600 words in 22½ minutes on television.

Q: *We often hear criticism of commercial television and the plea for it to become more of a hell-raiser. But isn't it possible that this is similar to the criticism made of advertising? We have a scapegoat: advertising is bad, ad-*

vertising leads to social injustice, and all that. But it is in the nature of our
system that we're supposed to get what we pay for. So if we pay for it,
whether "we're" General Motors, Pittsburgh Plate Glass, or myself buying
a commercial, we should get what we want in some way, shape, or form.
If you can accept all of those premises, then how can the situation ever be
corrected?

A: I'll correct you on something first. General Motors, Pittsburgh Plate
Glass, Marlboro Cigarettes do not pay; you pay, we all pay. They take it
off their income tax and those costs come right back to the consumer.
What they don't take off their income tax, they put into the cost of the
product that you and I buy. Now I would never knock advertising. It's
very difficult for me to knock advertising commercials. The agencies have
their own competitions for the best commercials — and they are simply
brilliant in terms of filmmaking. They communicate; they're artistically
made, although many of them are from other countries. Television commercials are a great discipline. But we come back to the question of the
function of television: Is it to entertain or to disclose? If you have to sell it,
it has to be entertainment. The British, the Germans, the French, the Cana-
dians all have an audience for documentaries. We have been so steeped in
America on television as entertainment that we aren't in the habit of looking to television to deal with serious subjects. You know the problem: People say, "Oh, it's some awful documentary about some social problem."
They might read an article in *Harper's* or *McCall's* or *Life* about the subject, but they are not likely to watch it on television because they don't
look at television as being that kind of source. They look at television as
being something quite different. They look at it as being the great relaxer,
the great entertainer; not as the informer. The television function as the informer has to be put back. But I don't know how you put it back.

As I said, I run the film program at Brandeis. I'm interested in trying
to create a new breed of people who are visual journalists, which is something we're desperately in need of in this country at the moment. The
problem is, you can turn them out, but where are they going to find work
if the networks don't want investigative reporting done by film? This is a
serious problem, but I think it is going to be changed by a technological
revolution: the cassette. I think the cassette concept — and it's on the
market — will be a major influence in American entertainment soon. The
cassette gives you the ability *not* to watch what the television network
gives you, but to go down to the local library or supermarket and either
rent or buy the films you want. So if you want to buy Bergman's films instead of watching all that junk you get on television, you go and buy or
rent "The Seventh Seal," and have your friends in and run it, and while
you are running it no commercials will be coming into your living room.

American television today is mostly trivia. They could get Jesus on TV and by the time he got out three thoughts, there would be the interruption, "Well, thank you for the Beatitudes, and now for a message from. . . ."

Q: *But it's some of the same people who are getting into the cassette field. So won't that end up the same way?*

A: You're a realist. I'm an idealist. Let me try to answer that; there is no answer. Still, people are hopefully getting better. When the present generation reaches 65 years of age, they will have spent 10 to 11 years in front of a television set. This is an appalling prospect. But surely we've got to try to teach people to see. Most people don't really see films. Most people have never been trained to see. This is why I'm so intrigued by "Sesame Street." There is really a great ethic involved in taking all of the techniques of the commercial and putting them to such use.

We're engaged in so many insanities in our society — I mean apart from the war and the ecological battle and the school system and the whole concept of the way we educate people and the methods by which we operate. But, to take one example: Medical schools. The methods of medical education are increasingly irrelevant. A person leaves with an M.D. degree, and within three years most of what he's learned is obsolete. To do a good job of closing such social insanities is what I would call ethical exploration — that is, digging into all the things which we have institutionalized and which have lost their rationale.

Q: *From an ethical point of view, you're saying that the answer to these "social insanities" is more disclosure. But the profit motive is basic to our total value system, and it is fundamental to the way in which the mass media are controlled. So what possible role do you see for television, newspapers, and the other media in "disclosing" these basic value systems?*

A: The financial aspects are not all that involved. I don't think the capitalist system *per se* can be said to have failed. Many people say it has failed. Many students say the whole system is shot. What they fail to realize is that ultimately you'll have to rebuild with some sort of financial structure; it is money that is going to make things work. Whether you're going to make films for a sponsor or a government agency, or whether you're just going to make them for the sake of making them, there's still going to have to be "bread" from some source, so I think pointing only at "capitalism" is wrong. The problem lies as much with the consumer as with the producer. You have to start with an elitist concept at some point and have that elitist concept — hopefully — filtered down.

On the other hand, I think we have to look for ways of improving our system. For example, this is the only country in the world that doesn't make an enormous profit out of its post office. The reason is that in every other country in the world you have the postal service and telegraph service and telephone service together. Now, they make a lot of money out of telegrams and far more out of telephones, and they lose money like mad on postage stamps. Here the only part that is the government is that part that loses money — postage stamps. It began like that because Bell invented the telephone and set up a company and made a lot of money. We started our television system in this country based upon the same thing — a private enterprise system. We made some basic philosophical decisions that radio and television were going to be privately owned. This is a mistake, and could probably be improved upon — as we see in many other countries in the world.

On the other hand, if you could take the best of American television, it's as good as anything else in the world. But the trouble is, I think, that it is so difficult to find the best because we have so much. In Chicago, for example, there are 11 channels going on for 18 hours a day. No one in his right mind can expect anyone to turn out 190 hours of decent programming a day. If you get one-half hour of good programming a day, you've done well. Bergman makes one movie a year.

Q: *Let's assume that television programming is based on — or at least reflects — what people want to see. Is it really what people want to see, or is it what people have been persuaded they want to see?*

A: You can take the average person to the Sistine Chapel and he'll walk through and say, "Okay, where's the next one?" But an artist or scholar can go and spend half his life and still not get to the bottom of how Michelangelo was interpreting Adam on the ceiling. Essentially we're dealing with the degree of education in the viewer. Many people find Bergman's movies hard to take or boring. People don't want to read difficult books; they would rather wait until they are made into movies. Movies and television programs communicate on many levels. Take a film like "Easy Rider": It is not a very good film; it has a rather indifferent script and very bad acting, but it is enormously germane to the contemporary American experience. It speaks to the heart of one of our problems. But take the average blue-collar worker who has had a couple of beers and goes in and sees that film and he'll say, "Why, those dirty kids should get haircuts and all be locked up or whipped." He doesn't see the problem.

If you get into the films of Antonioni, Bergman, or Fellini, you begin to deal with a very complex structure of film which involves you on an imagistic level, on a symbolic-religious level, and on a psychological level with a great deal of insight in it. Most people in America don't go to the movies expecting to have insights. Now these film-makers are not effete, impudent, eastern snobs. Their objective is not to keep the "masses" quiet. I think they simply accept what they are doing as something important and not just as a means of making money.

In any case, I think we are beginning to get an audience that is visually more aware, and beginning to look to films for more than just entertainment.

From an ethical point of view, I don't know what the answers are. But I do believe that what is needed in all these areas is leadership, and that leadership in all of these areas is political — just as censorship is political. It is the pursuit of excellence that is missing. And this is the ethical thing.

A Conversation with . . .

JUDITH CRIST
Film Critic

Q: *It seems to me that a critic of any medium, of sufficient stature, is in a position to influence that medium in several ways. Thus one could at least raise the question of some of the possible ethical or moral consequences of a critic's actions or non-actions. For example, aren't you in a position to make or break an individual's career? I would be very interested in how this consideration enters into your work, if at all. How do you go about looking at a particular performance and writing about it? What is in the back of your mind?*

A: I have never felt that in films you could really break people. I have felt you can make people. I have felt that by discovering someone or something and talking about it, you bring it to the attention of people who might be in a position to do something about it — whether a performer, a writer, or another movie-maker. In this country, you cannot really unmake a movie once the movie company has an investment and is determined to support the film, because you are not dealing with a selective audience in film. I believe that a survey would reveal that perhaps sixty per cent of moviegoers in this country go to see a movie because it's there. Moviegoers have to be post-critical because they have already paid. When a moviegoer buys his ticket, he has already voted his support of a film. Consider the case of "The Green Berets." There was no critic of any stature who gave that movie a good review. It got bad reviews for a variety of reasons. It wasn't even a good John Wayne movie. But "The Green Berets" made money. A critic is not going to be able to break John Wayne, because in addition to the indifferents — the non-selective audience — you have the people who are going to say, "No matter what it is, I'm going to see John Wayne." Or, consider "Valley of The Dolls." Across the country, critics with or without stature gave that movie bad reviews simply because it was bad; not because it was "dirty," but because it was just inane from beginning to end. But "Valley of The Dolls" was the big money-making movie of that year. I don't think a critic has the power of "death." I suppose that if a college boy by some streak of luck got his first movie into a little art house, I could "kill" him. But most critics don't bother to "kill" a little first-time-outer. The reason Robert Downey — who made "Putney Swope" — and I are still friends is that I did not review his first movie or his third. I thought they were atrocious; his intentions were good, but the films were so infantile I wouldn't have wasted anyone's time talking about them.

How many critics have raved about "The Beverly Hillbillies"? How many people rave about so many of the things that go on year after year after year just because people like them? People feel secure with these things; they turn the set on and watch them; they're like old friends.

So critics really don't have the power of life and death. However, let's pretend that they do. In a sense, if I didn't think that I did have, I don't think I could really function as a critic. If I didn't think that what I was saying was the truth of the matter and that it was so obviously validated in what I write, in my reviews, I believe I would begin to lose my validity as a critic. The person who brought this home to me most strongly was Bruce Atkinson, who was drama critic of the *New York Times* for many years. He said one night, "I'm not enjoying my work as much as I used to because shows are becoming very expensive and I find myself worrying when I sit down at my typewriter. I know the show wasn't any good. But if I really say this, there goes $100,000 down the drain. There are some quite capable stars and all those nice kids in the chorus. . . ." That's when he felt he had reached the point of retirement. I think that's one of the reasons why a critic rarely develops media relationships. I don't. With certain people I may develop a working or talking relationship, but I do avoid involvement in their particular concerns.

Q: *Could you talk a little bit about the bases on which you develop or formulate criteria for evaluating films, especially in regard to how people then might take these films into account, or how you feel they will take them into account?*

A: I don't go into a movie and say to myself, "Now, I am going to check out this movie — the theme, the acting, the camera work, the direction, the cinematography, the set design, costuming, etc." If you were watching a movie and said in the middle of it, "Oh, what a beautiful score," or "Look at that set," then the movie would be a failure, wouldn't it? A movie is a failure when you start seeing parts instead of the whole. In any case, I don't go in with an initial idea of what I'm going to look for in a particular movie. What happens is that I come out with a reaction. I think other critics function in this way, too. When I come out and say, "What a great movie!" then I have a terrible job of deciding what made this a great movie *for me.* Anyone who pretends there is objectivity in criticism is either quite dishonest, or foolish. There has to be this kind of subjectivity. The criteria I have for what is good may not necessarily be the same as those of other people.

Q: *How do you reconcile your reaction to a film you consider very bad, particularly when the public apparently finds it very worthwhile?*

A: Let's consider "The Sound of Music." It was a wild success. I have letters from all over the world from people who adored the album and the movie and there are people around who have seen it 50–60 times. It becomes a way of life with them. What I hopefully made clear in my review of that movie was that it is not a movie for a person of a certain level of sophistication. What I thought I had to do with "The Sound of Music" was to make it clear that, for a person of my kind, it was a saccharin, soppy, ersatz Cinderella story that even so would probably have a great deal of appeal for people of another kind, who want Cinderella on any terms. I had to concede, for example, that Salzburg had never looked so good; that the score, though it might be the worst of Rodgers and Hammerstein, was far superior to the average score; and that Julie Andrews was a particularly fresh and charming character at that time.

Once a person knows what he likes and why he likes it, then he should enjoy it. That is my ethic. Another critic said, in effect, that anyone who likes "The Sound of Music" is stupid. Well, you can't tell the five million ladies who read *McCall's* that they're stupid, particularly when four and one-half million of them liked the movie. I don't think it is the critic's function to pass judgment on moviegoers. Many young people do this in their reviews. They imply, "If you don't think the way I do about this movie, boy, are you stupid!" I take a different or diplomatic tack: I would have a tendency to say, "This movie is for the stupids among us. . . ."

Q: *If we assume that movies could make a difference in the culture at the level of moral or ethical behavior – or of ways of thinking about what's proper and improper – then the critic might at least make some sort of difference in what is acceptable and what is not acceptable. Is that in any sense a part of your rationale when you are working? Do you ever say to yourself: "I have a responsibility here which goes beyond the esthetic, which goes beyond an explanation of my own taste, and thus gets into the broader ethical or moral areas?"*

A: I think that I was more conscious of that kind of responsibility when I began. I began my critical writing when I was with the *Herald Tribune.* I knew my reader. He was of a certain level, and therefore I could, as I think any honest critic must, write for my peer. I wanted the reader to enjoy the play or the movie as much as my dearest friend would. I don't think you will ever get people interested in what you are saying if you are writing down to them or if you are writing up to them. There I was on very familiar ground. When I went on the "Today" show, my audience increased from around 350,000 readers to 8 or 9 million viewers, and I thought, "Gee! Have I got a responsibility! There are all of those nice innocent people out there and they are not sophisticated New Yorkers. What are they going to do when they hear this word in stereophonic sound or see this sight?" As I recall, that feeling lasted about three and one-half minutes. But I found that the proportion of people who would or would not go along with me was just about the same, whether on the quarter-million level of the *Herald Tribune,* the 8- or 9-million level of the "Today" show, or the 45-million level of *TV Guide.*

My interest in criticism, as I'm fond of saying, is as a teacher-preacher. I want people to like the things I like. I want them to be exposed to it. There was "Last Summer." I was overwhelmed by that film. I thought it was an excellent film about young people, that it had a perception, an honesty about teenagers, and that the entire ambiance of the film was right and real and that what it had to say was vitally important. What it said it said in shattering terms, and it dealt with a very broad and open question. The question was: Are you going to stand by yourself and do what you know is right, or are you going to go with the group, when you believe they are doing wrong? This is a question not just for young people. I think it is perhaps one of the most pressing questions in our whole society. Now, I thought this was a very fine movie, and I recommended it very strongly to people of all ages. I thought 15, 16, and 17-year-old kids would deeply appreciate this film. But from the Midwest I began getting letters. I got letters that said, "It certainly was a remarkable film — remarkably filthy. I don't know about the children in your jet-set in the East, but out here, in the boondocks of Ohio, we have decent young people!"

But what I'm saying is that I think people should maintain their own principles regardless of whom they are talking to, and this is what I try to do as a critic. This is a critical function we are all obligated to perform for our society, and we have to maintain our principles and not worry about our obeisance to the standards of others. For example, I have never used a script on NBC. No one has ever asked me what I'm going to say, and I wonder where the ethical responsibility is if they're letting me do what I choose. Is it because they are just great guys? Or are they letting me do it because the odds are that I'm not going to do anything horrendous? A critic can be only as decent and honest as his mouthpiece — his medium or his publication — is.

Q: *Let us take a specific case. Let's assume that young people who are supposedly impressionable might have seen "Easy Rider" and got from it the impression that the cool guys are the guys who are really in the "know," and that they also smoke marihuana. Mightn't they try to imitate that? Would you ever develop your review of such a movie with the thought that "I ought not to rate the movie as high as I think it is because teenagers ought not to go see it, or that movies of this sort ought not to be made"?*

A: I think "Easy Rider" is an ideal movie for teenagers. I think they're the only ones who can tolerate it. If you are going to push this imitation business to the logical conclusion, then all of those who want to pretend they are cool guys and start smoking marihuana are going to accept the fact too that they will wind up dead on the highway, like the "Easy Rider" heroes. This is not the first time young people have ever seen cool guys smoking marihuana. They've all been to the lavatory in their local high school.

This brings me to the basic thing about movies influencing people. It takes about two years typically — portal to portal — to make a movie from the day a guy says, "Hey, Sam, we've decided to produce your movie." It may actually take five years, because often they debate for three years about how or where or whether they are going to make the movie. But you see my point: Things change quickly in our society, and it simply can't be that movies set patterns. They reflect our society. Antonioni made a lot of money for MGM with "Blow-up," so they said to him, in 1967, "Make a great movie." Antonioni said, "I want to make a movie about what's wrong with America." So, in 1967, he goes out crossing the country, studying our culture, looking for unknown actors, and three years and five million dollars later he comes up with a movie called "Zabriskie Point." There is not a film critic around who will not concede that he has seen this movie made by a minimum of five undergraduates at the USC film school, ten undergraduates at the NYU film school, and about eight semi-underground film makers. The notion that the student radical is the only decent human being and everyone above the age of 30 is senile, that cops are pigs, that our entire civilization is going to explode any moment, might have had some impact three years earlier. But now we've gone past that notion, and even a campus radical or activist has a far different view of himself, his role in society, and of society as a whole. Hollywood's morality up until about 1960 was at least 30 years behind current moral behavior. And I don't mean just in sexual areas. Maybe at one time movies did set fashion and home-furnishing patterns: every woman wanted padded shoulders à la Joan Crawford or a ranch house because Doris Day had such a nice one. Beyond that movies certainly had little influence on what we were thinking and what we were doing in the real world (not our daydreams).

I don't know why we expect so much out of movies. How many great books are published every year? You know that movie-making is a commercial art. Occasionally there is a work of art, yes, but film-making is essentially an assembly line — people making movies not for the good of their souls or ours, but to make money.

Q: *I'd like to know what you think of the ethics of movie ratings and whose responsibility it is to decide who goes to what movie.*

A: I think it's your responsibility to decide what movie you go to. I think that until you reach the age of intelligence, it's your parents' responsibility to decide what movie you should or should not go to. I don't think that the man who manufactures the movie or his employees should decide about your maturity, your state of readiness, or anything else. I think the rating scheme is idiotic. I think it's a stupid form of censorship. I have known of cases where people were refused financing because their movies would have involved an "X." The "X" is applied indiscriminately to the cheap exploitation film and to the fine film. Films like "If" or "Midnight Cowboy" or "A Clockwork Orange" — and the not-so-fine but extremely interesting movies like "The Damned" or "Easy Rider" — are all lumped together with the despicable movies.

Actually the rating scheme has a negative effect. It attracts the wrong kind of audience. There is a beautiful French film about a ten-year-old boy who is shifted from foster home to foster home, very much in the school of "The Two of Us," and the direct translation of its title from the French would be "Naked Childhood." The distributor immediately changed it; the movie is now called "Me." He knew that if you had "Naked" in the name, you would get every freak off the streets who is looking for another glimpse of flesh. Every time there is an "X," there is a certain audience that goes.

"I am Curious (Yellow)" made an impact all across the country. It is a dreary movie, ugly, a disappointing movie. Even if you like dirty movies, it's a disappointing one; and I like dirty movies when they're good. It has made money because everyone *is* curious, and when a movie is "X," he thinks, "Gee, there's something I'm not supposed to see and I'm going to see it"; this is human nature. The Danes licked this thing; they took the position that if you want to see it, go see it.

The rating code is not for the good of the public. It was put in because the movie industry was scared stiff that there would be local censorship and there has been, because censorship and bluenosing spread. In some cities newspapers and other media refuse ads for X-rated movies, even the Academy Award winners. Big police chiefs come in and arrest the lady selling popcorn. This is very sad because the popcorn lady, who in small theaters is usually the one taking tickets, is the one who gets the police record. The distributor, nine times out of ten, who is interested purely in the buck, and who knows he is running a dirty movie, is hardly ever involved. I was in Jackson, Mississippi, some time ago where they even chopped chunks out of "Goodbye, Columbus." The local police chief did it. I think people have to stick to their own ethics. If you don't want to see naked women, you don't have to and no one is forcing you to. But I think you have to recognize that anyone who has lived in a house with a mirror may well have seen a naked body, and that there are worse things you could see. We pretend to be protecting "the children" by the ratings; they are already protected by anti-pornography laws. Actually we are trying to protect our middle-aged hung-up selves.

Q: *You referred to yourself as a teacher-preacher, and yet you have said you don't know where ethics begin and end. What do you feel qualifies you, then, to be a critic?*

A: I know where *my* ethics begin and end, and that is what is important. It is the job or the assignment that qualifies a person as a journalist-critic. There can be thousands of people sitting around who consider themselves critics, but you don't become a professional critic until you have an outlet, a public platform. If I were not qualified to express certain judgments on the basis of my experience and background, then I think that nobody would pay me any heed, let alone salary, and I would not be around as a critic. This is a very pragmatic thing, and I am a very pragmatic person. I consider myself a critic not only in my own concept of self but because others regard me as one — even those who follow me because they disagree with everything I say. I don't confuse mine with the word of god. Critics express only personal opinions, regardless of their pretensions. I want to be disagreed with because my ideal is that everyone should make up his own mind. I feel that a journalist-critic puts forth a view, and through it, experience. People know that this is my view and I want them to put theirs up against it, or beside it.

I think Walter Kerr is one of the finest drama critics ever to come into my experience. I disagree with him entirely on musicals; there his taste is not mine. He still serves as a fine critic for me because the critic with the voice is the one who takes a position and justifies it. I do that and people either agree with me or disagree with me, but apparently there is enough in my stated position to interest people and to stimulate them in some way so that hopefully they will clarify their own view. And this to me is the *raison d'être* for a critic.

Q: *Movie codes are changing. Do you think that film critics aid or play a role in those changes? Or, to put it in another way, do you think that society leads the critic, or that the critic leads the society?*

A: Critics are changing, too. They are changing not only through time, but also in their attitudes towards film. Also, there has been a great change in the attitudes of the other media toward film. Years ago, editors always used the sportswriter, when the horses weren't running or when the base-ball season was off, to review the theater and movies — or little old ladies were given the job. (Don't misinterpret me here; I think that 22-year-olds can be little old ladies, too.) Now we've all moved into a new phase, in which film criticism is a profession in itself. Further, American morality is changing and movies are reflecting the changes. I find myself, as a film critic, in open discussions with people about things I wouldn't have dared to whisper to my closest friends twenty years ago. Again, because the movie industry is a business, and not primarily an art, movies have had to catch up with the public, and that's why the movie codes are changing. I would like to think that critics have had a lot to do with it both in accept-ing the change in films ahead of the movie-going public and preparing them for it — and in urging the changes on the industry.

There was a Swedish movie several years ago called "Dear John," which I thought was a beautifully lyrical film. By the time it got to the Midwest it was dubbed into English, and when my own brother saw it, he thought it was a dirty movie. And indeed it had been vulgarized. But in its original form, it is a very tender story of two ordinary people, a sailor and a waitress, who find each other. There is a rather conservative county in upstate New York where we have a home and I have some devout fol-lowers. Two ladies there went to see "Dear John" on the basis of my rec-ommendation. When the first nude scene came along, one of the women said to the other, "My dear, I know it's your treat, but I think we should leave." And her friend said, "No. Mrs. Crist said this was a good movie, and I think we have to have faith a little longer." These two ladies con-fided to me later, their cheeks glowing scarlet, that they were suddenly caught up in it and that they did end up thinking that it was a very honest story about two grown-up people. So I like to think, yes, critics are mak-ing some inroads in making changes acceptable.

Q: *Do you find it more difficult to be positive about a movie which you think should be praised, as opposed to really panning a movie you think is terrible?*

A: There is a basic difficulty here that all of us have. I was up until 3 a.m. writing a column that would have normally taken me about 3 hours. This one took me six. It was simply because I was writing about three movies that meant a great deal to me. They had touched me very deeply and it was very hard to find synonyms to describe very lovely, heart-warming emotional experiences. On the other hand, it is extremely easy to write about a fourth movie I thought was dreadful. This is true of articulation about human relations and emotions in general. If you don't like someone, then you can go into all sorts of detail. But love makes us inarticulate. Young critics fall into this trap very easily. There is a notion that you can make a reputation by hating everything. But I think you can best make a reputation by hating what you hate and loving what you love.

Q: *You said, "Film is a business, not an art." When you write, do you think of that very often? Or do you go on the premise that it is an art or, if it isn't, that it should be?*

A: I see your point. Walter Kerr is supposedly a critic of an art form — the theater. But I would say that the majority of nights he spends on Broadway he doesn't feel like the critic of an art form. He is the critic of a commercial enterprise. Life is real. Life is earnest. I think people who babble about film "art" ought to go out and get jobs as critics — and become, as we must, unselective viewers. It's a humbling experience. Take the Walt Disney movies. You have to realize first of all that you don't need bulldozers to pluck daisies, that Disney fluff isn't polluting the nation. Secondly, there are people who adore Disney movies for their own very good reasons — and they too have a right to live, alongside the Kubrick or Truffaut or Godard worshipers. Walt Disney was never under the delusion that he was Ingmar Bergman. You have to meet things on their own ground, and you don't waste your time destroying a contrivance that is just great for a two-day double bill in the neighborhood theater — and that is how long it's going to last. But when even these films that don't aspire to be much beyond entertainment contain the unappetizing and the immoral and the insidious, then I think the critic has an obligation to take them on at quite another level. If Elia Kazan makes a horrifying soap opera called "The Appointment," this arouses me to fury because Elia Kazan owes me something besides a rotten soap opera. On the other hand, if Ross Hunter makes a rotten soap opera, I say to myself, "Well, what were you expecting, Fellini maybe?" If Helen Hayes does a rotten job, I think that is a sin. But if Joe Schmo does a rotten job, what did you expect?

Q: *You seem to be taking the position that when a good director fails, it's terrible. But when Ross Hunter fails, it's not so terrible. But isn't there a third position: Don't you want to say something about the fact that Ross Hunter makes movies at all?*

A: No. Everyone should have a right to do his thing. But this does not cancel my privilege to say what I think about it. The position you suggest would be very nice if only you and I were going to decide who went to see things and who didn't. Ross Hunter has made movies that made millions. He has a perfect right to manufacture movies. I just don't have to like them and you don't have to go.

Q: *Are you going to say that Jacqueline Susann shouldn't write because she is a lousy writer? Or what are you going to say about the author of "The Godfather"?*

A: That book is practically illiterate. I haven't even read anything so badly written. Yet you can't put it down. The author, Puzo, makes heroes of criminals. He insidiously makes you admire the wrong people, and he just writes badly. But he had a right, and the best that any of us can ever do is to say to ourselves, "Well, I don't have to read it" — and if you do read it, as I did, recognize it as immoral trash. And the same applies to the movie — enjoy it but recognize it for what it is.

Q: *It seems to me that you suggest several criteria for labeling a film immoral: One is that the film is less than aesthetically satisfying, or of poor quality. A second criterion you seem to have suggested is that it's immoral if it's manipulative — if it does something to you in spite of yourself. Are there other criteria you look for?*

A: Your first is not a question of morality but of aesthetics and art. Anyway, I don't know if these are criteria I look for. They are simply my own standards of aesthetics or ethics, and failure to meet them evokes my disapproval.

Q: *I guess what I'm asking for is an explicit statement of what your standards are.*

A: I just gave them to you. I think that the critical responsibility belongs to everyone. But while the layman can sit there and be mindless or inarticulate, the professional critic cannot.

Q: *You praised "Hud" because you said it was realistic when the good guys didn't win in the end, and this seems to me to contradict some of the other things you have been saying.*

A: No, because Hud himself is typical of a segment of our society, which the people who go to movies are unwilling to recognize, and that is the man whose only interest in life is material gain. The audience's heart is not with "Hud"; he is the villain. We all love old Melvyn Douglas. But "Hud" told people a very sad but true fact — life isn't a rhapsodic sound of music and that more often than not everyone you like winds up either dead or having to get out of town, and that there is the materialistic man who on many occasions does inherit the earth. I think the movie brought this unpleasant truth home, with particular impact in 1963; we've had so many anti-heroes since then their effect is less today — but Hud was the first not nice (but not criminal) man to win. I like movies that tell you things that aren't nice, because the more you know of things that aren't nice, the more you can appreciate the things that are. If your head's not buried in the sand, you spot the good as well as the bad.

Q: *Could you pick out one movie that stands out in your mind for any specific reason that you considered superior?*

A: There are many movies that stand out in my mind. We play this game constantly: You're shipwrecked on a desert island and can take one movie. Which one will it be? I wouldn't want to be shipwrecked on a desert island with just one film. But I know I wouldn't want to be on a desert island without "Citizen Kane." Beyond its content and artistry, that movie changed the entire face of movie-making. I have seen it perhaps 30 or 40 times, and each time I never fail to see a further richness in it, something I hadn't really paid enough heed to before. This is the kind of movie I would like to live with, as a constant intellectual enrichment. And "Rules of the Game" and "City Lights" and "Grand Illusion," "8½," "Winter Light," "Ikiru," "The Maltese Falcon," "The Bank Dick". . . . I think I would have to have about 30 movies, so I probably wouldn't make it to the island anyway!

A Conversation with . . .

MARTIN MAYER
Author and Journalist

Q: *You said once, I think, that all of the ethical and moral issues in your business — journalism — bottom on the obligation to question one's perceptions, and to fight against the degradation of their transmittal. Do you still hold to that position?*
A: I do. But in general the major ethical problem of the journalism business is that people become slobs, and that most people in it are slobs. That's the first sin.

The second, and this is also becoming increasingly common, is knowing what you are going to find before you go out looking. It is very tempting to take your own opinion seriously and to feel that you are paid to develop that opinion. I do not find it very interesting to develop an opinion. I think it is extremely important that two people who disagree with each other can both see what they believe in what you present, and it is by no means impossible to do this. I am very pleased when people on both sides of a dispute believe I agree with them, because it means I have touched the reality that both perceive. Epistemology 1: there is a real world out there.

The job of the journalist is not to write in such a way that people who read his stuff can find out what *he* thinks. It's much more important to help people find out what *they* think.
Q: *What are your feelings about journalism education?*
A: I sympathize with those who feel that journalism training was too

vocational in the past. I never did any of it myself. But it is interesting how angry a person gets if her name is Spelman with one "1," and you spell it with two. Now, that is an ethical problem. That's impinging upon people's personalities; that is not a joke. It may be a joke within the game that you get someone's name spelled wrong, but it is no joke to the person whose name you spelled wrong. So, if you want to talk about ethical obligations, one of them is to get people's names spelled right, because they are very attached to their names.

It seems to me that if journalism training has any purpose, it must first take care of adjusting the reporter's viewpoint so he can see where others stand — an adjustment which includes an understanding that the spelling of names is not trivial. Next would come a willingness and a capability to do the reading that underlies anything of a serious nature. Then, the development of ways to listen to people for what they are saying; too many journalists hear only what fits into their preconceptions of the problem. It's very hard sometimes to make sure that you understand how the person you're talking to perceives the problem he's talking about, but that's your job. If you are doing something in which there is an anthropological frame of reference, you need to read enough anthropology to get into the frame of reference the people you interview are talking from. Otherwise you never know what their words are supposed to mean. This is quite apart from the question of your opinions.

And without a knowledge of frames of reference you never know what's really interesting; you become a sucker for the theatrical. Important and serious things are happening in our political, economic, and social life, and are being treated in a trivial way, because both reporters and professors are lazy and use information in discrete units rather than seeking interconnections.

All sorts of things worth covering are going on in Washington every day, but people aren't really covering Washington. They're picking up press hand-outs and leaks and interpreting them according to the first approximations that popped up when the person or the situation first surfaced. Most reporters are not looking for the real stories. I suppose there are not enough reporters, and they are overburdened. I have heard that argument. But most of them don't have the habit of doing their own reading, or of interviewing to find out how the world looks to their interlocutor. You know the attitude: "No one will know anyway, except the people who are intimately involved, and I'm probably not going to get it straight anyway, so. . . ."

Q: *But don't you think that readers and viewers have some responsibility to themselves? If readers and viewers were responsible, they wouldn't let reporters get away with this kind of sloppiness.*
A: What does the reader care? The reader can pay attention to only so many things in any one day. His newspaper already has much more in it

than can possibly interest him. Our expectations of excitement and theater and color in the world has gone up enormously; the simulacrum of sensation is what the reader wants from the newspaper. All news is to some extent entertainment from the reader's point of view; it's passing the time. I don't think you can expect the reader to ask for much more, but you can expect the people who are doing the journalist's job to wish to live with themselves and with the stories they write, and to win the respect of those from whom they are getting their stories.

Just before an earlier printers' strike in New York, I went around and asked people what their feelings would be if the newspapers went on strike and there were no newspapers for six months. The overwhelming reaction of the people I talked to was — "Wouldn't that be great?!" The journalist can't look to these people for his rewards. He's got to please himself. Why don't clients please lawyers? Why don't patients please doctors? Why don't kids please teachers? Consumers aren't going to do that. We live, unfortunately, in a professionalized world — and a professionalized world can be defined as a world in which people's rewards come from peer approval, and not from results of their actions. And these "peer approval" standards are too low in all of the professions, including journalism. There are some individual exceptions, like the *Los Angeles Times*. They give their people a great deal of time and space on significant stories, and they permit their reporters to make their own definitions. They run stories of magazine length. This takes time, and you really have to put something into it, including thoughts about exactly why this story is worth the reader's time. Incidentally, a distinction should be made between the long *Los Angeles Times* take-outs, which are stories, and the long *New York Times* take-outs, which tend to be surveys of topics, a much less interesting form.

Q: *Do you feel that newspapers and broadcasters should disclose whatever information is available to them?*

A: There's no easy answer to that. We had a major riot in New York after the Martin Luther King assassination, which none of the newspapers carried. I don't know whether they were asked not to do so or not. But I do not feel morally outraged or ethically troubled about it. Sitting in their chairs, I don't know what decision I would have made. This is very much like the business with the Cuban missile crisis. It is a very hard problem. If competent people are asking you to be careful, maybe it's worth being careful about. I just don't know. My instinct would have been to run both the Cuban story and the riot story in New York. But I'm not going to criticize people who went the other way, because I do think that there are responsibilities involved, and I do not think there are absolutes in this world.

The bigger problem is coverage: "the information available" to reporters is in fact much greater than the information they use. We have not covered the degree of social disorganization in America, mostly because the people who could do so are too lazy to do their homework.

The ultimate laziness, of course, is "advocacy" journalism, which is nothing but the old theatricalism made to appear noble. It is neither necessary nor desirable to be ideological in one's treatment of what happened yesterday, which is the basic business of a newspaper.

Q: *Do you give readers what they want, or what you think they should have?*

A: That's first of all a television problem, because television is first of all in a reflexive business. The main reason why journalists should not work on their own opinions is that priorities are unidimensional, rank ordered, and we live in a multidimensional world full of matrices. When you say, "Should you give people what they want, or should you give them what you think they should have," you're taking an enormously complicated interactive mechanism and reducing it to something far too simple. What about movie reviewers? To whom does the movie critic have a responsibility — to the reader who wants to know whether or not he would like to see the picture, or to the art form of the film? Most people think newspapers are supposed to serve, to tell the reader whether he wants to go to a particular movie or not. Therefore the reviewer is supposed to have a stable point of view, so the reader can judge from his own experience, his degree of consonance with that point of view, the extent to which he can "trust" this critic. Monthly periodicals, by and large, are supposed to serve the art and the artist, and do more serious criticism.

But the question is unanswerable in the form you gave it. If you don't give people something of what they want, they are not going to read your stuff. And the guy who doesn't care whether people read his stuff is simply an egotistical fool. Many years ago, I covered TV for *Harper's* and learned to feel some compassion for the gaggle of capons who said they would give the public "what they want." But it seems to me that in the end you have to do what you think the story calls for. This comes back again to the basic problem of looking for the theatrical — the kid with the longest hair waving the biggest sign, the demonstration that is the most photogenic, the statement that makes the biggest headline. This I consider to be the great and continuing problem, and getting worse all the time, because people expect more and more theatricalism — more sensationalism. The lessened vulgarity of the modern paper reflects the risen social class of the community as a whole, not any significant change of attitude. I would say that this is indeed an ethical problem, but it may still be very much what people want.

Q: *What do you think the function of schools of journalism should be, then?*

A: I haven't kept up with journalism education. I came out of a journalism school called the *Harvard Crimson*. I have never been sure what the function of a school of journalism was supposed to be. I have come in recent years to feel very strongly that if you are looking for villains in our society, higher education is the place to find them. I can't tell you how strongly I feel that we must return to apprenticeship models for access to the profession, and we must not put everyone through the same cookie-cutter mold for 16 to 20 years of education. It's bad for them; it's bad for the institution. It's bad, period. At one time we had in this country something called an educational ladder. We no longer have that; now we have a series of educational hurdles that people have to get over, and it's playing hell with our entire social organization. To the extent that people now have to get journalism school diplomas to get jobs, I have negative feelings about journalism schools. It is probably true that we have fewer shyster lawyers and fewer quack doctors and that everyone is professionally a little better because we have raised educational values. But I doubt very strongly that these benefits are going to make up for the costs which are incurred.

So you ask me what I think of journalism schools. I think they are fine providing there are also other routes of access — getting a job as a copy boy and impressing someone somehow, or coming in through advertising sales, which used to happen too. We cannot give schools the exclusive franchise to license people to do the most interesting things in society. Even if they were better than they are, we couldn't do that, and the schools aren't much good because they too are unidimensional. They're always applying the same standards to people and very often these standards are quite irrelevant to the job that needs to be done.

Journalism schools should be teaching standards, and they should be turning young people onto the real world, rather than onto speculations about it. To the extent that I use the same standards for my own work that I use for others' work. I believe they come from a feeling of obligation to reality. I find the real world a great deal more interesting than speculation about it.

We ought to be getting away from the current fad of self-indulgence. One has only so much time, and one has an obligation to employ it, and one can employ it through work and still enjoy oneself. But one should not employ it in the sort of self-indulgence which is neither work nor enjoying oneself. And more and more of this unwholesome adolescent attitude comes from our universities.

Q: *In one of your books there is a paragraph in which you describe the way in which you build sentences. As I recall, you don't rely much on inspiration.*

A: It isn't a matter of inspiration at all. That doesn't bother me one way or the other. English is a word-order language and that's what makes it an extraordinarily rich language — not the enormous vocabulary, but the number of choices you are offered in the arrangement of your sentences. People like to think that short sentences are better. I happen to write very long sentences. If you write long sentences, then you have all sorts of options as to where you're going to put phrases, and you have to think through what you want to modify with a phrase, and where it can be placed. You need to consider both the rhythm of the sentence and the logic of the progression of what you are saying.

If I were designing educational systems for kids, I would have them learn to type very early because if you learn to type then you can edit. If you do everything in a sprawly hand, you never edit anything. You don't take a pencil to what you've handwritten: there's no *room* for it. If kids are going to learn to write, what they have to learn to do is to read their own stuff and to dislike it, to edit it. Most sentences that I write take a lot of time because I'm forever charging at the problem again. On the average, I write about a thousand words or a little less spread over perhaps four hours or so every evening. That's pretty slow. But something that I've written very quickly — and this happens too — I will normally put aside and reread three or four times. You may remember Yeats' advice to poets: If you feel that you've really expressed an important thought perfectly, and you've got something down as it has never been got down before, and it's going to be something of great value, then you have achieved your goal as a poet. You take that page and throw it away.

Q: *How much influence do you think owners and publishers and editors exercise on practicing journalists?*

A: These things vary tremendously. There are publishers who simply want to make money. There are others who want to impress their personalities upon the situation. There are others who want to reward friends and punish enemies. There are all kinds of patterns, and I don't think one can generalize. In my own case, I am not much bothered by publishers and editors one way or the other. If you are going to write a piece for *Commentary,* obviously you use language somewhat different from the language you use if you are going to write for *Better Homes and Gardens.* But when I do this, it is my conception of who is going to read the piece — not the editor's — that controls. I always have the feeling that I don't really understand how my colleagues work. But in my relations with an editor, I find that if he knows what bothers him, I have little problem translating it into something that ought to bother me too, and making the appropriate changes. Other people don't make changes in my stuff; I change my own stuff. As far as editors and publishers go, I simply want people I can work with. In working with magazines, I very often don't see the top editor at all. I may have an initial meeting with him, but I would much rather work with the guy who is putting out the pages of the magazine and who isn't involved with policy or image questions. I don't find that top editors or publishers get in the way of a piece. That may be because I am not eager to get my own opinions of something into what I do, and therefore I don't get into arguments with people who want to get their opinions in. I have heard from others that they have had such problems; I haven't.

A Conversation with . . .

LESLIE C. STONE
Current Affairs Commentator
BBC External Services

Q: *We've been talking about some of the ethical and moral issues faced by practicing journalists. What are your general feelings about this?*
A: I don't believe in moral absolutes — at least not to the extent that some people seem to. I find it very difficult to universalize and to make moral judgments which would apply to all broadcasters at all times in all societies. I think this is especially true for those of us who broadcast in the BBC World Service because we are in contact with a very wide range of audiences, from the Soviet Union to Vietnam, India, Latin America, and even parts of North America. So we talk to people with different backgrounds and different cultures. Often the only thing they have in common is that they are able to understand English.

In my own experience, I think it is important to try to relate to their society. When getting into very sensitive political areas, I have to retain some kind of credibility. And I have to do this across several levels. I have to try to inform, to some extent to try to persuade people to look at things my way, and at the same time to entertain — to hold their attention. And I think these are three fundamental aspects of all journalism that apply in all of the media — whether newspapers, radio, or television.

When a journalist tries to fulfill all three of these functions, I think certain tensions arise, and this can raise certain moral and ethical dilemmas, depending upon the priority one gives to each of these three components.

Q: *Are you talking about objectivity, or about telling the "truth"?*

A: One has to realize that no story can tell the whole truth. This applies especially in broadcast journalism where there are always limitations of time or space. No matter how good your intentions, no one can tell the whole story in a single dispatch or broadcast or filmed report. One can't tell exactly what was in people's minds when an event occurred. So the choices that the reporter or the cameraman or the editor makes about what to leave in and what to take out, what to emphasize, and so forth, creates some biases right at the outset.

At the same time, we have to realize that although people may be willing to sit in a lecture hall, or sit in a room and listen to a radio or read a newspaper, when it comes to television there seems to be a reluctance for people just to sit there and watch a newscaster tell a story straight for anything longer than 90 seconds. So broadcasters have come to feel that they have to spice it up somewhat to entertain and attract attention. For example, if one wanted to illustrate a story about the decisions made by the U.S. President or the British Cabinet, they would probably show photographs of the President or Cabinet Officers going in and out of a building in order to give an idea of the activity. But in doing so this could very well give a false picture of the kind of atmosphere in which the decision-making actually took place.

Then there is another kind of problem. How do you film the devaluation of the French franc or British pound? Usually it's done by showing people on the floor of the stock exchange in a high rate of excitement rather than simply showing pictures of the solid Central Bank. On the surface, this issue may seem to be trivial, but it also arises in discussion programs where I think there are all kinds of dangers. In Britain, we have a large number of discussion programs centered on public affairs, and often the producer is strongly tempted to pack the studio with as many people as possible. This gives a wide variety of faces and voices, which keeps the viewer interested. At the same time, it means that you have but two sentences at most in which to put your whole view, and you frequently have to shout loud — very loud — to get in. These kinds of discussions, in my view, typically generate more heat than light. They may have entertainment value, but I do not think they are very enlightening for the person at the other end who really wants to explore the issues.

And most of the big issues are terribly complex. The more points of view you try to bring to bear, the muddier the whole thing is, and the less enlightenment there is. I think there is a kind of ethical problem here — a problem of selection, of balance, of being fair to representatives of a wide variety of viewpoints, without provoking controversy just for the sake of controversy or slanting the program. The editor or the producer has to make a number of choices and decisions in which moral considerations are very much involved.

Q: *I take it, then, that you feel news broadcasts should essentially be informing, but they must also be entertaining.*

A: Yes. And this is particularly true for newspapers. As you know, news is what is new. News is what is unusual. News is people — a small number of people — going out to participate in a demonstration, not a large number of people staying home. If someone takes his clothes off and walks down the street, that is news — of a kind. If he remains fully clothed, that is not news and no one pays attention. So there is the whole problem of the exploitation of news items for purposes of other than informing. This is particularly true, I think, in politics. There is always the press secretary whose job it is to look for a gimmick. He needs to find something which will place the political candidate or office holder in a situation where he can grab the attention of the media. This is a dangerous tendency, and it encourages eccentricity. It encourages sensationalism. It downgrades the responsible. It downgrades the person who has integrity, and I think that today's journalist must ask himself more and more: Is he being used? Is he being deliberately exploited as a channel to relay certain information and news items for other purposes? Of course, we have always had the problem of the planted story. This is common in politics everywhere. This doesn't apply just to western politicians or to eastern diplomats; it applies to politicians and diplomats of all nationalities.

Q: *You mentioned earlier something of the problems of broadcasting to different cultures. Does this present any particular problem for you?*

A: Yes, it raises the whole question of universality of news. We broadcast to societies in various states of development, and having various kinds of political orientation. We have a great need to maintain a high tradition of accuracy, because we are also often heard by people who actually participated in the events we're broadcasting about.

Those of us in the BBC are often asked this in America, and I should answer it here. I have complete freedom to say what I like. I work for an organization which is supported by the taxpayer; the government does dispense the money, but it has no editorial control over program content. No pressure has ever been brought to bear on me to alter anything I've said on political grounds. What is more important for us, and this is what I was trying to get at earlier, is that certain moral and ethical problems arise about how one's views are going to be received by people in different cultures. During the Czech revolution, for example, I naturally wanted to relate exactly what was happening there. At the same time, there were obvious divisions within the Czech leadership, and I didn't want to get too much involved in those. So one had the problem: What does one say about individuals in this situation? Should you ask yourself: How is what I say going to affect their circumstances? If I go on the air and praise Mr. So-and-so, is this going to help him or hurt him? Do I limit what I really want to say about the situation? How does one deal with the situation where you feel that by praising a man you might make his circumstances more difficult for him?

I don't think there are any easy answers to these kinds of problems. The way in which they are resolved depends on the skill, the judgment, and the integrity of the individual journalist involved. This may sound trite and platitudinous. But reckless, irresponsible journalism is usually fairly easy to identify. It's much harder to spot instances where the reporter has been negligent or careless, when he simply hasn't done his homework or asked himself the right questions.

Q: *As you know, we've had a great deal of discussion in recent years about disclosure and privacy, about the First Amendment, and the like. Do you have any comparisons to make, or would you care to comment on this?*

A: Of course, we in Britain are always concerned about the question of intrusion into a person's private life. The most difficult case is the political one. If a politician is caught with his hand in the till, it is very clearly a journalist's duty to expose this, if one has positive information to that effect. But what about the politician's private life, or his moral behavior? Suppose he drinks too much, or has a mistress, or beats his wife, or something like that? How far does this relate to the public's right to know? I have always found it very hard to draw lines here. You may recall the case of the Christine Keeler memoirs. This was a case of rather sordid memoirs about public figures being exploited for private gain. The whole affair caused a great deal of discussion in Britain. It was argued that the affair should be dead and buried. Here is a case of a prominent politician who has already been made to pay very heavily for something that he did, and who has made a great attempt to start a new career in social work and has worked very hard with very little reward in a cause that everyone thinks is wholly admirable — and who is now going to be subjected again to great embarrassment and personal pain. The matter was referred to our Press Council. This is a body which is supposed to examine such ethical and moral issues relating to journalism, and make pronouncements on them. But personally I would find it very difficult in this area to lay down any absolute guidelines. In certain circumstances, I would deplore things on grounds of taste. It comes back again to the motives of the people involved. An excess of zeal in defense of the public interest can be excused. But all too often the motivating factor is the desire to increase circulation, attract bigger audiences, and make a lot of money. The meanderings of the gossip columnist, with the intrusions into privacy that these inevitably entail, may seem trivial. But they are apt to raise some fundamental moral considerations, as apparently trivial questions sometimes do. It is the same with the sensational treatment of a big crime story. For example, and this has more recently come up in your own courts, should a person be paid a large sum of money for his or her memoirs just after having been sentenced for some outrageous crime, or should their relatives be paid large amounts of money for this? We experienced this very vividly in the case of the great train robbery. The robber's wife was being paid 20,000 pounds for her account of how he evaded the police. Here is a case of someone being rewarded for their association with a crime, whereas the victim of the crime, the traindriver who was hit on the head and hasn't been able to hold a steady job since, gets nothing; in fact, no one seems to have been very anxious to get his story at all. I think there is a moral and ethical question here which every newspaper proprietor and editor and reporter has to ask himself. I don't want to propose how it should be answered, and I don't see how one could lay down absolute principles that would apply in all cases.

Q: *Have you in Britain been involved yet with the whole question of revelation of sources, with respect to matters of disclosure of materials reportedly vital to the national security?*

A: I think we have a very strict code in Britain regarding our political reporting; there are certain clearly understood ground rules about the revelation of sources, and these the journalist has to observe at all costs — at least not to give away the sources. Some ethical problems have arisen, nonetheless. There was a security leak in the Admirality some years ago. An Admirality clerk was found guilty of passing on information, and allegations were made against a number of government employees connected with the case. It came down to a matter of putting certain journalists on the stand and asking them to reveal the sources of their stories. Now, journalists are sometimes not able to give sources for stories, because there may not be any sources for them. They sometimes attribute to treasury officials an educated guess as to what treasury officials might be thinking. Or they might indeed have had a specific meeting with a specific treasury official at a specific time, during which specific things were said. We will never know the truth in this case, because the journalists involved refused to give evidence and to reveal their sources, and were therefore given prison sentences which they served. They certainly had very weighty ethical problems to consider.

Now, about the problem of national security. There are certain circumstances in which a journalist does come across information that relates to national security. In this, he is caught between his natural desire to print news to inform the public, and his desire not to reveal certain matters of national security which might affect the lives of large numbers of people, or the fate of the whole nation. We know that the *New York Times* had information regarding the events leading up to the Cuban missile crisis and the Bay of Pigs invasion; it withheld this information in the national interest. We do this somewhat differently in Britain, with a committee, which circulates to newspapers certain items of national security, so that the newspapers know about them, but are not allowed to print them without government permission. In the past this system has worked quite well — especially at times of great emergency. But in recent years it has come under strain, because of the feeling among journalists that too many items have been given an unnecessary "secret" label and that certain matters were being suppressed not in the national interest, but for partisan political purposes. In such an atmosphere, when the bonds of mutual trust are broken, the system tends to break down. I could give you all sorts of illustrations about the kinds of questions that come up: What should be printed and what should be withheld in the national interest? But, again, I think there can be no universal guidelines, and that often such things have to be dealt with on an individual basis. Some people have argued that the *New York Times* was right to hold back the information it had about the build-up to the Cuban missile crisis, but that it should have printed the facts prior to the Bay of Pigs invasion. But it is easy to make such pronouncements with the benefit of hindsight. There were no clear guidelines at the time.

Q: *You said earlier that you valued most highly your reputation for accuracy in the BBC. How do you maintain accuracy in a situation such as the Middle East conflict?*

A: The BBC in particular has to cope with these kinds of dilemmas all the time. In the case of the Middle East conflict, both sides make exaggerated claims for propaganda purposes and for reasons of psychological warfare. What does the reporter do, if he is not in a position to see an event, or to get verification of it? If he has at least a strong suspicion that facts are being exploited as political and emotional weapons, what should he do? Does he just convey the figures? My own feeling is that the best you can do is to present the claims made by each side, no matter how widely variant they may be, and leave it to the audience. I think that there is a journalistic obligation to report the rival claims. And by comparing the records for veracity of the two sides over a period of time — especially those occasions when there are neutral observers present and outside verification is possible — the listener soon learns which set of figures may be closer to the truth.

Q: *You said earlier that most of these questions bottom out in the integrity of the journalist involved. At the same time, we both realize that there is no such thing as objectivity in reporting — that every way of looking at a situation has its biases. So how does the journalist assure himself that he's reporting "the facts," and not just expressing his prejudices?*

A: Sometimes it's easy to do; other times it is not. Again, it would be impossible in my view to lay down immutable, universal principles. But there are some things that can be done to get closer to "the facts." To start with, I believe that every journalist should be an activist. By that I mean that he should have a foot in all estates — not just the so-called "fourth estate." I think it's an archaic notion that journalists should pretend to be above the fray — detached, nonpartisan, etc. No one is. We are all involved and committed to some extent. Journalists are not a special breed apart and they can't be political eunuchs. So it's essential for them to recognize and acknowledge their own prejudices. They need to identify these prejudices and recognize them when they are at work, because in reporting and analyzing the news it's sometimes necessary to counteract those prejudices and write against them. My test of a journalist's integrity is that he should have made a genuine attempt to do this. Of course, we all make mistakes. And often, when complaints of deliberate political bias are levelled against a reporter, these complaints are misdirected. In many cases he has simply made a mistake. Either he got the facts wrong or, for some reason or other he didn't get the full story. One of the requirements of a good journalist is that he should be regretful for his mistakes.

Q: *You spoke earlier of the age-old problem for the journalist of being used. What do you think can be done about this?*

A: This is what I mean by being an activist. I don't mean that journalists should tumble over themselves to embrace causes or candidates or immediately go out and run for office. But I do believe that journalists, who have at one time or another been involved in the political process, who have seen from the inside how a political campaign is run, will emerge from the experience with enhanced knowledge and, probably, a healthy scepticism. They learn to recognize the pitfalls. There is no way of acquiring complete immunity from the hazards of the planted story. To that extent the journalist is always in danger of being used. The cardinal sin is to allow oneself to be used, knowingly used.

Q: *What would be your feelings about a law which would protect journalists from having to reveal their sources?*

A: Just as I don't believe in my country right or wrong, I don't believe in my profession right or wrong. I don't feel that journalists should be defended at all times, and under all circumstances. I think this is just one of the hazards of the profession.

A Conversation with . . .

WILLIAM PRICE FOX
Novelist, Television and Film Writer

Q: *What are some of the kinds of ethical situations that a novelist might encounter, particularly one whose books are made into films?*
A: I've done four books so far, one of which has been produced on television, and two of the others have been bought for films. I haven't encountered any particular ethical problems, or any problems at all, unless you want to consider that the necessity of adapting to the fact that film producers conceive of what they do as a business rather than an art is some sort of problem. I don't think so; I think it is just a fact of life. This is not a matter of ethics; it is purely a matter of accommodation to the way things are.
Q: *Are you saying then that a film writer is not likely to encounter problems with his own conscience if he approaches his task as a businessman rather than an artist?*
A: No, I don't want to say that, because there is a lot of art in every good film. But if the film writer looks at his task completely as an artist, he is likely to create a lot of unnecessary problems for himself. There are always compromises that have to be made, and short-cuts that have to be taken simply because of the limitations of time, space, and money. But a writer can certainly be artistic within those limitations.
Q: *Does it seem to you that these sorts of compromises and accommodations do any violence to your work?*

A: No. The book and the film are simply two different mediums, and they require different things. We suffer from some old mythology — built on the assumption that sensitive artists like Fitzgerald and Hemingway went out to Hollywood and got screwed. I don't think there's anything to the old myth. The very nature of a screenplay is to shrink a book down to one-fifth of what it is in print. Once a writer accepts that fact, I don't think he has any problems from there on.

Q: *As a novelist and a screen writer, does it seem to you that you have any particular responsibility to the larger society?*

A: No, I don't think so. I suppose my own personal values come through, for good or for ill. But it seems to me that a writer has to work with particulars, not universals, and that if he begins to solve the world's problems, he ceases to be a good writer. When a writer develops particulars successfully, the values emerge.

Q: *Does it seem to you that your values, the ones which emerge in your own work, are fairly consistent with, say, some of the basic American values?*

A: No, I don't think so. I think I have more irreverence for things. I have a more critical view of things than many writers. Lots of people don't seem to pick this up, but it is there. I also have more appreciation for humor than most writers. It seems to me that a writer who doesn't have a feel for humor within the context of his characters is missing a whole lot. Humor should not be used as relief; it is fundamental to everything the novelist is writing about. Even death scenes can be humorous. Novelists who are not sensitive to the comic overtones in even the most tragic event are limited.

Q: *Do you have any axes to grind?*

A: None. In the case of particular relationships between blacks and whites that I might write about, for example, I want to show — not tell — that the black is, if not equal to the white, superior to him. But I don't see this as axe-grinding; I see it as the reality which I simply want to bring forth. But I don't set out to accomplish some ends like "social justice." I just try to write a good story.

Q: *In your books, you never seem to be much in the mainstream of current fashion in fiction. For example, you don't seem to have been caught up in the current fashions of writing about drugs, the "new sexual morality," etc. Is this intentional?*

A: In the first place, I don't think that that crop of novelists who exploit such current topics are really writers; they are only plotters. I guess they feel differently about writing than I do. I only write about stuff I really like. I wouldn't go to the trouble of writing a book just to make money. I guess I like writing too much for that. I think too much of writing to treat it in that way. I don't think these gimmick novelists are evil people. But I don't consider them as writers at all.

Q: *What you seem to be suggesting is that the ethical issues in writing bot-*

*tom out in the individual writer's commitment to his craft. Is that what
you are suggesting?*

A: Yes, I think so. I think a good writer always writes at the top of his
form. I don't think you can write left-handed. If a writer is not working at
the top of his form, at things which are of interest to him, he uses himself
up just for the buck. A writer has to work at the pace which is his top
form. Anything less than that is whoring.

Q: *Have you sensed any difference between book publishers and film producers — in terms of their ethical interests, and the kinds of ethical situations which might arise?*

A: I would say that there are producers and then there are producers.
There are the publishers who merchant sex, or some other gimmick which
is exploitable in fashionable fiction. On the other hand, there are publishers who work on the basis of some real feelings for the craft, and a
sense of responsibility for helping to develop it. The same thing is true of
film producers. There are those who will do anything for a buck, and there
are others who are serious, committed people. A good producer or director
thinks in terms of how much of his own life he has to invest in a film; if
he's serious about his work, he's going to select that property which measures his life in some satisfactory way. The other kind just measure what
they do in terms of dollars. That's the difference. Arthur Penn would never
do a Jacqueline Susanne movie.

Q: *We've talked about the novelist's situation, and a little about the role
of the publisher and the producer and director, and some possible ethical
implications of the way such things get set up. Do you have any feelings
about the role of the critic as far as ethical issues may be concerned?*

A: Critics serve a vital function. They cull out the crap. At the same time,
critics sometimes protect an established writer who bombs for one reason
or another. I think critics help to improve tastes a little bit, and this is an
admirable function. I think they are very necessary. Often when they call
attention to crap, the book still sells. But so does fertilizer and dog chow.

Q: *Within the fields of the novel and of film-making, there must be a relatively small sub-culture of people who have some strong philosophical
commitment to the craft, and who recognize each other and support each
other. Do you think this is good or bad?*

A: I think it is very healthy in some situations, and very sick in others. It's
sick when they get too supportive, and pump up some minor talent into
something enormous. But it can be very healthy when new talent is discovered and nourished in the early years. The whole situation can't be any
more ethical than the people involved are honest.

Q: *When you set about to write a novel or a screen-play, you don't begin
with the contemporary crises or issues. I take it that you have no interest
in exploiting them, or any direct sense of responsibility for solving them.
You work beside all of that. Is this correct?*

A: Absolutely.

Q: *Then would you offer that as an ethical prescription?*

A: Yes. When I wrote *Ruby Red,* I had no issues to solve, no axes to grind, but just a story to tell. For 300 pages, I wrote a story about a bootlegger. At that point, his girlfriend Ruby came in, and after the next 600 pages, I realized that the book was about her and not about him. So I went back and restructured it. If you don't structure it toward the market, or toward some polemic, you leave yourself free to work at top form. You leave open the possibility of surprises within your work. And a novelist's best work comes out of the surprises which emerge from his characters.

A Conversation with . . .

KENNETH MACDONALD
Editor, *The Des Moines Register* and *Tribune*

Q: *You're familiar with the discussions regarding "fairness" in the broadcasting industry. Does it seem to you that ethical problems are the same in the print medium as in the broadcast medium?*

A: The ethical problems of the print and the broadcast media are very similar, particularly the problem of access, but the solutions are necessarily completely different. As we all know, the broadcaster is licensed and required to operate in the public interest. Therefore government in the case of broadcasting is required by law to do what government in the case of the press is prohibited by the Constitution from doing — that is, regulate. As a newspaper editor I feel inhibited in discussing the ethical problems of broadcasting because newspapers are making slow progress in solving their own similar ethical problems. If newspapers cherish the First Amendment, they must find solutions, and they must hurry to find them before the government interferes. The fact that anyone who disagrees with the editing of *The Des Moines Register* has the freedom to start a newspaper of his own does not by itself convince me that no problem exists. Some progress is being made through press councils, ombudsmen, guest editors, in-house press criticism, etc. But more is needed.

Q: *Concern about the responsibility of the press is certainly not new. In your opinion, what is the present situation?*

A: The Constitution guarantees a free press. Who guarantees a responsible

273

press? The answer, of course, is no one. There can be no guarantee that a free press will be responsible, just as there can be no guarantee that a democratic government will be efficient. Keeping the press responsible, therefore, is the job of everyone — the readers, the owners, and the journalists who do the reporting and commenting and editing — particularly the journalists. Today, when all institutions are being challenged, there probably is more suspicion of the press, more feeling that journalists willfully distort news to suit their own prejudices, than ever before. This is ironical because the press as a whole in this country is more responsible now than it was in the days when most newspapers, openly or not, were party organs. The most serious weakness in today's newspapers, in my opinion, is not lopsided reporting or slanted editing. A greater sin is insufficient coverage, beyond easily available surface facts, of significant news which readers need in order to give them some measure of control over their own lives. In other words, the biggest weakness stems from an inadequate definition of what news it. Still, there are enough instances of one-sided reporting, of over-emphasis and under-emphasis, of questionable objectivity — to cause concern both to journalists and their critics.

Q: *You suggested that the burden of keeping the press responsible falls particularly upon the working journalist. Would you say a little more about this?*

A: One problem journalists have in dealing with their ethical sins is in recognizing them. Most transgressions in the ethical category are caused by carelessness, ignorance, or incompetency, and not by wilful intent to serve a private interest or aid a personal cause. As Donald McDonald observed in an article on objectivity in *The Center Magazine* of September/October, 1971: "Not many reporters get up in the morning and say to themselves, 'Today I am going to file a lying, incomplete, ignorant report of an event taken out of context.'" Not many editors approach their work in that mood, either. Journalists have developed codes of ethics. The Code of Ethics of the American Society of Newspaper Editors is one example. These can be useful in stimulating thought about ethics and they can be used as a checklist to monitor performance. But the heart of the ethics problem arises from the fact that no two persons see the same situation in exactly the same light. Codes are of little help here. Reasonable and responsible persons may agree completely on a general code of press conduct, but disagree on what constitutes fair coverage of a specific, complex, controversial news situation. If I think a certain point in the President's address is the most significant, and use that as a lead, but you think some other point is more significant, am I slanting the news or are you misjudging the significance? If I report in detail on a reprehensible crime, am I serving the public interest with realistic information, or am I pandering to base appetites? There is no definitive answer to such questions. There is no final arbiter of ethical issues. There can be none if the press is to remain free. Therefore, there cannot be final answers to ethical problems short of every person being his own editor. That, of course, is precisely the concept behind the Bill of Rights guarantee of a free press. If every person were free to print anything he wished to print without applying for a license, without interference or hindrance of any kind from the government, then whether everyone were responsible or not would be of relatively little consequence. Every point of view could be printed and everyone could make his own judgment on truth and fairness.

Q: *Do you believe that this concept of freedom of the press is as relevant today as it was at the time it was conceived?*

A: The concept is as sound now as it was then, but the problem today is how to give every person who has something to say access to a printing press. The manufacture of newspapers has become enormously expensive, and the custody of the printing press is in relatively few hands. As a personal reference, I am the editor of the only daily newspaper published in my state which circulates generally throughout the state. I don't think the fact that the First Amendment gives everyone the right to start his own newspaper is by itself an adequate answer to someone who disagrees with our editing. The concept won't work today unless newspaper editors and publishers voluntarily make certain that sizeable chunks of space are available in their newspapers for views other than their own. Progress has been made in this direction but not enough. Some newspapers allot generous space to letters from readers and give priority to those letters which are critical of the newspaper's views, or which question the newspaper's reporting. Most newspapers willingly print corrections, and some of them take pains to give the corrections the same prominence as the original errors. A few newspapers are experimenting with the ombudsman technique under various names. Two or three papers have in-house critics and give them space for critical articles about the press in general and their own newspaper specifically. All of these devices have merit, but it is obvious that they have not yet succeeded in allaying the suspicion of many readers that newspapers distort the news. Parenthetically, the fact that many readers, although they may not be conscious of it themselves, don't really want objective news because they want support for their own beliefs merely complicates the journalist's problem.

Q: *You didn't mention press councils. Does it seem to you that this technique might have some real promise?*

A: Certainly press councils might prove beneficial to both the press and the public, but they have not been adequately tested. Since the report of the Hutchins' Commission on Freedom of the Press was issued in 1947, the press-council concept has been widely discussed as a device for monitoring newspaper performance and correcting errors of omission or distortion. There has been far more discussion than action. A few small cities have experimented with press councils in various forms and a state-wide organization was set up in Minnesota. A few editors and publishers have urged establishment of press councils, some on a local or regional basis and some on a national basis. Many others have opposed any experimentation. Some of the opposition is self-serving, but a number of responsible journalists oppose the press council idea because they fear it would lead ultimately to some measure of control over the press by official or quasi-official bodies. Unfortunately, in much of the discussion of press councils there is at least an implication that the council would adjudicate controversies. This alarms many serious, thoughtful journalists. The right to adjudicate implies the right to enforce. I believe the press council concept would be more acceptable if all implications of adjudication were dropped, and efforts were concentrated on devising a forum where representatives of the public might question, study, and comment on press performance, without any assignment to agree on conclusions or to force corrective measures. Perhaps "press forum" would be a better and more descriptive term than press council.

Q: *It is your opinion, then, that there has to be some alternative to government regulation — and that too much government regulation would be destructive of press freedom?*

A: Journalists learn early in their careers that, if they are to survive and remain honest in their work, it isn't possible to please all of the readers. This sometimes makes them slow to respond to public concerns. Whether the current widespread suspicion of the press is justified or not, and some of it is, the press cannot afford to ignore it. If the press does not find ways to give the public greater access to the mechanics of communication, the government will step in to enforce access, and that will be the beginning of the end of press freedom. There are cases in the courts now seeking to force newspapers to accept advertising under certain conditions. A serious but horribly misguided proposal has been made to the American Civil Liberties Union which would make that organization an advocate for compulsory access to newspaper advertising columns. If newspapers lose control of their advertising columns, can they hope to maintain control of their news and editorial columns?

Q: *Are there any other developments on the contemporary scene that will alter the ethical situation either now or in the future?*

A: Yes, there are two developments largely unrecognized outside of the communications industry which may remake current newspaper circulation patterns and thereby place the problem of ethics and access in a different perspective. These developments are the rapid advances in printing technology, and the fragmentation of metropolitan areas into separate suburban populations. High manufacturing cost is the primary reason for the sharp reduction in the number of newspapers during the early part of this century. Current developments in photo-composition of type, electronic editing and typesetting, offset printing, etc., should reduce these costs substantially in the next few years. At the same time, the movement of people within huge metropolitan areas into distinctive neighborhoods or suburbs creates audiences with increasing local interests. This makes it difficult for the large newspapers to meet all the needs of readers in a wide geographic area, and invites the development of more local-interest publications. These two developments are largely responsible for the recent increase in the number of suburban newspapers and are to some extent responsible for the proliferation of the underground press.

Q: *You're assuming, of course, that increasing the number of newspapers would also increase the variety of points of view brought to the reader. But that is not necessarily so, is it?*

A: There is no assurance that increasing the number of newspapers will solve ethical problems or provide greater access to the press for the general public. But it is possible that the day will come when there will again be a multiplicity of newspapers as there once was in this country, but with the important difference that perhaps many of them will be healthy enough financially to maintain their independence.

EDITORS' COMMENT

The author acknowledges the use of a number of organizational devices to improve the atmosphere surrounding press-public relationships, and the encouragement of responsible journalism, in particular.

Perhaps the most significant statement can be found in the acknowledgement of social and technological developments that may result in placing ethical problems in a different perspective.

Specifically, MacDonald argues that the advances in print technology and the fragmentation of metropolitan areas into separate suburban populations may raise new questions concerning the availability and accessibility of newspapers.

He says, in effect, that neither individuals nor single institutions make the conditions under which we must face questions of journalistic responsibility, but that these conditions are the result of a changing society to whose *tempo* and direction we must adjust in the most imaginative and creative way. Thus, while press councils and ombudsmen may serve a useful purpose in the context of present-day attempts to provide a healthy degree of accountability to the public, it becomes essential that those concerned about issues of press responsibility continue their search for the best possible solutions in close contact with the developments in the field of mass communication.

The introduction of computerized newsrooms and rapid delivery systems of information, for instance, suggests the availability of more information in the storage of editorial computer systems as well as the possibility of control exercised by fewer journalists than before. More decisions must be made regarding the use of information to provide for a more rapid preparation of news items and interpretations of chains of information "bits" that are accessible. This progress also places additional importance on the selection of journalists; professional competence in subject matter area as well as in editorial decision-making processes along with an understanding of the relationship between press and public are desirable prerequisites for positions in modern press enterprises.

The establishment of suburban communities with their own identities or the desire to create distinct physical and social environments makes different demands on those who participate in the mass communication systems that serve these areas. In order to provide necessary and useful information, journalists will have to learn much more about their readers than they have in the past. They must develop the skills of an interested observer, not unlike social scientists, who are able to obtain a sense of what makes a community through careful observation. Such an approach requires empathic skills, knowledge of the environment, and ability to translate series of events into statements about the nature and function of suburban communities. If successful, the journalist will become an important contributor to the definition of suburban life.

In summary, one can argue that the future of journalism depends on the recognition of those forces that shape the future of the field of mass communication as well as on the development of professional sensitivity that allows journalists to listen and to comprehend the communities they serve.

A Conversation with . . .

RAYMOND RUBICAM
Co-founder, Young & Rubicam

When asked for his views on the ethical and moral issues in advertising, Raymond Rubicam provided these responses:

To me, the best years of advertising creatively, and morally and ethically, were the years when *The Saturday Evening Post, Ladies' Home Journal, Good Housekeeping Magazine* and the *New York Times* maintained a censorship over advertising copy claims.

True, those media could do it successfully in those days because the best national advertisers wanted to be in those publications, but the result, and that's what counts, was a higher code of ethics in media generally than had ever before prevailed, and surely far higher than prevails today.

Those higher standards were primarily the result of the personal attitude of four men — Cyrus H. K. Curtis, George Horace Lorimer and Edward Bok, all of Curtis Publishing, and Adolph Ochs of the *New York Times.*

Earlier in the history of print advertising it had gone through, as everybody knows, a long period of "anything goes," but it won its highest public respect and public confidence in the years of the leadership of those men and those publications. This inevitably had an enormous influence on what advertisers did and tried to do in other publications, on what the other publications themselves did, and on what agencies did and tried to do.

I have to report, regretfully, that when the Depression of the '30s came, there was a weakening of standards, especially with respect to testimonials for a *quid pro quo*.

In all my 21 years in Y&R, however, we never once ran a paid testimonial for any product or service. Contrast that with the constant TV parade today of celebrities testifying that they use products everybody knows they do not use except for pay, and perhaps not even then.

Question: Does that help advertising? I know it doesn't help the character of the nation . . .

I wish we did not have the most commercialized TV among the nations. I wish in the print field for a rebirth of the spirit of Cyrus Curtis, George Horace Lorimer, Edward Bok and Adolph Ochs.

May we who live in the land of the free not end up in slavery as a result of our own excesses. . . .[1]

Freedom Has Limits

. . . It has been said that every good thing holds within itself the seed of its own destruction through excess — and this is certainly true of freedom — especially of those freedoms granted to minorities so that they may be exercised for the welfare of majorities. Liberty stretched to license can destroy itself and destroy those persons who have enjoyed it. General welfare must be the final test of democracy as well as other governments, and sometimes customs have to be changed in order that principles may remain in effect.

Nobody believes more strongly or more sincerely in the value of advertising than I do. I mean that I believe in its worth to the buyer as well as the seller, and in its considerable contribution to the general welfare.

Nobody believes more strongly than I in the infinite desirability of the American ideal of freedom, whether spiritual or economic, whether for capital or labor, whether for you or for me.

But freedom of public activity must necessarily be limited by the necessity to serve, or, at least, not to violate, the public welfare. Whether the press likes it or not, this, in the final analysis, must be a condition of the continued freedom of the press. Whether advertising likes it or not, this, in the final analysis, must be a condition of the continued freedom of advertising. If the activity is in the main sound and good, the public is patient, practical and fair enough to overlook the offenses of a few. But a general decay of the sense of responsibility can bring only one end — the loss of freedom. . . .[2]

. . . Television advertising is like a man who plants himself squarely between you and your girl and tells you at great length what a great guy he is. And then brings up a friend and tells you what a great guy *he* is. And another, and another.

With newspaper and magazine advertising you have a choice: you can look or not look, you can read or not read as you wish. At first blush this seems an advantage for television, since in their case you are a captive audience. But with 19 ads in a half hour — or even 10 — and with your mind on the program they took away from you, you can be not only inattentive but resentful. It is difficult at such moments to be thankful that you got the whole program free.

That's one reason why, back in the early days of radio, I instructed Y&R's great media buyer, Tony Geoghegan, to battle the networks against the build-up of more and more commercials. A losing fight.

It is also a reason why, some years later, I wrote an article for *Saturday Review* (which was re-printed in the *Congressional Record*) in favor of educational television and in favor of "pay-as-you-see" television. Educational television (without advertising) became a reality; pay-as-you-see, after several trials, failed to win its way financially.

This last is understandable as I see it, because in my opinion the networks have done an admirable job of originating and furnishing good and varied entertainment for most people, and that is what their job is. It is hard to see how they could do better for their diverse mass audience. True, there have recently been large injections of smut in some programs that can spoil the record if continued — but I like to think that there will be successful pressures on the networks to curb it.

My quarrel is with the commercials — their length, their number, their theatricality, their absurdity, and their seemingly endless repetition.

Because television is largely theatre, largely entertainment, and is the most popular medium of the day, it has affected all media. Even the once sober *Wall Street Journal* is giving its news stories a jumbo shot of entertainment.

Because of television, more and more newspaper reporters today see themselves as not just reporters, but as feature writers — even if they don't know how to write and don't know their subject.

Even the television commercials are a form of theatre, but, unfortunately, there is only one plot and one outcome, and that plot and outcome are repeated over and over, with slight variations, for all products, and then repeated some more for each product. A great thing for the performers and ther residual compensation, but not so great for the audience, and maybe not for the advertiser in the future if the overloading continues.

Young & Rubicam has given me a list of television and radio regulations in 13 European countries. It shows that four of them have no advertising at all on TV or radio and that the other nine have placed strong and specific limitations on it.

There are many more countries where broadcasting is yet to come. In the interest of all the equities of civilization I fervently hope that it will not be so dependent on and pre-empted by the sellers of goods.[3]

SOURCES

[1] From *Advertising Age,* January 5, 1976.

[2] Excerpted from *Advertising Age,* December 21, 1959, from a speech made by Mr. Rubicam in 1938 in accepting the Annual Advertising Award Gold Medal for 1937.

[3] From *Y&R International Report 4,* Winter/Spring 1973.

A Conversation with . . .

T. GEORGE HARRIS
Magazine Editor*

Q: *As a magazine editor, Mr. Harris, what do you believe the basic re-sponsibilities of an editor to be?*
A: My concern is a bit different from the standard one. A legalistic ap-proach to ethics, in the press as other areas of life, misses the major issue, which is the positive fulfillment of the press's mission. The pharisees are not the only ones who brag that they are not as other men, while failing to deliver the minimum. And the self-righteous young, like the self-righteous old of the Nineteenth Century, tend to confuse virginity with virtue. My central thought is a very simple one. It came out of the black insight into institutional racism, and relates to what I've seen in many newspapers and magazines. When the editor hides behind his editorial purity, he washes his hands of his organization's responsibility for what it does. The important decisions that control the publication, and ultimately its contents, get dele-gated to the business managers. The editor, like the king, can do no wrong, which as in the divine rights doctrine means that he cannot do any-thing important.
Q: *Magazines sustain themselves generally from advertising revenue.*

---

* At the time this "conversation" was developed, Mr. Harris was Editor-in-Chief of *Psychology Today*. He is now affiliated, among others, with *New York Magazine*.

Don't the advertising salesmen therefore confront ethical problems on a daily basis?

A: The advertising sales staffers of most magazines refuse to read the publication they work for. Their view of its editorial content has probably been colored by a barroom encounter with an editor, who put on his preacher hat and condemned them as sinners. I worked on one large magazine where most of the salesmen and also the publisher considered the magazine's best work to be communistic. You can imagine how well they served it.

Lacking any insight into the magazine's function, or any personal reason to desire insight, the salesmen and their marketing people take the magazine's demographics, invent a rationale of readership that fits the numbers and pleases prospective advertisers. This statistical invention is a lie, for it has little to do with what the editors publish to the readers. But life eventually imitates art, for the editor or his successor becomes a partial captive of the rationale invented by the marketing people.

Q: *You're suggesting, then, that editors are more likely to be influenced by their sales and marketing staffs than by their subscribers?*

A: Yes: What I just said about the marketing department is true for the circulation department, only worse. The most moral contract in publishing is that between the reader and the editor — the subscription order-blank. But most circulation promotion is done by that peculiar breed of specialist, the Golden Mailboxer. Yes, the poets who write direct mail solicitation get together once a year in convention; the one of their number who has created the most dazzling results of the year, in junk mail, gets a Golden Mailbox Award. Perhaps he should. Upon his craft depends the survival of many a magazine. His performance gets tested by the toughest statistical measures in any field of behavior testing. You can measure his results down to the hundreth of a per cent on response ratio. And he, too, usually works with no direct knowledge of what the editor is trying to do. Because the editor is too busy keeping his legs crossed. Result: The reader gets hooked into a pitch that does not represent the magazine. Nobody is lying. It's just that the editor is too busy being pompous to make friends with the Golden Mailboxer, and thus have a chance to corrupt him into representing the magazine honestly — for what it is. Second result: Because the reader's perception is first shaped by the marketing letter, everything that the editor says is distorted by the original set.

Q: *What you're suggesting is that an editor who doesn't know what he stands for is likely to get corrupted. Is that right?*

A: The honest editor has to go out to influence the advertising and circulation groups, rather than fear that he will be corrupted by them. It is a dangerous practice, because he will note things that reduce his innocence. On one occasion, I was about to run an article that would cost us, I knew, 14 pages of advertising. The Advertising Director, a close friend with whom I had had many good fights, hounded me day and night to kill the article, revise it, or at least postpone it. I listened to every argument he made, really listened, not just to make answers. In the end, there was only one choice: I ran the article, as it was, on schedule, and we lost the 14 pages. Maybe next time I would have fudged for survival's sake. But I don't think so. The Director was proud of the way it turned out, and he came to have great pride in knowing that we held the line. He was, like most advertising men, a secret moralist who led his salesmen out into holy battle once he knew that I would not cheat for him.

Q: *Is it your view, then, that an "honest" editor is one who assumes responsibility and leadership for more than just the editorial aspects of the magazine?*

A: Yes. Otherwise, he is a victim of the irresponsibility of his own innocence. If the editor knows nothing about the economics of the magazine, he becomes the jolly little elf in the back room. He abrogates responsibility for what his institution does, and eventually gets choked by his own chastity belt. If I'm going to knock off 14 pages, I want to do so with full realization of the consequences of my choice. In most magazines, where the editors lap up praise of their "creativity" (meaning they don't know when to come in out of the rain), the business side develops a reliable underground for finding out what is going in the magazine, and for killing the articles that would cost advertisers or readers. (And a sell-out to reader prejudice is perhaps more destructive than advertiser catering, because you promise the reader your honesty.)

Q: *Would you feel that editors who place primary value on "objectivity" or on "creativity" actually create many of the ethical situations they encounter?*

A: The great newspapers and magazines came out of editor-owners, who put the product first but knew all about the rest of the publishing institution. They did not, as today's bureaucratic publishing tends to do, hang the whore label on their business people and force them to act the part. They did not crawl into the editorial hole and claim innocence of the institution's circulation and advertising. They initiated business programs as honest extensions of the editorial concept. They understood the difference between virginity and virtue.

Bibliography

SOME SOURCES ON ETHICAL AND MORAL ISSUES
IN MASS COMMUNICATION

Prepared by Richard L. Johannesen

Agee, Warren K., ed. *Mass Media in a Free Society*. Lawrence, Kan.: University of Kansas Press, 1969.
    Contains essays which examine the social responsibilities of the mass media by Ben Bagdikian, Bill Moyers, Carl Rowan, Theodore Koop, Stan Freberg, and Bosley Crowther.
Baker, Richard, and Gregg Phifer. *Salesmanship: Communication, Persuasion, and Perception*. Boston: Allyn and Bacon, 1966.
    Chapter 5 explores the ethics of salesmanship.
Baker, Samm S. *The Permissible Lie: The Inside Truth About Advertising*. Boston: Beacon Press, 1971.
    An expose of advertising ethics based on the author's extensive experience in the advertising industry.
Bedell, Clyde. *How to Write Advertising that Sells*. 2nd ed. New York: McGraw-Hill, 1952.
    Pages 471–494 probe ethical issues and standards in advertising.
Blythin, Evan. "Improbable Claiming." *Western Journal of Speech Communication*, 41(Fall 1977), 253–259.
    An interdisciplinary empirical analysis of deceptive advertising of sex-oriented ads in Las Vegas.
Bok, Sissela. *Lying: Moral Choice in Public and Private Life*. New York: Pantheon Books, 1978.
    A thorough and well-documented study of how "lying" has been thought of

and assessed over the ages. Although the author does not specifically deal with the media, she touches upon many forms of truth telling and deception that are pertinent to mass communication.

Bourke, Vernon. "Moral Problems Related to Censoring the Media of Mass Communication." In *Problems of Communication in a Pluralistic Society.* Milwaukee: Marquette University Press, 1956. Pp. 113–137.
Probes relationships between issues of ethical mass communication and constitutional rights of free speech.

Boyenton, William H. "Enter the Ladies — 86 Proof: A Study in Advertising Ethics." *Journalism Quarterly,* 44(Autumn 1967), 445–453.
An ethical case study of female-oriented hard liquor advertising.

Burke, Kenneth. "The Rhetoric of Hitler's.'Battle.'" In Burke, *The Philosophy of Literary Form.* Rev. abridged ed. New York: Vintage Books, 1957. Pp. 164–189.
A critical analysis of the nature, effects, and responsibility of Hitler's approach to propaganda described in *Mein Kampf.*

Chesebro, James. "A Construct for Assessing Ethics in Communication." *Central States Speech Journal,* XX(Summer 1969), 104–114.
An adaptation of Kenneth Burke's rhetorical theory (dramatism and the pentad) as a framework for assessment.

Christians, Clifford. "Fifty Years of Scholarship in Media Ethics." *Journal of Communication,* 27(Autumn 1977), 19–29.
A critical survey of major publications, trends in ethical standards, and unresolved issues.

Christians, Clifford G., and Michael R. Real. "Jacques Ellul's Contributions to Critical Media Theory." *Journal of Communication,* 29(Winter 1979), 83–93.
Includes an interpretation of Ellul's stance on the ethicality of propaganda.

Cirino, Robert. *Don't Blame the People: How the News Media Use Bias, Distortion, and Censorship to Manipulate Public Opinion.* New York: Vintage Books, 1972.
The title of this book is quite descriptive of its focus.

Davidson, W. Phillips. "Diplomatic Reporting: The Rules of the Game." *Journal of Communication,* 25(Autumn 1975), 138–146.
Among the "rules" described are the ethical standards which seem operative for news reporters covering international diplomacy.

DeGeorge, Richard T., and Joseph A. Pichler, eds. *Ethics, Free Enterprise, and Public Policy.* New York: Oxford University Press, 1978.
Especially see the essays by Burton M. Leiser, "The Ethics of Advertising," and by Phillip Nelson, "Advertising and Ethics."

Dieterich, Daniel, ed. *Teaching About Doublespeak.* Urbana, Ill.: National Council of Teachers of English, 1976.
Contains 24 essays designed to assist teachers at the elementary, secondary, and college levels in developing student abilities to understand and evaluate the ethicality of political and commercial doublespeak. Of special interest is Dennis Gouran's "Guidelines for the Analysis of Responsibility in Governmental Communication."

Ellul, Jacques. *Propaganda: The Formation of Men's Attitudes.* New York: Vintage Books, 1973.

The ethics of propaganda are discussed on pages xv, xvii, 27, 38, 166–170, 174–175, 197, 217, and 250.

Evans, Laurence. *The Communication Gap: The Ethics and Machinery of Public Relations and Information.* London: Charles Knight, 1973.
A professional, whose experience includes the Local Government Information Office, explores ethical issues and standards for public relations in English government and commerce.

Felknor, Bruce. *Dirty Politics.* New York: Norton, 1966.
In this fascinating sourcebook of examples, the former director of the non-partisan Fair Campaign Practices Committee examines the ethics of political campaigning.

Finman, Ted, and Stewart Macaulay. "Freedom to Dissent: The Vietnam Protests and the Words of Public Officials." *Wisconsin Law Review,* Vol. 1966(1966), pp. 632–723, espec. pp. 694–723.
The authors suggest ethical guidelines to govern statements by government officials which might impair citizens' rights of freedom of expression.

Finn, David. *Public Relations and Management.* New York: Reinhold, 1960.
Pages 145–165 discuss the issues and problems characterizing the struggle for ethics in public relations.

Gardner, John. *On Moral Fiction.* New York: Basic Books, 1977.
Argues that current literature suffers most of all from a plain failure of morality. "Moral" fiction attempts to find out what best promotes human fulfillment, human possibility. Our experience of literature and ourselves is undermined because so much present-day fiction fails to be moral in this sense.

Garrett, Thomas, S.J. *An Introduction to Some Ethical Problems of Modern American Advertising.* Rome, Italy: The Gregorian University Press, 1961.
Pages 39–47 are of special interest because they offer suggested criteria for assessing the ethics of advertising.

Gerald, J. Edward. *The Social Responsibility of the Press.* Minneapolis: University of Minnesota Press, 1963.
Discusses means for citizens to better evaluate mass media performance, proposals for media improvement, and media critics.

Griffin, Emory A. *The Mind Changers: The Art of Christian Persuasion.* Wheaton, Ill.: Tyndale House, 1976.
Chapter 11 discusses the mass media and Chapter 3 presents an ethic for the Christian persuader.

Hardt, Hanno. "The Dilemma of Mass Communication: An Existential Point of View." *Philosophy and Rhetoric,* 5(Summer 1972), 175–187.
Examines how the mass media promote "inauthentic" communication and lessen the probability of what Martin Buber calls communication as "dialogue."

Harrison, John M. "Media, Men and Morality." *The Review of Politics,* 36(April 1974), 250–264.
Through using examples such as the Pentagon Papers, the Eagleton Affair, and the Watergate Affair, Harrison balances freedoms and responsibilities in exploring guidelines for fairness, decency, and honor in journalism.

Haselden, Kyle. *Morality and the Mass Media.* Nashville, Tenn.: Broadman Press, 1968.

Haselden advocates what he terms "authentic" Christian morality in judging mass media, a position somewhere between the extremes of rule-bound legalism and the relativism of Joseph Fletcher's *Situation Ethics.*

Henry, Jules. *Culture Against Man.* New York: Random House, 1963.
In Chapter 3, anthropologist Henry examines the ethics of advertising assumptions and techniques.

Herzog, Arthur. *The B.S. Factor: The Theory and Technique of Faking It in America.* New York: Simon and Schuster, 1973.
Contains illustrations of suspect persuasive strategies and techniques appropriate for analysis to determine degree of ethicality.

Hiebert, Ray, *et. al.,* eds. *The Political Image Merchants: Strategies for the Seventies.* 2nd ed. Washington, D.C.: Acropolis Books, 1975.
Section VII on ethics of the New Politics contains essays by James M. Perry, David Broder, and Samuel J. Archibald.

Hulteng, John L. *The Messenger's Motives: Ethical Problems of the News Media.* Englewood Cliffs, N.J.: Prentice-Hall, 1976.
An author with both professional and academic journalistic experience utilizes profuse actual examples of obvious and borderline unethical practices to illustrate five fundamental ethical standards (p. 23) for electronic and print news media.

Johannesen, Richard L. *Ethics in Human Communication.* Columbus, Ohio: Charles E. Merrill Publ. Co., 1975; reprinted Avery Publishing Group, 1978.
The author explores the decline of confidence in truthfulness in public communication, explains seven perspectives for ethical evaluation (religious, legal, utilitarian, political, ontological, dialogical, situational), discusses twelve basic ethical issues, and presents fourteen examples for analysis. An appendix reprints four complete ethical case studies and a bibliography contains over 180 items.

Johannesen, Richard L. "Perspectives on Ethics in Persuasion." In Charles U. Larson, *Persuasion: Reception and Responsibility.* 2nd ed. Belmont, Cal.: Wadsworth, 1979, Chapter 9.
Discusses potential perspectives for ethical assessment, explores issues basic to judging communication ethics, and examines in detail possible ethical standards for political persuasion and commercial advertising.

Johannesen, Richard L, ed. *Ethics and Persuasion: Selected Readings.* New York: Random House, 1967.
Contains 13 articles and essays which suggest diverse standards for assessing the ethics of persuasion and which probe ethical issues in mass communication.

Kail, F. M. *What Washington Said: Administration Rhetoric and the Vietnam War 1949–1969.* New York: Harper Torchbooks, 1973.
An analysis of the shifting grounds and rationalizations used by several Administrations to defend America's role in Vietnam.

Kelley, Frank K. "Ethics of Journalism in a Century of Change." *Nieman Reports,* XXII(June 1968), 12–15.
Advocates a two-fold ethic for reporters, broadcasters, and editors: (1) thorough and complete reporting, including a warning of incomplete information where appropriate; (2) active, aggressive investigation and exposure of societal

problems demanding solution (not passively "waiting for the news to break").

Key, Wilson Bryan. *Subliminal Seduction: Ad Media's Manipulation of a Not So Innocent America.* Englewood Cliffs, New Jersey: Prentice-Hall, 1973.

An attempt to document and expose advertisers' uses of "subliminal persuasion" techniques.

Ladd, Bruce. *Crisis in Credibility.* New York: New American Library, 1968.

A documented indictment of the federal executive branch (pre-Watergate era) for lying, unwarranted secrecy, and misleading news manipulation.

LeRoy, David J., and F. Leslie Smith. "Perceived Ethicality of Some TV News Production Techniques by a Sample of Florida Legislators." *Speech Monographs,* 40(November 1973), 326–329.

An empirical investigation of the question, could members of a news medium's audience define what constituted ethical journalistic behavior?

Levitt, Theodore. "Are Advertising and Marketing Corrupting Society? It's Not Your Worry." *Advertising Age* (October 6, 1958), 89–92.

Argues that the advertiser's goal should be to efficiently and successfully sell products, not to save souls, promote spiritual values, elevate taste, cultivate human dignity, or enhance consumer self-respect. (For a rebuttal by Clyde Bedell see *Advertising Age,* October 27, 1958, 101–102.)

McGaffin, William, and Erwin Knoll. *Anything But the Truth: The Credibility Gap — How News is Managed in Washington.* New York: Putnams, 1968.

This book's title is quite descriptive of its focus.

Marietta, Don E., Jr. "On Using People." *Ethics,* 82(April 1972), 232–238.

The author examines circumstances in which it might be ethical to "use" communication participants as "things" and "means" and suggests guides for ethical communication in such contexts.

Marston, John E. *The Nature of Public Relations.* New York: McGraw-Hill, 1963.

Pages 346–359 examine issues in public relations.

Marston, John. *Modern Public Relations.* New York: McGraw-Hill, 1979.

Of special interest is the section on "Right and Wrong in Professional Public Relations."

Martin, Thomas H., Richard D. Byrne, and Dan J. Wedemeyer. "Balance: An Aspect of the Right to Communicate." *Journal of Communication,* 27(Spring 1977), 158–162.

For public communication media, the authors advocate an ethic embodied in the communication "rights" of access, redress, and public accountability.

Merrill, John C., and Ralph D. Barney, eds. *Ethics and the Press: Readings in Mass Media Morality.* New York: Hastings House, 1975.

Ethical foundations for electronic and print media are explored in 11 essays. Ethical problems in mass communication are assessed in 25 essays.

Moran, Terence P. "Public Doublespeak: 1984 and Beyond." *College English,* 37(October 1975), 223–227.

Moran's guidelines for distinguishing genuine communication from pseudo-communication also can be viewed as standards for determining ethicality in human communication.

Newsom, Doug, and Alan Scott. *This is PR: The Realities of Public Realtions.* Belmont, Cal.: Wadsworth, 1976.

Pp. 174–187 examines the ethics of public relations and pp. 265–293 reprint professional codes of ethics for public relations, advertising, jouranlism, and broadcasting.

Nilsen, Thomas R. *Ethics of Speech Communication.* 2nd ed. Indianapolis: Bobbs-Merrill Co., 1972.
A provocative blend of the political, dialogical, and ontological perspectives for judging the ethics of mass and individual communication.

Packard, Vance. *The Hidden Persuaders.* New York: McKay, 1957.
Chapter 23 explores the ethics of advertising, public relations, and political campaign persuasion. Packard pinpoints eight difficult questions to be resolved by senders and receivers of such communication.

Preston, Ivan. *The Great American Blow-Up: Puffery in Advertising and Selling.* Madison: University of Wisconsin Press, 1975.
A detailed analysis of the nature and functioning of one type of commercial persuasion which often is ethically suspect.

Quinn, Francis X., S.J., ed. *Ethics, Advertising,* and *Responsibility.* Westminster, Md.: Canterbury Press, 1963.
An anthology surveying problems of ethical and moral responsibility in advertising.

Rasmussen, Karen. "Nixon and the Strategy of Avoidance." *Central States Speech Journal,* 24(Fall 1973), 193–202.
The ethics of Nixon's mass media "strategy of avoidance" during the 1972 presidential campaign is condemned by Rasmussen through applying criteria derived from concepts of essential political values and of communication as dialogue. (Reprinted in Johannesen, *Ethics in Human Communication.*)

Rivers, William, and Wilbur Schramm, eds. *Responsibility in Mass Communication.* Rev. ed. New York: Harper and Row, 1969.
This anthology contains a number of essays which explore ethical problems related to the various mass media.

Rubin, Bernard. *Questioning Media Ethics.* New York: Praeger, 1978.
Case studies prepared under the auspices of The Institute for Democratic Communication, providing "insight" into the ethical/moral issues faced by media practitioners.

Samstag, Nicholas. *Persuasion for Profit.* Norman: University of Oklahoma Press, 1957.
Pages 102–103 and 187–195 examine ethical issues in advertising.

Sandage, C. H., and Vernon Fryburger. *Advertising Theory and Practice.* 9th ed. Homewood, Ill.: Irwin, 1975.
Chapter 5 on ethics and truth in advertising discusses various types of advertising which the authors judge unethical.

Schwartz, Tony. *The Responsive Chord.* Garden City, New York: Anchor Books, 1973. Pp. 18–22, 31, 33, 97.
Schwartz argues that the concept of "telling the truth" is a "print ethic, not a standard for ethical behavior in electronic communicaton" such as political and commercial advertising on television.

Smith, Samuel V. "Advertising in Perspective." In Joseph W. Towle, ed., *Ethics and Standards in American Business.* New York: Houghton Mifflin, 1964. Pp. 166–177.
Probes ethical problems and standards in advertising.

Taplin, Walter, *Advertising: A New Approach.* 1st Am. ed. Boston: Little, Brown, 1963.

　　Chapters 4 and 6 scrutinize the ethics of advertising.

Thayer, Lee, ed. *Communication: Ethical and Moral Issues.* New York: Gordon and Breach Science Publ., 1973.

　　Includes essays, some directly on mass communication, by such scholars as Jurgen Reusch, Anatol Rapoport, Hugh D. Duncan, J. L. L. Aranguren, Martin E. Marty, Kenneth Boulding, William Stephenson, Frank E. X. Dance, Alfred G. Smith, Kenneth Burke, and Lee Thayer.

White, Ralph K. "Propaganda: Morally Questionable and Morally Unquestionable Techniques." *Annals of the American Academy of Political and Social Science,* 398(1971), 26–35.

　　White discusses major categories of what he views as unethical and ethical propaganda appeals.

Wise, David. *The Politics of Lying: Government Deception, Secrecy, and Power.* New York: Random House, 1973.

　　A pre-Watergate analysis of varied ethically suspect communication practices of the federal government.

Witcover, Jules. "The Indiana Primary and the Indianapolis Newspapers — A Report in Detail." *Columbia Journalism Review,* VII(Summer 1968), 11–17.

　　Castigates the ethicality of the Indianapolis *Star* and *News* in their coverage of Robert Kennedy's campaign for blurring the line between news reportage and editorial viewpoint.

Witcover, Jules. "William Loeb and the New Hampshire Primary: A Question of Ethics." *Columbia Journalism Review,* XI(May–June 1972), 14–25.

　　Questions the ethicality of publisher Loeb's treatment of candidate Edmund Muskie in Loeb's newspaper, the Manchester *Union Leader.*

Wright, John S., and John E. Mertes, eds. *Advertising's Role in Society.* St. Paul, Minn.: West Publ. Co., 1964.

　　Part VI contains eight reprinted essays, including a provocative one by Theodore Levitt, which examine or advocate various ethical standards appropriate for advertising.

Wright, John S., and Daniel S. Warner, eds. *Speaking of Advertising.* New York: McGraw-Hill, 1963.

　　Chapters 37, 40, 42, and 48 are essays focusing on ethical standards for advertising.

Wrighter, Carl P. *I Can Sell You Anything.* New York: Ballantine Books, 1972.

　　The author, a "renegade adman," vividly explains the "weasel words," claims, demonstrations, and emotional appeals characteristic of successful commercial advertisements. This is a storehouse of potential examples for ethical analysis.

Index